Ric

Richard's bicycle

new revised and expanded edition
Pan Books London and Sydney

Length/distance		Weight		
$\frac{1}{16}$ inch	1.59 mm	1 ounce	28.4	grammes
$\frac{1}{8}$ inch	3.18 mm	8 ounces	226.8	grammes
$\frac{1}{4}$ inch	6.35 mm	1 pound	0.45	kilogrammes
$\frac{1}{2}$ inch	12.7 mm			
1 inch	25.4 mm			
12 ins/1 ft	30.48 cm			
36 ins/1 yard	91.44 cm			
100 yards	91.44 metres			
1 mile	1.61 kilometres			

First published in Great Britain 1975 by Pan Books Ltd,
Cavaye Place, London SW10 9PG
Revised editions 1976, 1977
Revised and expanded edition 1979
11th printing 1982
© Richard Ballantine 1972, 1975, 1976, 1977, 1979
ISBN 0 330 25805 2
Printed in Great Britain by
Richard Clay (The Chaucer Press) Ltd, Bungay, Suffolk

Mechanical illustrations by John Batchelor;
old bicycles and cycling scenes from the author's library,
with contributions from Heywood Hill and Sherry Rubin.
Cover bicycle by F. W. Evans Ltd, London

This book is dedicated to
Samuel Joseph Melville, hero

'PRIMROSES'

Contents

'Rational Dress.'

Foreword

Fair notice: I am an American, and despite Scottish and English grandparents and an English mother, some of my notions differ from those of the British, just as Italians can be distinguished from Swedes.

A daring and foolhardy feat was performed by a bicyclist the other afternoon at Cabin John Bridge. The place is a general pleasure resort about twelve miles from town, over the military road built by Jefferson Davis while Secretary of War. The bridge is said to be the largest single span of masonry in the world. It is 125 feet high, and about 200 feet long, a single magnificent arch spanning a deep and rocky gorge. A good many people go out there to see the bridge, and the man who keeps the little hotel known as Cabin John, just at the end and across the bridge, does a good business, especially on Sunday. Every nice Sunday the sheds about the place are crowded with vehicles of every description, and sporting men, family parties, wheelmen, and gentlemen of leisure, are loafing about the house, getting country dinners or picnicking in the wild gorge below the bridge. As at all such places, there are always a few wheelmen lounging in and out, and a number of machines were stacked in the yard that afternoon, and a lively party within could be heard telling stories and boasting of their personal skill on the road. In the midst of the hilarity one young man suddenly came out alone, and, singling out his machine, mounted, and without a word rode towards the bridge. There is a brownstone coping on the three-foot wall on either side of the roadway. This coping is about a foot broad, and is bevelled on the two upper edges for an inch or two. On the inside of these walls is the solid roadway above the duct. On the outside is a perpendicular descent of about 125 feet in the centre of the bridge, and no less than 75 feet at either abutment. The young man stopped and dismounted at the end of the bridge and lifted his machine upon the coping. The act was noticed by a couple of gentlemen smoking under the trees, but it was looked upon as a freak, and no particular attention was paid to it. The next moment there was an exclamation of horror, for the young man was seen mounted upon his bicycle deliberately riding along the narrow coping. The sight froze the blood of the ladies and children picnicking in the gorge below, and was enough to appeal to the stoutest heart. The gentlemen in front of the hotel started to their feet and called to the other wheelmen within. It was too late. The young man was already in the centre of the bridge. He never swerved a hair's breadth from his seat. From the end of the bridge he seemed a toy machine running by mechanism, so erect and motionless he sat, and so evenly he rode. 'Let him alone,' cried one of his companions, 'he could ride it if it was a rope.' Nevertheless, the fear that interference might hasten the horror that all wished to prevent left the party rooted to the spot. In two places the coping makes a zigzag by the widening of the roadway, and at these places the rider must steer his wheel through a very narrow space at nearly right-angles with his course. The daring fellow had passed the first of these ticklish spots, and, when he carefully wore round the second, not a single one of the horrified spectators could draw a breath for fear. From thence to the end was a short and straight run, and in another moment the young man had completed his dangerous ride, dismounted, and was waving his hand laughingly at the frightened men and women and children who had witnessed it. The young fellow calmly remounted his wheel and rode on towards the city as if he had done a very common thing not worth mentioning. He was induced to undertake the feat because someone had doubted whether he had the requisite ability and nerve to perform it.

Bicycling News, 10 October 1886

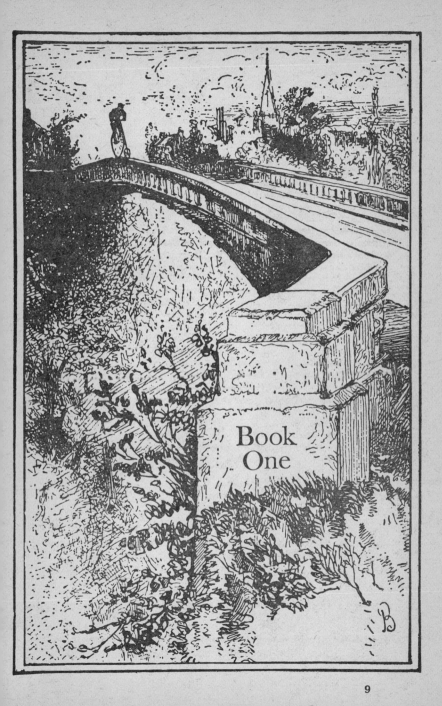

Book
One

1 Get a bike!

The bicycle is of age. Called by Stuart S. Wilson the most
important modern invention (*Scientific American*, March 1973),
it is selling in boom quantities throughout the world. In America,
trading in the bicycle business was for a while like being first in line
at the 1849 California gold rush: annual sales climbed from 4.4
million in 1960 to a peak of nearly 17 million in 1975, and then
subsided to the present average of between 10 and 11 million per
year. Over 100 million Americans ride on two wheels. In the
Netherlands 75 per cent of the population own bicycles. In Japan,
over 47 million bikes are in use, and congestion is so severe that if
one parked bike in a line falls, the resulting chain-reaction of falling
bikes can last for several minutes, and travel a block. In China there
are no private motor vehicles, only public lorries and buses.
Everybody rides a bicycle. The output of just one Chinese bicycle
factory is listed as 14,000 bicycles per day!

And there is a boom in Great Britain, too. The pattern is unique
and distinctive. In America, for example, the typical pre-World
War II bike was sturdy but cumbersome. Equipped with a single
pedal-operated coaster brake and one low, slow gear, these 'balloon
tyre bombers' hit the scales at about 5 stone plus. Used primarily by
youngsters not old enough to drive, they were wonderful workhorse
machines tough enough to withstand jolting rides over kerbs and
through fields, frequent nights out in the rain, and a generally high
level of abuse. Fond nostalgia permeates memories of these bikes,
but for the most part only people who had no other alternative used
them. Pre-World War II sales could not have exceeded 500,000 per
annum. In contrast, in much smaller Great Britain, 1935 was the
heyday of the bicycle, with a record sale of 1.6 million. The bicycle
was then a transportation staple in widespread use. The basic design
established by 1910 had been subject to a long evolutionary series of
minor improvements. Most machines were middleweights with
lightened frames, roller lever rim brakes, and 1½-in tyres, and

Sandy Lane near Petersfield.
A MEMORY OF MY BOYHOOD.

fancier models had calliper cable-actuated rim brakes, gears, and $1\frac{1}{4}$-in or $1\frac{3}{8}$-in tyres. Tipping the scales at 45 to 50 pounds, they were dubbed 'English Racers' by Americans because of their startlingly better performance over the domestic product. Here, they were just the ordinary ride-around bike for local use, to and from work, shopping, mail delivery, police work, light touring, and the like.

The bottom dropped out of the market after the war. Although in America the 'English Racer' provided the foundation for the growth of cycling as an adult sport and means of transport, after World War II sales in Great Britain dropped below 500,000 per annum. Britain went car-crazy, and the bicycle went the way of the Dodo bird. Roads, car parks, petrol stations, motorways, and cars, cars, cars proliferated, so that now Britain is a world leader in number of cars per mile of road, and many of her towns and villages have been transformed into mazes of one-way motordromes. Some of the traffic and parking schemes are marvellously efficient, but serve only to perpetuate the motorcar and further refine a continuous, gigantic traffic jam.

Re-enter our Dodo bird the bicycle. In 1972 sales were 700,000. In 1976 they were 1.1 million.* And while a fair number of bikes in use today are old middleweight workhorses, the new bikes come in a sparkling variety of shapes and sizes. There are sporty 10- and 15-speed racing and touring bikes which weigh about 20–25 pounds and are almost incomparably faster and easier to ride than other bikes. The standard 3-speed is now a lightweight at about 35 pounds. Shoppers and commuters are whirling around on natty mini-bikes. Folding bikes are another hit. And to get mounted on a new machine you can spend anywhere from £40 to £500.

Why? How come the bicycle is coming back like Mrs Grundy's spinach? For the moment, let's concentrate on the personal advantages of cycling and discuss broader social benefits later. A full list of the vastly extended applications and uses for lightweight bikes would be dull. The main ones are:

Economics

With even moderate use a bike will pay for itself. Suppose you use a bike instead of public transportation or a car to get to work and back. Figure public transport costs at £1 a day. Say it rains once a week† and you lay up the bike from December through February. That's 4 days × 4 weeks × 9 months × £1 or £144 which buys a very nice bike. On a 10-mile round trip (the national commuting average) at 14p a mile, a car costs £1.40p a day. Using a bike four days a week saves £200. And eliminating the car altogether saves £252 per annum. These are conservative figures, for a 14p per mile cost is calculated over all types of driving, including motorways. The

* Statistics are nasty things. A critic might point out that while the number of cycles in use is increasing, so is the population, and hence the *per capita* use is declining (at about 5 per cent per annum). But population growth is slowing down and bike sales, steadily increasing, will catch up sooner or later. In towns such as Stevenage, where there is special provision for cyclists, the decline in *per capita* use has fallen to 2½ per cent.

† A generous allowance. There is no measurable rainfall twenty days a month. Cycling is out of the question only fifteen days a year. And in the time between 8–9 a.m. and 5–6 p.m. it rains only twelve days a year. In towns such as Stevenage where cycles are a popular form of transport, the variation in use is at most 5 per cent, and is not related to the weather.

1885 Rover Safety

man who drives five miles to the station and pays parking fees as well is shelling out a lot more. Two hundred and fifty two pounds will buy two to four bikes, each guaranteed for anywhere from one to five years. Annual maintenance costs should be under £15.

Travelling to and from work is just one application. Bikes are just dandy for visiting friends, light shopping, nipping down to the cinema, and so on. You save money every time and it can add up to an impressive amount. Besides easing many of your chores and tasks, bikes are worthwhile in themselves, so that a bike easily 'pays for itself' in rides taken just for fun and pleasure.

Convenience

Speed. In heavy traffic you can expect to average 10 mph, and in lighter traffic 15 mph. I used to ride from my London flat near Westbourne Park Grove to Oxford Circus in 20 minutes, usually less. The bus or Tube usually took about 35 or 40 minutes. (And in these days of deteriorating public services you can set out for the bus or Tube and not have the bloody thing come at all. A bike is not only faster, but also more reliable.) When I lived in New York City, a regular $2\frac{1}{2}$-mile ride from the Lower East Side to midtown

Manhattan took less than 15 minutes as against 30 to 40 for the bus and 25 to 35 for the Subway. It used to be my delight to race Subway-travelling friends from 120th street to Greenwich Village – about 6 or 7 miles – and beat them. The story is the same everywhere. There have been many bike versus bus, Tube and/or sportscar contests in many cities, and in each case I know about the bike has always won.

One reason a bike is so fast is that it can wiggle through the traffic jams that now typify cities and towns. Another is the fact that a bike is door-to-door. Use of public transportation involves walking to the local stop, waiting around for the bus or train, possibly incurring a change with another wait, and then a walk from the final stop to your destination. Cars have to be parked. On a bike you simply step out the door and take off. No waiting, no parking problems.

The bike's capabilities make it a real freedom machine. Your lunch hour: tired of the same company cafeteria slop or local sandwich bar? Cycling to a new and interesting café a mile or so away is a matter of minutes. Or how about a picnic in the park? Lots of errands to do? A bike can nip from one place to another much faster than you can hoof it, and has a car beat hollow in traffic and for parking. What might ordinarily take an hour or more is only 15 minutes on the bike. And if there is a lot to lug around, it is the bike and not you that does the work. Last-minute decision to catch a film or visit friends? Boom! Ten minutes and you're there before the Tube even gets going. If, like me, you are at all nocturnal,

A country postman

a bike is a tremendous advantage. Trains and buses tend to become elusive as the wee hours approach. There is also a powerful contrast between a journey on a noisy and often dirty train or bus, and a graceful rhythmic ride in which you glide through calm and silent streets or through the stillness of a country night under the moon and stars.

Medical

All right, you say. So it takes less time than the Tube. But I've got to work for a living and the Tube is easier, takes less out of me. You expect me to get up in the morning and crack off 5 miles? Finish a day of hard work and do another 5? I'd never make it.

Get this. Even a moderate amount of exercise makes life *easier*. It gives your body tone and bounce which makes daily work and chores a breeze. Simply put, this is because exercise increases your range of possible effort, putting daily activities towards the centre rather than the peak of your capabilities. So as you go through the day you are just cruising. It's something like the difference between a 25- and 100-horsepower automobile engine. At 60 mph the 25 horse is working hard but the 100 is just loafing. It is important to realize that you can get this increased bounce, verve, and good feeling with relatively little time and effort. Bicycling will make your work and day easier, not harder.

Are you familiar with 'cleaning out' a motor vehicle? Cars today often operate in stop-and-go traffic for long periods of time. The engine becomes clogged with carbon and other residue. The car stumbles and staggers, it works harder than it needs to, and petrol consumption goes up. The best thing for any such car is to be taken out on a motorway and run fast, for at higher speeds the engine cleans itself out. Your body is a machine with exactly similar characteristics, and you will literally become more fagged out and tired just sitting still than if you run around the block a few times.

According to Eugene Sloane in his *Complete Book of Bicycling*, if you get in some sort of regular exercise you can expect:

to live for up to five years longer;
think better (more blood to the brain – and if you think this is crazy, go out and run around for a while and then think it through again);
sleep better, and in general be more relaxed;

be stronger and more resistant to injury;
reduce the incidence of degenerative vascular diseases responsible
for or associated with heart attacks, strokes, and high blood
pressure.

As cardiovascular problems account for over 50 per cent of all
deaths each year, this last point is worth some elaboration. The
basic deal with the cardiovascular system is movement, the flow of
blood through your heart, veins, arteries, and so forth. The heart
normally pumps about 5 quarts per minute and, during exercise, up
to 30 quarts per minute. If this flow is sluggish and slow, the system
clogs up. In arteriosclerosis, for example, the walls of the system
become hardened and calcified. This decreases the bore of the
arteries and veins, resulting in a diminished capacity to carry blood.
The heart must therefore pump harder and higher blood pressure
results. High blood pressure is a cause of stroke or rupture of brain
blood vessels. Arteriosclerosis happens to everybody, but extent is
governed by the rate of flow of the blood. Exercise stimulates the
blood flow, and does not permit calcification to occur as rapidly.

Atherosclerosis is a related malady. This is when fatty substances
are deposited on the lining of the blood vessels. Clots in the blood
may be formed as a result, and these can jam up the system at
critical points, such as the brain or heart, causing a stroke or heart
attack. Again, exercise by stimulating the blood flow helps prevent
fatty deposits.

So, the main benefits of regular exercise are first, that it will help
keep your blood circulatory system cleaned out; secondly, the heart
muscle, like any other, responds to exercise by becoming larger and
more efficient, so that each heartbeat delivers more oxygen to the
body; and thirdly, lung-filling capacity is restored or enlarged. In
short, you can do more, and recover more quickly from doing it.

Bicycling, in particular, is a complete exercise. Not only are the
legs, the body's largest accessory blood-pumping mechanism, used
extensively, but also arm, shoulder, back, abdominal and
diaphragmatic muscles. At the same time there is enough flexibility
so that muscle groups can be worked individually, and of course
pace can be set to suit the rider.

A word about weight control. Bicycling or other exercise will help
your body's tone and figure. But for weight loss, eat less food. A
brisk ride does not entitle you to apple pie and ice cream. Regular

cycling burns about 300 calories per hour and hill climbing or racing about 600 per hour. Your body uses up about 150 calories per hour anyway, and so in the case of regular cycling this means a burn-up of an extra 150 calories per hour. At 3,600 calories per pound, it would take 24 hours of riding to lose this amount. It's much simpler just to eat less. Curiously enough, cycling may help you to do this. Regular exercise can change the metabolic balance of the body and restore normal automatic appetite control so that you eat no more than you actually need.

A serious health hazard for the urban cyclist is the breathing of highly polluted air. See Traffic jamming for more information on this subject.

Ecology

Great Britain is literally drowning in pollutants and many of them come from transportation machinery. In cities the internal combustion engine is a prime offender, contributing up to 85 per cent of all air pollution,* and of an especially noxious quality. The effluents from petroleum engines hang in the air and chemically interact with other substances and sunlight to form even deadlier poisons. Living in a major city is the same thing as smoking two packs of cigarettes a day.†

All city transportation contributes to pollution. Trains run on electricity generated in plants fired by fossil fuels or deadly atomic reactors. But as anyone who has been lucky enough to live through a taxicab strike or vehicle ban knows, cars and buses are the real problem. I shall never forget a winter many years ago when a friend and I came driving into New York City late at night after a holiday in Canada. To my amazement, the lights of the city shone like jewels and each building was clear and distinct. From the west bank of the Hudson river I could for the first (and perhaps only) time in my life see Manhattan and the Bronx in perfect detail from beginning to end, and even beyond to Brooklyn and her bridges. As we crossed the George Washington Bridge the air was clean and fresh, and the city, usually an object of horror and revulsion, was astoundingly beautiful and iridescent. The explanation was simple:

* Reinow, L. & L., *Moment in the Sun* (Ballantine, New York).
† Commoner, Barry, *The Closing Circle* (Jonathan Cape, London).

enough snow had fallen to effectively eliminate vehicle traffic for a couple of days. No vehicles, no junk in the air. A better world.

Arguments against motorized transport are usually dismissed as idealistic and impractical and on the grounds that the time-saving characteristics of such vehicles are essential. The fact is that even pedestrians are easily able to drone past most traffic, and of course bicycles can do even better. A saving in physical effort is realized, but few of us are healthy enough to need this, or dismiss inhaling the poisons (equivalent to two packs of cigarettes a day) which necessarily accompany the internal combustion engine.

Walking, roller-skating, or riding a bicycle is an efficient use of energy and reduces wastage. Professor Rice in *Technology Review* has calculated that a cyclist can do 1,000 miles on the food energy equivalent of a gallon of petrol, which will move a car only some 20 or 30 miles. His figures are based on a 40-pound bicycle, and could probably be doubled for a 20-pound lightweight. Facts and figures be as they may, utilizing a 100-horsepower, 3,000-pound behemoth to move one single 150-pound person a few miles is like using an atomic bomb to kill a canary. Great Britain runs neck and neck with the United States in its ability to consume and waste, and in relation to the size of her population utilizes a disproportionately large proportion of the world's resources. For example, we import fish meal from African countries where people are starving, to feed beef herds, and then wonder why people down there don't like us. Great Britain's dependence on imports needs no documentation. The point is, many of the commodities we take for granted are gained at considerable expense to a world hurting badly for food and other necessities. Using a bicycle is a starting antidote to the horrors of consumerism.

Which brings us to the most positive series of reasons for trying to use bicycles at every opportunity. Basically, this is that it will enhance your life, bringing to it an increase in quality of experience which will find its reflection in everything you do.

Well! You have to expect that I would believe bicycling is a good idea, but how do I get off expressing the notion that bicycling is philosophically and morally sound? Because it is something that *you do*, not something that is done to you. Need I chronicle the oft-cited concept of increasing alienation in our lives? The mechanization of work and daily activities, the hardships our industrial society places in the way of loving and fulfilling relationships and family life, the tremendous difficulties individuals experience trying to influence political and economic decisions which affect them and others?

Of course there will always be people who say that they like things the way they are. They find the Tube really interesting, or insist on driving a chrome bomb and rattling everybody's windows. But the fact is that trains are crowded, dirty, impersonal and *noisy*, and nearly all cars are ego-structured worthless tin junk (with bikes the more you pay the less you get).

The most important effect of mechanical contraptions is that they defeat consciousness. Consciousness, self-awareness, and development are the prerequisites for a life worth living. Now look at what happens to you on a bicycle. It's immediate and direct. *You* pedal. *You* make decisions. *You* experience the tang of the air and the surge of power as you bite into the road. You're vitalized. As you hum along you fully and gloriously experience the day, the sunshine, the clouds, the breezes. You're alive! You are going some place, and it is *you* who are doing it. Awareness increases, and each day becomes a little more important to you. With increased awareness you see and notice more, and this further reinforces awareness.

Each time you insert *you* into a situation, each time *you* experience, you fight against alienation and impersonality, you build consciousness and identity. You try to understand things in the ways that are important to you. And these qualities carry over into everything you do.

An increased value on one's own life is the first step in social conscience and politics. Because to you life is dear and important and fun, you are much more easily able to understand why this is also true for a Vietnamese, a black, or a Tobago islander. Believe it. The salvation of the world is the development of personality and identity for everybody in it. Much work, many lifetimes. But a good start for you is *Get a bicycle*!

2 Choosing mounts

What kind of bike for you? The main points are covered here, but
you should also look over the sections on riding, fitting, touring,
and racing to get the best idea of what's going on and what your
particular needs may be before arriving at a final selection. This
chapter is broken down into three sections: adult full-size bicycles;
other bicycles; and children's bicycles. Technical information given
for adult bicycles applies to any bicycle and will not be repeated in
each section.

Adult bicycles

Bicycle categories by function break down into six slightly
overlapping groups:

(1) The balloon tyre bomber, built entirely of steel, with a heavy,
robust frame, wide 2-in tyres, and a 1- or 2-speed rear hub equipped
with pedal operated coaster brake. This is the classic American bike
for really tough work like riding on beaches and fields, newspaper
delivery, collisions, and absolutely no care. With a weight of up to
65 pounds it can be mighty hard pedalling on anything but dead
flat terrain.

(2) The heavy roadster, also built entirely of steel, with wide 1½-in
tyres, roller lever rim brakes, and 1- or 3-speed hub gears. Weight
about 50 pounds. This is the European version of the balloon tyre
bomber, and is sometimes called an 'Africa' model because of its
popularity in developing countries for transporting heavy loads,
bouncing across deserts and through jungles and the like. They were
used extensively by the North Vietnamese for transporting supplies
during their last war with the Americans. A frame and forks designed
for taking the sting out of bumps make them particularly steady
and graceful, and for this reason they are also very popular with
Netherlands housewives. The Netherlands are mostly flat however,
and pedalling them where there are any kinds of hills is hard work.

GRIFFITHS'S UNIVERSAL CYCLES.

CLYDE WORKS.

"IXL," Price £15.

"CLYDE," Price £18.

Telegraphic Address :—
GRIFFITHS,
Clyde Works,
Wolverhampton.

PRICE LISTS
ON
APPLICATION.

"SPECIAL," Price £10.

"UNIVERSAL" No. 1, Price £14.
"UNIVERSAL" SAFETY No. 2, Price £10 10s.

"UNIVERSAL," Price £18.

S. GRIFFITHS & SONS, Heath Town, WOLVERHAMPTON.

(3) The sports roadster, also called tourist model or English racer, with lighter steel frame and mudguards, $1\frac{3}{8}$-in tyres, calliper rim brakes, and 1-, 3-, 4-, or 5-speed hub gears. This is the bike for utility use such as local errands, shopping, lots of stop-and-go riding, short trips, and gives good durability with minimal maintenance. Weight about 35 pounds.

(4) The lightweight tourist can be as the sports roadster above, but with 5- or 10-speed derailleur gears, or it can be as the touring/commuting bike below, with a truly lightweight frame, $1\frac{1}{4}$-in tyres, and steel or alloy components. In either case it usually features flat handlebars and a wide mattress saddle. Weight from 25 to 35 pounds. It is a hybrid intended to give the light weight and gear range of the touring/commuting bike with the riding position of the sports roadster, and is suitable for local errands, commuting, and short ride touring up to 25 miles.

(5) The touring/commuting bicycle features a lightweight frame, steel or alloy components depending on model, $1\frac{1}{4}$-in tyres, calliper rim brakes (sometimes a disc brake is fitted to the rear wheel), 5-, 10-, 12-, 15-, or 18-speed derailleur gears, narrow 'racing' saddle, and dropped handlebars. Weight from 21 to 35 pounds. These bikes are for general use, hilly terrain, and for tours of over 25 miles. Far more lively and responsive than the sports roadster, the frame is still designed for reasonable riding comfort over rough ground and easy directional stability.

(6) Racing bicycles are as the touring/commuting bicycles above, but usually feature narrow-profile tyres, close-ratio gears, and a 'stiff' frame designed for quick handling and maximum translation of pedalling effort into forward motion. They are thus relatively more fragile and harsher riding than the touring/commuting bicycles, but on smooth roads in the hands of an experienced rider can be both comfortable and exceptionally swift. They are inappropriate for most commuting and utility use. Weight as little as 19 pounds.
Racing bicycles for use on wooden tracks are utterly stark greyhounds, with a single fixed gear, no brakes, and a weight of 16 to 17 pounds. Only the most expert of riders can use these on roads.

For the sake of simplicity I am going to speak of 3-speed bicycles, by which I mean those with 3- to 5-speed internal hub gears; and

10-speed bicycles, those with 5- to 18-speed derailleur gears. If this is Greek to you, hold on for just a bit.

I hope your decision will be to get a 10-speed bicycle. They can be set up to suit nearly any rider, job, or purpose, are dynamic, responsive, and vibrant, the most comfortable, and give the most speed for the least effort so that you will get more out of riding and will be encouraged to do even more. They are also the easiest to service. Initial cost may seem high, but experience has shown that most people who start with a heavyweight or sports roadster soon find themselves desiring (and acquiring) a 10-speed bike. It takes no longer than the first time such a machine sweeps by them going up a hill. My advice is to save money by buying a 10-speed bike in the first place. You get the most fun and turn-on for your money, and you get it right away.

Assigning utility functions to a 3-speed bike, and touring and racing functions to a 10-speed bike, is only broadly accurate. Actually, a 10-speed can be set up for almost any job or purpose except beach riding. The same machine, with minor modifications, can compete in a race, go on a camping tour, be ridden cross-country through streams and muddy fields, and haul groceries or newspapers. It can even pull a trailer. The only crucial difference between the 3- and 10-speed is the method of operation for the gears: the 3-speed can be shifted to the correct gear at any time, the 10-speed must be shifted while the bicycle is in motion. It's easy once you get the knack, and the 10-speed's efficiency outweighs the disadvantage of initial unfamiliarity. If you get stopped in a 'wrong' (inefficient) gear, it is easy to shift once you are under way again.

A 3-speed hub

Rear derailleur and freewheel for a 10-speed bike

The question of durability is largely a function of bicycle model and weight and rider sense. Ten-speeds range from ultra-light (20 pounds) alloy models to heavy (35 pounds) steel models. My first 10-speed was a sturdy machine with steel wheels which I not only rode hard and fast over bumpy streets, but also used for games of bicycle tag in the woods and fields, as well as just plain cross-country and back-trail riding. It held up just fine.

The classic down-swept handlebars of the 10-speed are not a requirement; you can equip or buy such a bike with conventional tourist handlebars, although it wouldn't be to your advantage to do so (more on handlebars later). With the exception of the cheaper models, 10-speed bikes have the much better centre-pull calliper brakes, rather than the coaster or side-pull calliper brakes usually supplied with 3-speed bikes. Comfort is sometimes cited in favour of the 3-speed. The fact is that the 10-speed has a wider variety of riding positions, allows you to utilize more muscles to greater advantage, and is therefore much less tiring to ride than a 3-speed.

The choice of bike is therefore largely governed by the type of person you are and how heavy you want to get into bicycling, the contents of your purse, and real-life physical factors such as the quality of your neighbourhood and the number of stairs you climb every day. It is the first of these which is the most relevant, and what you must assess is how much consciousness you want to bring to bicycling. Not everybody is interested in the boiling scald of blood through their veins as they sprint up the highway, or the eerie desolation of a chill night. Get a 3-speed if: you are not terribly interested in bicycling and just want something you can stick in the shed or basement to use for local jaunts once or twice a month (if you're really in this category and can do so, rent machines); you or the prospective rider are not at all mechanically inclined and don't care to be; you need a knock-around bike for use by several different people or just want a worry-free machine. There is nothing degenerate about this last state of affairs. There are times when I prefer the totally casual spirit of the 3-speed, where one can just drop it on the spot, bash it around, and in general not think about what is going on. But this is the exception, not the rule. Over the long haul, the 10-speed is just so much better, so much more rewarding, that it will surely overcome any diffidence you feel about bicycling and make you an enthusiast.

Expense is a consideration only if your absolute maximum is £20, which restricts you to a serviceable used 3-speed. If you have £25 to £30 you can buy a used bike that at least has 10 speeds, if nothing else. More on this later.

Most of the more pragmatic considerations in type of bicycle are physical:

For hilly terrain get a 10-speed, no matter what.

If you live at the end of a long and rocky road you may want a sturdier model 10-speed. This is also a question of rider weight. For example, many years ago I gave a 100-pound cousin a Peugeot UO-8. At 27 pounds this is closer to an ultra-light 20 pound racer than a 35 pound heavyweight. My cousin lived at the top of a steep, winding, rocky dirt road about one-eighth of a mile long, and his idea of fun was to blaze down the hill as fast as he could. The Peugeot held up fine but with a heavier rider would have shown noticeably greater wear and tear. Bear in mind that 'sturdier' bikes are built

Rushing a rise

that way in order to overcome inherently inferior materials and manufacturing techniques. The amount of extra strength gained is debatable, and only at cost to the power to weight ratio.

Rider sense and skill also affect durability. I have ridden racing bikes equipped with lightweight tubular tyres through fields and woods. It is just a question of watching where you go and not overstressing the machine. A rider who sits on his saddle like a sack of oats when his bike hits a bump needs a machine that can absorb punishment; a rider who moves with his bike, allowing it to pivot underneath him over the bumps, can use a lighter, more responsive machine.

Stair climbing apartment dwellers need to consider weight if they intend to keep their bike at home, oftentimes a necessity if the bike is not to be stolen. The two sensible answers are a 10-speed, or the Bickerton Portable (see Folding Bicycles). Other folding bikes, mini-bicycles, and 3-speeds run 35 and 40 pounds, and are a clumsy nuisance to lug up two to four flights of stairs.

Using a car or public transportation to get to a departure point for a trip is also part of carrying. Any 10-speed is easier to take apart than a 3-speed, and a good quality 10-speed will have quick release wheels which come off at the flick of a lever. The only thing easier is the Bickerton Portable, which in under 60 seconds folds into a bag 30 in × 20 in × 9 in. This makes it a hands down winner when storage space is limited. Next in line is the 10-speed. With the wheels off it can be hung in a closet. It is light enough to be hung from the ceiling or a wall via brackets or pulleys. It can be kept in the bathtub or shower stall. Under any circumstances it will be easier to deal with than a 3-speed.

For frequency of repair the 3-speed has it all over the 10-speed. All the 3-speed hub will need for years is a monthly shot of oil. Once it does go however, it is much too complicated to fix, and most bicycle shops will simply replace it. It is also considerably less efficient than the 10-speed design, and transmits less pedal effort to the rear wheel. The 10-speed, while more efficient, requires more frequent adjustment and servicing. However, because the parts are all quite simple and out in the open where they are easy to get at, this is easy to do. In fact, it is part of the fun of riding. The vitality and responsiveness of the 10-speed is such that you come to enjoy fine-tuning your bike.

Perhaps now you have started to form a notion of what kind of bike you would like to have. But there are still more types: mini-bikes, folding bikes, tandems, tricycles, and prices for this bewildering array vary from £40 to £700. I will discuss these under Other bicycles, but first here is some technical information to guide you through the maze and help you to get your money's worth.

The significant components of a bicycle are the frame, brakes, rims, tyres and hubs; gears and gear-changing hardware, chain-wheel, cranks, and pedals; and stem, handlebars, and saddle. According to the grade of component selected by the manufacturer, the price for a 3-speed will range from £50 to £100, from £70 to £180 for production line 10-speeds, and £180 and up for custom-made bikes. Manufacturers tend to assemble rather than manufacture bicycles, getting the components from a number of independent companies. Hence, two bikes in the same price category from two different brand name 'manufacturers' sometimes have exactly the same parts.

The frame

The frame is the heart and soul of a bicycle. It is the determining factor of bicycle weight, and the more you pay the lighter the weight for the same strength. Frames are not meant to be rigid or unyielding, but rather to absorb irregularities from the road surface.

seat post

top tube

head tube

seat stays

seat tube

forks

drop outs

down tube

chain stays

bottom bracket
shell

drop outs

Called resiliency or twang or flex, this is a function of quality of materials and manufacturing methods, and gives better bikes more springiness and vitality. There is no way to improve a cheap frame. Other components can be modified or changed but the frame endures, and it should be the first focus of your attention when considering a prospective bike.

Inexpensive coaster brake, 3-speed, and cheap 10-speed bikes use seamed tubing, made by wrapping a long, flat strip of steel into a tube and then welding it together (electrically) at high temperature. Better bikes use a seamless tubing which is even in bore throughout. The best bikes use special, cold-drawn alloy steel seamless double-butted tubing. Double-butted means that while the outside diameter of the tube remains constant, it is thicker on the inside at the ends, where greater strength is needed.

Conventional Tubing

Double-butted Tubing

The method by which the frame parts are attached to each other is important. Bikes with seamed tubing are usually just stuck together and welded, leaving a smooth joint. This is the commonest and weakest type of assembly. The welding, done at high temperatures, robs the metal of strength. High-carbon bike tube steel becomes brittle and subject to fatigue when heated. With better bikes the frame is lugged and brazed, rather than welded.

lugged   smooth

Lugging is the addition of reinforcing metal at stress points, and brazing is done at lower temperatures than welding. Make sure that the job has been done cleanly and neatly on any prospective bike you examine.

The very, very best frames are Reynolds 531, Columbus, or Falk, double-butted, with Reynolds generally considered the finest. Reynolds 531 comes in several grades. Read the label to see what you are getting:

Only the top tube, seat tube, and down tube are Reynolds 531 plain gauge tubing.

All the tubing is Reynolds 531 plain gauge.

Only the top tube, seat tube, and down tube are Reynolds 531 double butted tubing.

All the tubing is
Reynolds 531
double butted.

All the tubing is
Reynolds 753 double
butted.

All the tubing is
Reynolds 531 Special
Lightweight double
butted.

Reynolds 531 Special Lightweight tubing used in place of
Reynolds 531 double butted will give a frame approximately 1
pound lighter in weight. There is no point to using this material
unless you spend the money to equip the frame with
ultra-lightweight components – say about £300 or more. Reynolds
531 Special Lightweight and 753 tubing are so light that tolerances
in frame assembly and brazing temperatures are absolutely critical.
The slightest error can result in a pile of junk. Do not buy a frame of
these materials unless it is from a top quality master builder.

Chances are you will not be getting double-butted tubing unless
you have elected to spend upwards of £160. However, you should
at least get seamless lugged tubing, which is used even on low-cost
quality bikes. Here are three tests for frame quality. Differences
between price ranges should be evident.

(1) Weight. Electric welded tubing and joints are heavy in order
to overcome inherent weaknesses of this type of construction and
materials.

(2) Lift the bike a couple of inches and bounce it on the wheels.
Better frames have more twang and bounce.

(3) Stand to one side of the bike. Hold nearest handlebar with one
hand and saddle with the other and tilt bike away from you. Place
one foot on end of bottom bracket axle and give a *gentle* push. A
good frame will flex and then spring right back. Try several different
bikes to get the feel of it and be careful, the idea is to find frames
that will give with a gentle push, not bend anything you may
encounter. If enough force is applied cheap frames will bend –
permanently.

Bicycle frames are also available in aluminium, aluminium and
graphite, and titanium. These frames are very light and very, very

expensive. I do not advise buying such a frame until you have owned at least a couple of bikes, and know exactly what you are getting into.

The design and geometry of a bicycle frame varies according to its intended purpose and weight and type of rider. The commonest design for touring and general use is 72° parallel. This means that the angle to the top tube formed by the seat and head tubes is 72°.

This is the standard design and gives an excellent combination of road holding, shock absorption, and power transmission. It is very good for bumpy urban streets. Many variations are possible. The frame built by Jack Taylor for his Superlight Tourist model uses a 73° seat and 71° head. It is designed for stability and comfort with heavy touring loads. Road and track racing frames use steeper angles, such as 73°, 73½°, 74°, or 74½° parallel, or combinations like 74° head and 73° seat. The ride is stiffer, but more power is transmitted to the wheels. Some riders use these frames for touring and around town sprinting, but they are inadvisable for anything but very smooth roads. Out-and-out racing frames use shorter fork blades and seat and chain stays to bring the wheels in closer, and cannot be fitted with mudguards. The rake of the front fork, e.g., the distance between the front wheel axle and a line formed by extending the head tube downwards, is usually less on racing

fork tube

fork crown

arms

drop-outs

trail or rake

frames than on touring frames, and this also contributes to a stiffer ride and brighter handling.

Rider weight must also be taken into account. A frame and forks that are stiff for a person weighing 10 stone may be soft for a person weighing 13 stone. Frame design is a complicated subject, well covered by Albert Eisentraut in 'The Frame', a chapter in Tom Cuthbertson's *Bike Tripping* (Ten Speed Press, Box 4310, Berkeley, CA 94704 USA), and by Joe Kossak in *Bicycle Frames* (World Publications, obtainable from Selpress Books, Suite 413 4th Floor, 16 Berkeley Street, London W1X 6AP, and The Cyclists' Touring Club, 69 Meadrow, Godalming, Surrey GU7 3HS).

Summary

One of the most satisfying and important features of a good bike is responsiveness and whip-like flex that you can feel with your whole body. The main determinants of this quality are the frame materials and construction.

In 10-speed bikes expect the following:
Under £80   – Seamed, smooth-joint frame.
£80 to £95   – Seamless, lugged-joint frame.
£95 to £130 – Seamless, lugged-joint frame, with main tubes of
                 531 plain gauge or equivalent.
Over £130   – Seamless, double-butted, lugged-joint,
                 low-temperature brazed frame.

The brakes

It is the nature of bicycling accidents that the bicyclist more often runs into something than is run into. Good, well-adjusted brakes are vital, and especially in traffic. There are three basic types of brakes: pedal or hand operated hub or coaster brakes; hand operated disc brakes; and hand operated calliper rim brakes.

Pedal operated coaster brakes are only for small children who lack the necessary strength to actuate hand levers. Although they are easy to apply, they are hard to control and can lock a wheel, causing a skid. They do not have actual stopping power. It's a skid or next to nothing. Skidding is a bad way to stop since (a) it takes too long; (b) at high speeds it is excessively exciting; and (c) wear and tear on the tyres is very high. A coaster brake has poor heat dissipating qualities, and can burn out in the middle of a long downhill descent. The sole advantage of a coaster brake is that it remains effective in wet weather, when calliper rim brakes may lose up to 80 per cent of braking power.

Disc brakes are powerful, and effective in wet weather. They are often fitted to tandems and tricycles. The disc brake is a heavy unit however, and for this reason is not commonly used on lightweight bicycles. The exception is the light and very beautiful Phil Wood disc brake which costs over £100 and is not worth fitting to any but the finest machines. I would advise disc brakes only for tandems and tricycles, very heavily loaded touring bicycles, off road woods and BMX bicycles, and possibly, commuting bicycles used often in wet weather.

Hand operated calliper brakes come in two types, centre- and side-pull.

Side-pull brakes come in two versions: inexpensive, for use on less costly bikes, and expensive, for use on fancier racing and touring bikes. The inexpensive side-pull brake is, in Americanese, strictly from hunger, and cannot be compared in performance to a good

brake blocks

centre-pull   side-pull

quality side-pull or centre-pull brake. It works, but only just, and requires constant adjustment.

Far superior is the centre-pull brake, which pulls from the centre and thus works in balance, and is more even, precise, and powerful. The good quality side-pull brake is built to a different purpose from the centre-pull. It has a rigid design which affords precise control at high speeds. The centre-pull is softer and less rigid. The brake lever-pressure necessary for a complete stop is less than that for a quality side-pull, but at high speeds the centre-pull can 'snatch', e.g. exert more deceleration than necessary or, for a racing bike, safe. Both types stop equally well; the quality side-pull is better for speed control.

Quality side-pull brakes start at about £20 per set, and can cost up to £75. They are only worth considering for bikes costing £160 and up. For ordinary road use the much less expensive (about £12) centre-pull design is perfectly suitable, and since required force on the levers is less, even preferable for touring and utility cycles. Bear in mind that distinctions between the two types are quite fine; the winning bicycle of the 1977 Tour de France was equipped with centre-pull brakes.

Good brand names are Campagnolo, Shimano, Modolo, Dia-Compe, Weinmann, Universal, and Mafac. Be sure that the levers on the brand you select fit your grip. Some brakes are supplied with a second 'touring' or 'safety' lever set underneath and in line with the top, straight section of the handlebars:

These increase the number of positions from which the brakes can be operated, and this can be very useful in traffic or for comfort when making long downhill descents. However, safety levers require a relatively greater length of travel in order to actuate the brake mechanism. If the brakes are not adjusted to close tolerances, it is possible under hard braking for the safety lever to bang uselessly on the handlebar while you carry on to destruction. Under these circumstances a safety lever is a liability rather than an asset.

I therefore recommend safety levers only for those riders able to keep their brakes adjusted to close tolerances.

One development for the mechanically feeble-minded is self-adjusting brake mechanisms and levers. These units are heavy and mechanically complex, and are more trouble than they are worth. Any cyclist, at the minimum, should know how to adjust his or her brakes.

Until recently, one unnerving characteristic of rim brakes was that in wet conditions, braking power was reduced by up to 80 per cent. To compensate, manufacturers redesigned brake block patterns and materials. Wet braking power is much better but now, in dry conditions, over-zealous application of the front brake can pitch the rider right over the handlebars. Anyone who has slithered helplessly down a long hill in the wet will not mind developing the ability to handle modern rim brakes in the dry. Once the skill is mastered, for ultimate braking power I recommend fitting Mathauser brake blocks (about £8 from Scott/Mathauser Corp, Box 1333, Sun Valley, Idaho 83353, USA). Less dear, but effective, are Carrea brake blocks.

A variant of the centre-pull is the cantilever brake, which pivots on a boss brazed on to the fork blades and seat stays:

Cantilever

Powerful, and less likely to 'whip' (where the whole brake assembly judders back and forth), cantilever brakes are good for the heavily laden tourist, cyclo-cross, and tandems and tricycles. There is also a saving of six ounces in weight over the conventional centre-pull. However, only cyclo-cross and custom-made frames are likely to have the requisite brazed-on bosses necessary to mount cantilevers.

Rims, tyres, and hubs

There are three types of rims. The Westwood, for use with $1\frac{1}{2}$-in tyres and roller lever brakes, is seen only on heavy roadsters and utility bikes. Modern bikes use Endrick rims, with wire-on $1\frac{3}{8}$-in to $1\frac{1}{4}$-in tyres (called 'clinchers' in the United States), or sprint rims, with tubular tyres ('sew-ups' for Americanos and 'singles' for Aussies).

Wire-on tyres are available in a wide range of weights, and are more durable and far easier to repair than tubular tyres. Tubulars offer the ultimate in light weight and minimal rolling resistance, but are expensive (£5 to £25) and puncture easily. Because the tube is sewn into the tyre it is impractical to repair on the road, necessitating the carrying of a spare tyre which must be glued onto the rim. This is actually a quick process, but it is a drag to lug the spare tyre with you wherever you go, since it cannot be left on the bike when parking on the street.

wire-on

casing tube bead rim

tubular

Wire-on tyres are available in a range of models from heavy-duty knobby speedway through to high pressure (90 lb/sq in) narrow profile. These latter will match the performance of a heavy tubular, so only the lightest tubulars are worth using, and then only for racing and very fast day rides. Wire-on tyres are the sensible choice for any other use.

Both wire-on tyres and tubulars fitted with a two piece Presta valve can be made puncture-resistant through the injection of a liquid sealant, adding about 2 ounces to the tyre weight. The tyre is then proofed against direct punctures, as from a nail, but not against slashes or cuts, as from glass. The sealant can also be used to repair an existing puncture. Sealant is well worth considering if you ride regularly on littered urban streets, and on long tours. At the time of writing sealant is not yet obtainable in the UK, but can be ordered by post (about £1) from

The Palo Alto Bicycle Shop
171 University Avenue, PO Box 1276, Palo Alto, CA 94302 USA.

Rims are made either of aluminium alloy or steel. Less costly bikes feature steel rims, which are the most heavy and durable. Better bikes feature aluminium alloy rims which are lighter but of course more fragile. Really brutal riding over bumpy terrain may require steel rims but I have found the alloy wheels entirely satisfactory. An important consideration is that in the wet aluminium alloy rims offer much better braking power than steel rims.

Hubs also come in steel or aluminium alloy. They may use conventional bolts, requiring the use of a spanner to remove the wheel, or quick-release levers which work instantly. This is a desirable feature for bikes that will be stored in the closet, transported by automobile often, or left locked on the street (you take the wheels with you).

The hub illustrated is a high-flange design used for racing and sport riding. The flange is the part with all the holes where the spokes are attached. A low-flange design requires longer spokes and gives a softer ride. It is often used for touring and commuting bikes.

A recent development are hubs with sealed bearings which do not require lubrication or adjustment. In ordinary service these units are durable. However, very wet, muddy, or dusty conditions may make servicing a requirement, and this can be difficult to do. Good sealed bearing hub brands are Weyless, Phil Wood, and Hi-E (£20 to £45). The new Viscount hubs are OK, but avoid at all costs the old Viscount known as Lambert. Campagnolo, Shimano, OMAS, Normandy, Sunshine, Zeus, and Sun Tour are all good brand names for conventional design hubs (£10 to £60).

The hubs, after the frame, are perhaps the most vital component of a bike. Cheap hubs run rough, wear out quickly, and are inclined to promote spoke breakage. Get the best hubs you can afford.

Beeston Humber Tandem

Gear-changing mechanisms, cranks and chainwheel, and pedals

Nearly all 3-speed bikes use Sturmey-Archer, Sun Tour, or Shimano multi-speed hubs, no matter what price range. At the core of the design of the 10-speed bike are the derailleurs, which shift the chain from sprocket to sprocket. Differences between brands are to be found in weight, smoothness and precision of shifting, and durability. However, each manufacturer offers several different grades of derailleurs in two different categories, competition and touring. For example, the Campagnolo Nuevo Record (competition) and Rally (touring) are top of the line products of irreproachable beauty and performance, as well they might be with price tags of about £26 each. Campagnolo's Vallentino economy model on the other hand, has not been well received, and there are plenty of other inexpensive units which are better.

Simplex is a popular brand noted for smooth shifting and lightness. Newer models feature main bodies of alloy rather than of delrin, a plastic that was prone to disintegrating. Huret is another popular brand, although some models are constructed so that just a little dirt and oil will gum up the works. They have to be kept clean. A most attractive new Huret model is the Duopar, which uses a double parallelogram design instead of the conventional single parallelogram. The result is exceptionally easy shifting, particularly under heavy loads such as generated by tandems and touring bikes. The Duopar is made of aluminium alloy and titanium and weighs only 11 ounces complete with mounting bracket. At the time of writing the Duopar leaves a massive £40 hole in the pocket, but a new model sans titanium parts is anticipated and should go for a more reasonable price.

The Japanese have justifiably cornered the derailleur gear market for some years. Shimano produces a comprehensive line of derailleurs. Their low cost Lark and Eagle models are reliable but heavy. The medium cost Titlist and 600 series derailleurs are much lighter and give excellent performance. The Dura-Ace and Crane units are fully competitive with the best European units, and have the edge on price. Shimano also produces a semi-automatic derailleur called the Positron, which positions the chain correctly for any gear selected, thus avoiding missed shifts and chain grind. I have found the Positron a good unit for novice riders who are all thumbs.

Best value for money today are the Maeda Sun Tour series derailleurs, popular with tourists and a good choice for beginning riders. They have wide range, and positive shifting under load, e.g. when pedalling pressure is maintained while shifting. This is a common novice error, and a recurrent problem for heavily laden tourists climbing hills. Campagnolo and Shimano units perform perfectly when shifted correctly, but can jam up and grind when shifted under load.

Gearing is a major factor to consider in the choice of derailleurs, and this subject is covered under Fitting. Read this chapter before purchasing a bike.

There are four different places on a bicycle commonly used to mount the levers for shifting derailleur gears:

down tube

stem

top tube

handle bar

Each method has advantages and disadvantages. In my own opinion, simplest is best. Down-tube mounting allows the use of short cables giving maximum feel and quick response when shifting. Stem and top-tube mounts are more convenient when flat or all-rounder handlebars are used, but in a crash can dig you nastily in the gut or crotch. Handlebar-end mounting requires long cables which give a sloppier response. It also requires the drilling of holes in the handlebar, and I know of instances where this led to corrosion and a complete snapping apart of the handlebar while the rider was under way. Down-tube mounting is simplest and safest.

bolts

Cranks and chainwheels are made of aluminium alloy or steel. Design varies in the method of fastening to the bottom bracket axle:

one-piece   cottered   Ashtabula

Fine bikes use cotterless cranks and chainwheels of dural, an aluminium alloy. Campagnolo and Shimano are the top brands, with prices to £90. Best value is the Sugino 'Maxy' (about £18). Zeus, Stronglight, TA, SR, and Williams are all good makes. Less expensive bikes use steel cotterless, or alloy cottered, cranks and chainwheels. Cheap bikes use cottered steel. A one-piece design called the Ashtabula is used on many American-made bikes. A freewheeling chainwheel by Shimano which allows derailleur gear shifts without pedalling may be useful for beginning riders. However, it is mechanically complex, and of too recent development for a reliability rating.

A sealed-bearing bottom bracket unit with a titanium axle is available from OMAS (about £45) to fit Campagnolo, Dura-Ace, and SR Royal crank arms. Less dear is the Stronglight 651 bottom bracket (about £22). Sealed bearings require no adjustment or lubrication in ordinary service. In very wet or dirty conditions servicing may be required, and this can be difficult to do.

An elliptical chainwheel known as the Durham is available as an accessory (Durham Bicycles, 3944 Marathon Street, Los Angeles, CA 90029 USA, about £15).

Elliptical chainwheels are not as effective as circular chainwheels when used for racing. However, at low speeds and under load, as when hill climbing or in frequent stop-and-go traffic riding, they can have a power advantage. Elliptical chainwheel enthusiasts claim that over long distances the lowered cadence rate (pedal revolutions per minute) is less fatiguing. Other cyclists disagree. There seems to be no hard and fast rule. It is something you have to try for yourself. One limitation of current elliptical chainwheel designs is that no front gear changer can be used, so that the maximum possible number of gears is seven with a derailleur system.

Pedals come in three basic types (1) the classic rubber-tread platform; (2) cage design; and (3) metal platform.

1   2   3

Cage and metal platform pedals can be used with toe clips and cleats, rubber platform pedals cannot. Metal platform pedals offer good foot weight distribution. The thin cage design can induce foot cramps on long tours. Pedals may have no ball bearings, adjustable bearings, or sealed bearings. Pedals with no ball bearings are found on only the cheapest and most chintzy of bikes, and should be avoided like the plague. Adjustable ball bearing pedals are found on low cost quality bikes through to superbikes, and range in price from £3 for the good value Lyotard to £60 for the Campagnolo Super Record road pedals with titanium spindles. Sealed bearing pedals are lubrication and maintenance free, but only to a point. In very wet or dirty conditions even a sealed bearing pedal (or hub or bottom bracket) will require maintenance. In this event, adjustable bearing pedals are easier to service. But in ordinary conditions sealed bearing pedals will not require lubrication or adjustment. A top quality sealed bearing pedal is the Barelli Supreme (about £23), which features replaceable platform cages. Another excellent sealed bearing pedal is the Cinelli M71 (about £30), which uses a special shoe plate that locks on to the pedal thus obviating need for toe clips and straps. It is only for racing use.

Mattress

Racing

Saddle

Three-speed bikes generally have a mattress design wide saddle
with coil springs. Racing bike saddles are long and narrow to
minimize friction between the legs.

Less expensive saddles are of plastic, the best of leather, with
Brooks the acknowledged leader. A choice between the two depends
somewhat on the type of riding and conditions. Leather wants a
minimum of 500 miles of riding to become supple and properly
broken in, but once done the fit is so good you will keep the saddle
from one bike to another. Plastic needs no breaking in, and is
impervious to weather, making it a good choice for cyclo-cross
machines and bikes that will be left out in the rain. A plastic saddle
such as the Unica (12 oz) is half the weight of the leather Brooks
Pro (25 oz), and this is a decisive factor in short-distance and
track-competition events. The problem with plastic is that in warm
weather it has you slipping about in your own sweat. A compromise
has been sought in models such as the Milremo Super de Luxe,
which are plastic covered with foam and leather, softer to ride, and
a good choice for riders who will cover a lot of rough roads or paths.
Also popular and comfortable are suede covered saddles.

I own and ride a number of different cycles, and have not got the time to switch my Brooks Pro from bike to bike, or break in half a dozen saddles. I find the suede covered plastic Milremo Professional excellent. Other good brands are Cinelli and Unica.

People with problem posteriors should consider an Avocet saddle, obtainable in 10 different models by post from:

The Palo Alto Bicycle Shop
171 University Avenue, PO Box 1276, Palo Alto, CA 94302 USA.

Avocet saddles come in men's and women's designs in different grades of racing and touring models. They are orthopaedically engineered and feature padding at the pressure-points where the pelvic bones contact the saddle. Price about £10 to £20, depending on model.

In leather saddles only the good ones are worth buying. But whatever kind of saddle you buy, don't skimp. If you buy a bicycle and the saddle is of poor or unsuitable quality, exchange it immediately for a better one and pay the price difference. You will spend many, many miles and hours on your saddle, and if you pinch pennies you will be so oftimes reminded, for truth, by a sore behind and inflamed crotch.

Handlebars

Handlebars come in four standard designs:

Maes

Pista

Porter

Randonneur

47

The Maes pattern is the most common downswept version, and is suitable for either touring or racing. The Randonneur and Pista patterns are more specialized, and respectively are for touring and racing. On inexpensive bikes the bars are of steel, and on better bikes of aluminium alloy. The virtues of downswept bars as opposed to flat bars are discussed in Fitting.

General summary

There are many different bicycle brands, and each manufacturer usually produces upwards of a dozen or more models in different price grades. As you move from the under £80, all steel bike with seamed, smooth-joint frame, to the £400 and over superbikes, you find an increasing use of aluminium alloy for all parts of the bicycle, except the frame, which in quality machines is of cold-drawn alloy steel, and increasing sophistication of manufacture, such as lugged and brazed frame joints, double-butted frames, and cotterless cranks.

Broadly speaking, bicycles divide by function into: hub gear utility bikes designed for a soft ride and very stable handling; derailleur gear touring and commuting bikes also designed for a soft ride and stable handling, but with definitely brighter performance and lighter weight than the utility bike; combination touring and racing bikes designed for a medium ride and fairly brisk handling, and suitable for fast day rides or touring on smooth roads; and racing bikes designed for maximum speed, giving a stiff ride and very quick handling.

Now, clearly if most of your riding will be commuting on rough tarred city streets, your interests will be best served by a bike with a long wheelbase 72° parallel (73° at maximum) frame with $1\frac{1}{4}$-in tyres mounted on sturdy rims with 14-gauge spokes. Such a machine will also suit touring of a type where you frequently wander off into the boondocks down unpaved roads or paths. Suppose you are more interested in fast tours and sport riding. A stiffer frame with narrow profile high-pressure tyres will best suit your needs.

I find that beginning riders make two common errors: they under- or over-buy with respect to their needs. They are interested in cycling, but 'don't need all that fancy stuff'. So they buy an all-steel machine which turns out to be good enough for local use, but just gives a taste of what is possible when touring or racing. Two or three years later they are back at the shop laying down the money for a better quality machine.

Alternatively, a prospective cyclist wants 'the best money can buy'. He purchases a lightweight racing bike for regular commuting and quickly tires of a sore behind, endless punctures, and buckled rims. The bike goes off to moulder in a shed.

Evaluate and understand your own needs carefully, and then try to buy a bike that has some potential in reserve. For example, a 3-speed is perfectly adequate for local utility use, short commuting trips, and off-road use. A sturdy 10-speed will serve all these functions *and* be suitable for moderate touring. A lighter combination touring/racing bike can still, with careful riding, be used for commuting and even off-road riding.

Conversely, do not buy more machine than is comfortable. Own the bicycle rather than having the bicycle own you. An expensive touring/racing bike requires a certain amount of maintenance. It wants to be ridden with some degree of sensitivity. It needs protection against theft. If you know for a fact that you just want a thrasho utility bike to get you from here to there, then buy that sort of machine. A bike should be used, not be an object of deification and worry about investment.

The first B.S.A. Safety Bicycle, 1884

Recommended bicycles

I can't possibly cover and evaluate every available bike and therefore am going to make recommendations by category only, and largely to set standards. The bikes that I list are fair value for the money. Diligent shopping may net you a better buy. Many bike shops have one or two specials where you may compromise on colour or some other consideration for a good break in price. In any case apply and use the technical information I have given you. There are many fine bicycles which are not listed here and you will be doing yourself a disservice if you pass them by.

In standard 1- and 3-speed bicycles the large manufacturers offer good quality and value. In 10-speed bicycles the products of smaller firms that specialize in this kind of bicycle are usually better. Decent 10-speed bicycles are fairly refined and exact pieces of machinery, and while the use of mass production techniques for their manufacture is far from impossible, it is difficult. Bicycle dealers, mechanics, and riders report that 10-speed models from large manufacturers are sometimes poorly prepared, and are subject to breakdowns. Products of the smaller, more specialized firms are more likely to come from the factory properly assembled and ready to go, and give less trouble in service. They are also more likely to have quality features such as leather saddles and ball-bearing pedals.

On the other hand, there are many bicycle dealers and riders who swear by the large firms, and say their products are the best value in any model or price range. In the next chapter I tell you where and how to buy a bicycle, and extol the virtues of your friendly local bicycle shop. I suggest you be guided by the shop. If they say that a big brand bike is good, and are willing to back that statement up with a service guarantee, that is a very important consideration. Many, many are the miles I have gone on popular brand name bicycles. For the more esoteric racing and touring machines – say over £100 – I personally would favour a smaller company whose main business is this sort of bike. In any case, I repeat, use the technical information I have given you. In any given model there is often little to choose between three or four different manufacturers, as the components supplied (brakes, derailleurs, chainsets, and so forth) may be exactly the same.

Do not be put off if the bike you find on a showroom floor has a slightly different specification than listed here. The desirability and/or availability of components can change rapidly. Manufacturers will generally provide the best components affordable within a given price range.

For further information try the quarterly news-stand publication *Bicycle Buyers Guide* (75p), which provides road test reports on selected bicycles, and a catalogue of currently available machines.

Heavy-duty roadster

Raleigh 'Superbe'. Sturmey-Archer 3-speed gears, brazed frame with cutaway lugs, side-pull calliper brakes, dyno lighting which functions even when the bike is stationary, roller lever brakes, 26-in special section Raleigh rims, lockable steering, enclosed transmission, rear hold-all, and prop stand. Frame sizes: 21 in or 23 in. Colour: green. Weight 45–50 pounds. A modern museum piece. Very rugged.

Sports roadster

(1) Hercules Balmoral AW. Single-speed or Sturmey- Archer 3-speed gears, side-pull calliper brakes, mudguards, and pump. Sizes: men's 21 in and 23 in, ladies' 21 in. Colour: green.

(2) Raleigh Wayfarer. Single-speed or Sturmey-Archer 3-speed gears, side-pull calliper brakes, mudguards, holdall bag, pump, and chainwheel protector. Sizes: men's $19\frac{1}{2}$ in, 21 in, 23 in, ladies' $19\frac{1}{2}$ in and 21 in. Colour: blue. Dyno hub lights available.

(3) Puch Touring. Styria 3-speed gears, side-pull calliper brakes, mudguards, sprung rear carrier, pump, and chainwheel protector. Sizes: men's 20 in, $21\frac{1}{4}$ in, $22\frac{1}{2}$ in, colour green, ladies' 20 in, colour salamander.

(4) Raleigh Esquire. Sturmey-Archer 3-speed gears, side-pull calliper brakes with self-adjusting levers, reflectorized pedals, mudguards, holdall bag, pump, and chainwheel protector. Sizes: men's $19\frac{1}{2}$ in, 21 in, 23 in, colour bronze, ladies' model Caprice in sizes $19\frac{1}{2}$ in and 21 in, colour mauve. Dyno hub storage lights available.

(5) Puch Elegance. Styria 3-speed gears, side-pull calliper brakes, chrome mudguards, reflectorized pedals, sprung rear carrier, tool bag, and chainwheel protector. Men's size $21\frac{1}{4}$ in colours red or green, ladies' 20 in, colours bronze or green.

All of the above with flat bars, mattress saddles, and 26-in $\times$ $1\frac{3}{8}$-in tyres. Straightforward utility bikes suitable for town use, moderately pitched terrain, and light touring. Price range £70 to £100. Choice of bike is pretty much a matter of sorting out which accessories you need, particularly with regard to lights. See Accessories for a detailed discussion of this subject.

Lightweight tourist
(1) Raleigh Sprite DL90 and DL95. Huret 5- or 10-speed derailleur gears, self-adjusting side-pull calliper brakes, flat handlebars with stem mounted gear shift levers, vinyl mattress saddle, alloy rear carrier, 27-in steel wheels with low flange bolt-on steel hubs. Sizes: men's $21\frac{1}{2}$ in, $23\frac{1}{2}$ in, 25 in; ladies' $19\frac{1}{2}$ in, $21\frac{1}{2}$ in, $23\frac{1}{2}$ in. Colours: red, coffee, and yellow (not all sizes). Basically a sports roadster with derailleur gears and not a true lightweight. Will stand rough use.

(2) Raleigh Super Tourer DL140. Frame, forks, and stays of Reynolds 531 double butted tubing. Huret Jubilee 10-speed derailleur gears, Weinmann alloy side-pull calliper brakes, cotterless chainset, alloy flat handlebars with stem mounted shift levers, 27-in alloy wheels with high flange quick release alloy hubs, leather mattress saddle. Sizes: men's $21\frac{1}{2}$ in, $23\frac{1}{2}$ in, $25\frac{1}{2}$ in. Colour: green. A proper lightweight suitable for commuting and limited touring.

(3) Falcon Model 88 and 89. Frame of Reynolds 531 plain gauge tubing. Shimano 5-speed derailleur gears with down tube mounted shift lever. All alloy components throughout, including Sugino cotterless chainset, Weinmann centre-pull calliper brakes, flat handlebars, and 27-in wheels with low flange bolt-on hubs. Mattress saddle. Sizes: men's 21 in, 22 in, 23 in, 24 in, 25 in; ladies' 21 in.

Colour: black or red. The Falcon 88 has a very good finish and excellent handling qualities. It wants only dropped handlebars, a narrower saddle, and a double chainwheel, for conversion to a long-distance touring bike.

The Falcon is especially nice. While retaining a conventional saddle and handlebars, these bicycles offer the advantage of derailleur gears and light weight (about 25 lb). Perfect for around town use and light touring. The extra cost of £15 to £20 over a sports roadster is amply repaid in easier and more enjoyable cycling.

Five-speed derailleur

(1) Eddy Merckx Tour de L'Avenir Model 118. Sizes: $19\frac{1}{2}$ in, $21\frac{1}{2}$ in, $22\frac{1}{2}$ in, 24 in. Shimano gears. Steel chainset. Alloy: Weinmann SP brakes, S/F hubs, bars and stem. Reflector pedals. Quilted saddle. Short mudguards. Colour: orange.

(2) Coventry Eagle Supersonic Model 36. Sizes: $19\frac{1}{2}$ in, $21\frac{1}{2}$ in, 23 in, $24\frac{1}{2}$ in. Shimano gears. Alloy: Sugino cotterless chainset, S/F hubs, Weinmann SP brakes with dual levers, bars and stem. Quilted saddle. Stainless steel full mudguards. Colours: lavender or green.

Nine-speed bicycles

These are created by combining a 3-speed freewheel with a 3-speed hub. The complete kit for this conversion, consisting of a 3-speed freewheel, derailleur, and shift lever and cable is manufactured and sold by the Cyclo Gear Company.

The disadvantage of this system is the inherent inefficiency of the internally geared hub. The advantage is that gears can be shifted quickly and positively through a wide range whether the bike is moving or not. This can be handy for people who are fumble-fingered, and for cyclo-cross types riding through fields and woods where most of the attention goes into staying upright. Here are the gear ratios commonly obtained through this conversion. Look up the section on Gearing if you do not understand the meaning of the numbers. A 36T front chainwheel and 26-in wheel gives:

3-speed hub	freewheel		
1st	30.5	40.7	54.3
2nd	36.9	49.3	65.7
3rd	43.9	58.5	78

and a 40T front chainwheel and a 26-in wheel gives:

3-speed hub	freewheel		
1st	33.9	45.2	60.3
2nd	41.1	54.7	73
3rd	48.7	65	86.7

Five- to twenty-one-speed derailleur, commuting, touring, and racing bicycles

A word for ladies. A ladies' pattern frame is structurally weaker and less responsive than a men's frame. They are not available in all models, frame sizes are limited, and often a mattress saddle and flat handlebars are supplied in place of the racing saddle and downswept bars supplied with the comparable men's model. You will get better value and performance from a regular 'men's' bike.

In ladies' bikes best recommendations are the Eddy Merckx Club Special 109 (21 in, Shimano gears. Alloy: Weinmann CP brakes, Sugino chainset, bars and stem. Plastic saddle. Colour: orange); the Dawes Fleur (21 in, Huret gears. Alloy: Weinmann SP brakes, hubs, bars, and stem. Steel: chainset and rims. Quilted saddle. Colours: blue or aqua); the Falcon Black Diamond 71 (19½ in or 21½ in, specification below); the Viscount Sebring (specification below); and the Peugeot UE-18 (20 in, Simplex gears. Alloy: quick release hubs, Mafac CP brakes. Steel: chainwheel, mudguards, bars and stem. Mattress saddle. Carrier rack, pump, toolkit, and dynamo lights. Colours: blue or gold). In men's bikes small-size people are limited to the Eddy Merckx 118, Coventry Eagle Supersonic, Falcon Black Diamond, and Viscount Sebring and Sport. For a high-quality bike with a Reynolds 531 or 531 double butted frame you will need a custom builder. If you want to tour, I suggest specifying a slightly raked top tube. This allows adequate bottom bracket height, a comfortable straddle when stationary, and, because a longer head tube can be used, increased frame flexibility (small frames tend to be stiff).

And a word for everybody. If you have less than £80 to spend I recommend strongly the purchase of a used machine (see next chapter). You can get an acceptable 10-speed for as little as £35, and £40 to £50 will net you something unquestionably worth riding.

I have looked at a lot of low-priced new bikes for around £70, and they are mostly junk. Here, manufacturers have given in to un-principled consumerism and cut-throat competition. Many people don't know much about bikes. They want, say, a 10-speed with chromed fork tips and quick-release wheels, and look for the bike with these features at the lowest price. They don't know if the frame is made with old lead pipe. Spotty bright paint and glitter hide the truth. Wheels are out of true. Saddles are liquid, floppy plastic. Bearings bind. Derailleurs are low-grade units that either slip or jam or break quickly. Brakes are often crummy. You get on one of these machines and things are such a grinding painful torment that in a short while you decide the whole idea is worthless. Where is Old Invincible Ironsides you ask, that faithful heavyweight that at least works? It doesn't always happen this way. There are some shops, too proud to sell junk, that will patiently spend the hours and hours necessary to put a cheaperoo bike right from the way it came from the factory – but there is nothing they can do about low-grade components. Most reputable shops will tell you to avoid the £70 10-speed bikes as pain and grief for everybody – you and the shop, where you will spend a lot of time if you buy one of these machines.

Anyway, the problem is not to save money, but to be sure you get what you pay for. Don't get duped by avaricious manufacturers who 'give in' to market pressure and deluge you with colourful brochures filled with pictures of happy types sporting about on garbage machinery. Ignore the junk. Know the fundamentals in this chapter and buy a bicycle that really will bring you joy and pleasure.

The bicycles recommended below are grouped in arbitrary price ranges of £80–£100, £100–£140, and £140–£200. Prices will change; the idea is more to indicate what to expect in basic, medium, and high quality grades of bicycle.

Basic quality bicycles

(1) Coventry Eagle Supersonic Model 36. Specifications above.

(2) Falcon Black Diamond Model 70 and 71. Sizes: men's 19½ in, 21½ in, 23 in, 24 in; ladies' 19½ in or 21½ in. Seamless frame. Shimano gears. Alloy: Weinmann CP brakes, Sugino cotterless chainset, bolt on hubs, bars, and stem. Stainless steel mudguards. Plastic saddle. Toe clips and straps. Colours: silver or purple.

(3) Viscount Sebring. Sizes: 19½ in, 21 in, 23 in. Seamless frame. Shimano gears. Alloy: Shimano CP brakes with dual levers, SR cotterless chainset, bolt on hubs, bars and stem. Plastic mudguards. Quilted saddle. Colours: blue or red.

Falcon bicycles (which include the Coventry Eagle and Eddy Merckx brands) consistently offer quality features at good value for money, and careful assembly at the factory so that in-service problems are minimized. The Black Diamond is a touring bike also suitable for commuting. The Sebring, sans mudguards, is a touch sportier. Both will stand rough use.

Medium quality bicycles

(1) Viscount Aerospace Sport. Sizes: 19½ in, 21½ in, 22½ in, 23½ in, 24½ in. Frame: chrome–molybdenum alloy steel cold-drawn seamless double-brazed lugless, with full chrome forks. Shimano gears. Alloy: Viscount CP brakes with dual levers, Sugino cotterless chainset, Q/R hubs, bars, and stem. Spokes: 14 gauge. Plastic saddle. Colours: blue or red.

The Sport has a frame geometry suitable for both touring and club racing. The hubs and bottom bracket utilize sealed bearings which do not require adjustment or lubrication. These are durable in ordinary service, but in severe conditions may need maintenance, and this is difficult to do. The sealed bearings, dual action brakes, and strong 14-gauge spokes are of particular interest to the tourist or utility rider, and racers will find the Sport lively and responsive.

(2) Falcon Olympic Model 78 and 79. Sizes: 21 in, 22 in, 23 in, 24 in, 25 in. Frame: Reynolds 531 plain gauge. Shimano gears. All alloy components. Sugino cotterless chainset. Weinmann CP brakes. Bolt on hubs. Stainless steel mudguards. Vinyl covered saddle. Colours: blue or green.

(3) British Eagle. As Olympic above, but Q/R hubs and padded saddle.

The Falcon Olympic and British Eagle are touring bikes also suitable for commuting. Considering the Reynolds 531 main tubes and specification, they are excellent value for money. A better bike will cost a good bit more.

High quality bicycles

(1) Dawes Galaxy Deluxe. Sizes: 21 in, $22\frac{1}{2}$ in, $23\frac{1}{2}$ in, $25\frac{1}{2}$ in. Frame: Reynolds 531 plain gauge. Sun Tour gears. All alloy components. Cotterless chainset. Weinmann CP brakes with dual levers. Q/R hubs. Brooks B-17 saddle. Plastic mudguards. Rear pannier carrier. Toe clips and straps. Colours: brown or green, with glisten or coloured mudguards.

Bicycle made by T. & H. King, blacksmiths,
Wimborne, Dorset, 1872

The Galaxy is the standby favourite quality touring bicycle. Workmanship and finish are to a high standard. Handling is excellent, even on rough surfaces.

(2) Peugeot PR10L. Sizes: 20 in, 21 in, 23 in, 24 in, 25 in. Frame: Reynolds 531 plain gauge. Simplex gears. All alloy components. Stronglight 49D cotterless chainset. Mafac CP brakes. Q/R hubs. Ideale Leather saddle. Tubular tyres. Toe clips and straps. Colour: white.
A very good basic racing bike which has claimed many victories.

(3) Claude Butler Competition. Sizes: 21 in to 24 in. Frame: Reynolds 531 plain gauge throughout. All alloy components. Campagnolo GS gears and high flange Q/R hubs. Super Champion sprint rims, Weinmann 500 SP brakes, and Royal GT suede covered plastic saddle. Toe clips and straps. Colour: silver.
A racing bike also suitable for very fast day rides, but not touring or commuting.

(4) Dawes Double Blue. Sizes 21 in to 25 in. Frame: Reynolds 531 d-b main tubes, 531 plain gauge forks. All alloy components. Shimano 600 series cotterless chainset, gears, low flange Q/R hubs, and SP brakes. Narrow profile, high pressure wire-on tyres. Milremo suede saddle. Colour: blue.

A nicely set up, value-for-money, high-performance bike that will suit fast day rides, lightly laden touring and, with care, commuting. Please note that at the time of writing Dawes Cycles has just changed owners, and the Galaxy and Double Blue models may or may not continue in production; I have included them in this listing in the hope that they will – for both are excellent bikes.

Twelve-and fourteen-speed derailleur
Twelve or fourteen speeds are obtained by using a 6- or 7-cog freewheel gear cluster on the back wheel. In the ordinary way, an extra cog requires additional 'dishing' – offsetting the hub into the rim so that the middle of the cluster is in line with the middle space between the front chain-rings. The wheel is thereby slightly weaker, and not the best choice for the heavily-laden tourist, or for the commuter riding on rough surfaces. One way around this problem is to fit the new Sun Tour 'Ultra' chain and freewheel, which uses components reduced 1.1mm in width from standard, so that a 6-speed gear cluster can be fitted without modification to hub,

'Nottingham Sociable.'

wheel dish, or derailleur. Even better, though not yet available
in the UK, is the new Shimano 600EX Freehub, which offers
the 6-speed facility while at the same time actually reducing wheel
dish. A 12-speed gear system can be very attractive, offering
narrower steps between gears and easier shift sequence, or a
super-low 'Granny' gear. A very comprehensive article on the
subject by Frank Berto appeared in the American magazine
Bicycling, May 1978 (PO Box 10098, Palo Alto, CA 94303 USA).

Fifteen-speed derailleur

Fifteen speeds are obtained by using triple front chainrings.
Experienced tourists are the main users of this arrangement, because
it gives a very wide range of closely spaced gears. Wide range
10-speed gearing usually leaves large gaps between each gear. But
15-speed gearing also has drawbacks: shifting requires more skill,
and the chain will sometimes fall between chainrings; the chain is
required to deflect greater distances from side to side, increasing
chain wear and often rubbing the chain against various parts of the
gear system; and the selection of components must be exactly right if
the whole system is to work at all. Only an experienced cyclist who

has to handle severe mountain gradients and/or very heavy touring loads should even consider a 15-speed system.

A very comprehensive series of articles about 15-speed gear systems was done by Frank Berto in the March, April, and May 1977 issues of the American magazine *Bicycling* (address above). I strongly suggest reading them before undertaking a 15-speed project.

Custom and bespoke bikes

In a price range of £175 and up are the offerings of small manufacturers and custom shops. Several are listed in the next chapter. They have models for touring, road racing, hill climbs, time trials, track, cyclo-cross, etc. Frames are hand built, and price depends on specification (grade of components supplied). The usual range is £220 to £400, with super de luxe models costing over £500. The design and specification of these bikes reflect considerable experience, and they can be a most worthwhile investment for a keen cyclist. Often gear ratios, fittings, and colour will be done to suit your own particular needs.

For about £200 and up you can construct your own bike. A factory produced double-butted frame runs about £60, with handmade jobs starting at about £85. For about £100 you can have a frame custom built to order. If the frame builder knows his business, and many do, you can have a bike that fits you and your kind of riding to absolute perfection. It is grand fun to have a superbike, but I would advise leaving this until you are an experienced cyclist and know exactly what you want – any mistake will be expensive.

Other bicycles

Small-wheel bicycles

These are mini-bikes with 16-in or 20-in wheels, available with a variety of options, including hinged, folding frames. Their virtues are: (1) easy storage; (2) good luggage capacity; (3) manoeuvrability; and (4) easy adaptation to any size rider. Their drawbacks are (1) relatively high price, ranging from £70 to £90 depending on number of gear speeds and accessories selected; (2) a weight of 40 to 50 pounds which makes them heavy to carry and hard to pedal; (3) an unstable ride due to the small wheels so that oil slicks, manhole covers, and gravel patches are likely to throw you; and (4) poor brakes, even in the calliper versions. This last is critical, since the net effect of the mini-bike's design is to restrict it to short local trips in urban areas where good brakes are premium.

Many people who take up cycling for the second time around get a mini. It's new. They like the crisp looks and easy way it goes. But if you are in this category I want to caution you specifically that these bikes are good for some things and not for others.

For getting the groceries it is hard to beat one of the shopper versions with baskets front and rear that come off quickly to carry around with you in the store. The manoeuvrability and small size of the bike make handling and parking easy. On the other hand, a conventional 10-speed with touring panniers will carry as much and more – *and* go touring. For shopping, the mini wins simply on grounds of convenience because with the 10-speed there is always a certain amount of fumbling as purchases are packed away in the panniers and/or boxes are lashed on the rack. Some of the better panniers like Karrimor's have been designed however, to go on and off the bike in seconds, so you'd better check the section on touring and luggage before opting for the mini – which won't go touring very well.

Any of the small-wheel jobs have a darting manoeuvrability that is very handy for exploring urban locales. They will U-turn and turn right and left as fast as thought. You can get on and off hundreds of times effortlessly. They encourage spontaneity – nipping down a mews to look at an old house, pulling over to study a bookshop window, even hi-jinks cutting around obstacles. The price is paid in unsteadier handling at speed and sudden dumps on slippery surfaces like oil or leaves. Mini-bike brakes are just adequate so long as the sun shines and the rims and brake blocks are dry. While in the wet any rim brake tends to piffle out, the mini-bike's brakes go down to near zero. As a choice for steady, all-weather commuting, or habitual use by a rider weighing more than 12 stone, they are just not on.

Most mini-bikes come with quick-adjust seat and handlebars. This can be a very useful feature if several members of the family will be using the same bike.

In sum, the mini-bike is a local use machine with characteristics that give it the edge for multi-rider use, light shopping, urban exploring, and zesty handling. It is not so good for commuting or longer tours.

The best – and most expensive – 20-in bikes are the Dawes Kingpin series. They are light, have a slight edge in handling characteristics, and have quality features such as ball-bearing pedals and better grade saddles.

(1) Dawes Kingpin 500C. Sturmey-Archer 3-speed gears, side-pull calliper brakes, rustless Feran mudguards. Rear carrier bag and prop stand, reflector pedals. Colours blue, green, brown, or purple. Variant models are Kingpin Shopper as 500C but with front carrier and quick-release shopping basket. Kingpin Folder as 500G but without rear carrier bag. Dynamo lighting optional.

(2) Puch Pic-Nic. Styria 3-speed gears, side-pull calliper brakes, prop stand, chrome mudguards, sprung rear carrier, and whitewall tyres. Colour: yellow. Variant is: Folder – as above but red. Tall people may find the handlebar reach on the Pic-Nic more to their favour.

(3) Peugeot UNS40. Tyres 22 in. Simplex 5-speed derailleur gears. Chrome mudguards. Centre-pull calliper brakes. Adjustable seat and handlebars. Chainguard rack. Optional: dynamo lighting and front carrier wire shopping basket. Colours: blue or orange.

Folding bicycles

In all the world there is only one folding bicycle to consider seriously – the Bickerton. Conventional folding bicycles weigh 40 to

50 pounds and are bulky and difficult to manage. The Bickerton, constructed of aluminium alloy throughout, weighs only 18 pounds (20 pounds for the 3-speed model) and folds down in 45 seconds to an astonishing 30 in × 20 in × 9 in – about the size of a small suitcase. A stout canvas bag fitted on the front handlebars will hold up to 40 pounds of groceries or whatever, and also doubles as a carrier for the folded bike.

The portability of the Bickerton has to be experienced to be believed. It is no trouble at all to take along in a taxi, train, or bus. Two Bickertons will fit into the boot of a mini. More importantly, the Bickerton obviates security problems. There is no need to bother with locking it up, because you can take it wherever you go. A folded Bickerton will slide under a desk or workbench. It can hang from a cloakroom coat-hook. Storage in a flat or home with limited space is a snap.

The portability of the Bickerton is a great asset for touring. Hopping by train, bus, airplane, or car from one interesting touring area to another is easy. On country tracks the Bickerton can be carried in a backpack when the going becomes too rough for riding.

In performance a Bickerton will keep up with anything short of a flat-out racing or touring bicycle. The very light weight gives quick acceleration and easy uphill pedalling. Design and materials give the frame a surprising flexibility, so that despite the use of small wheels, the ride is very comfortable.

Of course the Bickerton is a mini-bike, and the handling is quick. Rapid downhill descents are unnerving. Very powerful pedalling from a standing start can 'bounce' the front wheel. The initial riding sensation on a Bickerton is distinctly odd. But once the distinctive characteristics are mastered the Bickerton becomes a very tractable and enjoyable bicycle to ride.

Price is about £130 for the 3-speed, and if this seems steep, remember that most 20-pound derailleur gear bikes cost £250 and up. And the Bickerton cannot even be compared to conventional folding bikes. It is in a class of its own for combining portability, easy riding, and load carrying ability.

Tandem bicycles

A tandem bicycle offers a number of advantages and disadvantages over a conventional solo bicycle. Two strong riders can move a tandem along very briskly, as overall bicycle weight is less, and wind resistance is cut in half. A tandem will outrun a solo on a downhill run. Uphill, a tandem is slow. But over gently undulating terrain the greater mass of the tandem increases momentum, 'ironing out' small hills.

Two riders of unequal strength can have rest periods for the weaker rider on the easy parts of a ride, and put in the muscle together when climbing hills. Togetherness is a very definite positive feature of tandem-cycling; it is easy to talk, and there is something very pleasant about the shared physical effort. The rear rider, or 'stoker', is free to enjoy the scenery to the maximum. Disadvantages include awkward handling in traffic, which riding should be done only by experienced cyclists, and the sheer size of a tandem, which necessitates a roof rack for transport by automobile, and generous storage space.

Only a lightweight (35 to 45 pounds) derailleur gear tandem is worth owning. The heavyweight (90 pounds) models are just too much work to pedal. At double the weight of a solo bike, a tandem requires first rate brakes. At the minimum it should have cantilever rim brakes with oversize blocks, or with Mathauser blocks. This would be for a lightweight racing tandem for use by experienced riders. Touring tandems should have drum brakes or disc brakes, or better still, cantilever rim brakes and a drum or disc brake.

Invincible Tandem

Tandem tyres take a beating. Tubular tyres and $27\frac{1}{4}$-in wire-on high pressure tyres are suitable only for racing or ultra-fast day riding. The technical editor of *Bicycling*, Fred DeLong, who has racked up many thousands of miles on tandems, recommends the sturdy 650-B tyres and rims for durability, comfort, and stable handling even on unpaved roads.

A good tandem is expensive – £350 to £1000 – but think of it as one bicycle for the price of two. Do not compromise on quality. A tandem must be soundly engineered and constructed in order to withstand the stress of two riders. My personal favourites are the tandems manufactured by Jack Taylor Cycles, Church Road, Stockton-on-Tees, Teesside TS18 2LY. Another quality builder is Bob Jackson, 148 Harehills Lane, Leeds LS8 5BD. Two shops specializing in tandems are

Beta Bikes   and   The Tandem Centre
275 West End Lane   281 Old Kent Road
London NW6 1QS   London SE1

and technical advice and help are available from

The Tandem Club

25 Henred Way Abingdon, Oxon OX14 2AN

Tricycles

These are popular items in retirement areas. They usually have
20-in wheels to keep the weight down low and are quite stable as
long as they are not driven briskly. A large rear basket-carrier,
handy for carrying groceries, gold bricks, golf clubs, or whatever, is a
popular accessory. People with poor balance or coordination, brittle
bones, or other problems, should seriously consider a tricycle.
But bear in mind also that many old folks do just fine with
conventional two-wheelers, and in fact there are a number of
bicycle clubs whose members are all over seventy.

One type of tricycle has a fixed gear on which there is no
free-wheeling and the pedals turn when the wheels turn. People who
have limited motion in their legs have sometimes found that the
exercise provided by this type of machine helps recovery of leg
mobility. Cost is about £100. For hilly terrain get a 3- to 10-speed
freewheel and expect to spend about £125.

People with a taste for the unusual might want to consider a
lightweight racing or touring tricycle with 26-in or 27-in wheels. In
no way is this an old age toy. Many an experienced bicyclist has
come a cropper first time out on a trike. It must be steered around
a corner, a sensation completely at odds with the handling of a
bicycle, and rider weight must be counter-balanced to the inside
on even a moderate bend. It is quite easy to lift a wheel, and

Humber Gripper Tricycle

downhill bends in particular must be approached with caution.
Changes in the camber of the road also easily upset balance.

At first I enjoyed trikes simply because I found them challenging.
Now that I am more familiar and comfortable with their handling
characteristics a number of advantages have emerged, and
in fact the 'family' cycle is a tandem trike. It has very good
load-carrying capacity, does not require a dismount when stopped,

Higgins Ultralight. *c.* 1950

will park without having to be propped up, and will stay upright under slippery conditions. The baby's seat is located between the two rear wheels, giving some measure of protection should there be an accident. When the next little 'un comes along it will be easy to add another seat. All in all, the tandem trike works out as a very comfortable family bike for relaxed and social cycling. The handling does not inspire rapid downhill descents, but this is immaterial on a family bike.

A lightweight solo trike costs about £200 and up, and a tandem about £300 and up. Solo and tandem models are available from Ken G. Rogers, 71 Berkeley Avenue, Cranford, Hounslow, Middlesex TW4 6LF, and solo models from Jack Taylor Cycles, Stockton-on-Tees, Teesside TS18 2LY.

In Britain a trike is known also as a 'barrow', and there is a dedicated fraternity of adherents banded as

The Tricycle Association
Sec. J. H. Mills, 58 Townsend Avenue, West Kirby, Liverpool
L11 8ND.

Another racing tricycle is the recumbent, a Japanese design included here out of sheer interest, as at this writing it is not available in the UK. The rider lies parallel with the ground, head at the rear. Two front wheels are steered through a system of rods and levers. The low centre of gravity increases cornering ability, and the streamlining contributes to a high cruising-speed. With a low riding position they are suitable only for racing. Very exciting to ride, and in Japan, at least, very popular.

At the opposite end of the scale from the recumbent design is the utility tricycle, weighing in at about 100 pounds. These feature a rear platform with a load capacity of 500 pounds, and have a great variety of industrial and commercial uses. A few examples would be: moving gardening equipment and lawnmowers around estates and parks; moving TV sets (or lawn furniture, or lace undies, or bags of cement – anything that a human being can pick up) around a warehouse; mounting a hot dog, ice cream, or vegetable stand; collecting rubbish from small litter bins. The great point in favour of the utility trike is that it is highly economical, and uses only the amount of power appropriate for the job at hand. It is also noise and pollution free. If you can think of and suggest an application for a utility trike where you live or work, you will be doing yourself and everybody else a big favour. One utility trike is called the Pedi-Porter, made by Alco Cycle Products, 451 3rd Street SE, Largo, FLA 33540, USA.

Quadricycles

These are 4-wheel cycles with seating for one or two persons. They generally aim to provide protection from the weather, and good load carrying capacity. To date they have been too heavy for practical urban use, but research and development continue, and the near future may well see such vehicles available to the general public. A fun quadricycle popular in holiday resort areas is the Graziella Rickshaw Bench Seat Tandem, which comes complete with a fringed awning top.

Sailing bicycle

The Rans Company, East Highway 40,
Hays, Kansas 67601, USA, manufactures
and has sold about 350 sailing tricycles.
Their product looks well made, and like a
lot of fun. It is literally a tricycle with a
(30 sq ft) sail just like on a boat, and will do
up to 50 mph. The Windhawk model sells
for about £250, and the Eagle V model for
about £350. Just be sure you have a lot of
room.

Unicycles

These are becoming increasingly popular with kids, and one of
these days I'm going to get one myself.

Flying machines

Human-powered airplanes have been designed, and in some
instances built, virtually since the invention of the bicycle. Few got
any appreciable distance off the ground until the epic *Gossamer*

Gossamer Condor

Condor, which in 1977 captured the £50,000 Kremer Prize by flying a figure of eight course around two poles half a mile apart. In comparison to previous flying machines, *Gossamer Condor* requires relatively little power input; it has been flown by a grandmother! The inventor of *Gossamer Condor*, Dr Paul MacCready, is now in pursuit of the next Kremer Prize of £100,000 for flying a human-powered vehicle over the English Channel.

Pedal machines
Machines using human pedal power include a garden tractor, lathes, food processing equipment, water pumps, lawnmowers, sewing machines, electric generators, hoists, cider presses, and many more. Particularly in developing countries where fuel and complex technology can be expensive, pedal power machines are often the most efficient in terms of energy expenditure and ease of application. An excellent book on the subject is *Pedal Power*, edited by J. C. McCullagh (Rodale Press, Emmaus, PA 18049, USA; £2.95).

Children's bicycles

One attitude towards buying clothes, toys, and other materials for children is something like, 'Well, the kid'll grow out of it soon, so let's not waste money. Just get him/her something good enough.' Another ploy is, 'Well, let's first see if she/he is really interested – then we'll get him/her something better.' The victim of this faulty reasoning is the helpless child, who is saddled with some worthless or even painful piece of junk and who is expected to be grateful for it. The price difference between a good bike and a cheap one is at most £5.00. The cheap bike is difficult and unpleasant to ride, and shoddy workmanship and materials guarantee that it will grace the junkpile within a year. Result: total financial loss and total lack of stimulation for the child. The better bike is not only a pleasure to ride, thus ensuring your child's fun and interest, but will also survive for a number of years through the hands of several children. It can be passed down in the family or sold for at least half the purchase price. Result: happier *children*, and less net expenditure. If you would like to save money or are on a tight budget, check the classified adverts in local papers and put up cards advertising for what you want at newsagents, laundromats, school meetings, etc., and buy a used bike for £5 to £15.

Incidentally, the use of training wheels will only make learning to ride more prolonged and difficult for your child. He has to learn how to balance, and training wheels only postpone and make harder the inevitable. The best way to teach anybody, young or old, to ride is to let them do it themselves. Lower the seat so that they can comfortably touch the ground with their feet when mounted. All they need to do is push themselves along with their feet, like scootering. Balance and steering ability will come quickly.

Children are ready for their first two-wheel bicycle at about the age of five, depending on the development and coordination of the individual child. The first bike for a child aged five to seven should be a small-frame 20-in wheel featuring:

Pneumatic tyres for a comfortable ride, easier pedalling, and effective braking. Solid rubber tyres are three times harder to pedal, provide a jolting ride, and give bad braking.

Steel steering head bearings. The plastic sleeve bearings used on cheap bikes result in bad handling and steering characteristics, and wear out quickly, compounding the problem.

A sturdy frame with at least two permanent members welded to the steering head. Anything less won't take the punishment kids dish out.

A large seat range adjustment so the bike can grow with the child.

A desirable feature is a coaster (foot-actuated) brake, as small hands sometimes experience difficulty in managing calliper brakes. Coaster brakes are rare on British kids' bicycles however, and since most children can manage a calliper brake this is not a problem – just check and make sure.

Going up to six- to nine-year-olds, the Raleigh Tempo, a 15-in cantilever frame with 20-in wheels is good, as is the Raleigh Chicco, available with either 14-in or 16-in frame and 20-in wheels. Children aged seven to nine can also manage the Raleigh Jeep, an 18-in frame with 24-in wheels and available with 3-speed gears. Athletic eight-year-olds and children between the ages of nine and twelve should have a small frame 26-in wheel bicycle with 3-speed gears. Children over twelve years can use adult bikes.

I recommend increasing wheel size as quickly as possible. There are any number of children's bicycles in wheel sizes from 14 in to 20 in, and while a number are mechanically satisfactory, they are subject to the limitations of small-wheelers. On the other hand, a machine like the

Dawes Kingpin 18. Frame 14 in, tyres 18 in. Ball bearings throughout, pump, PVC-coated rear carrier with lamp bracket and fitted bag, and 3-speed gears,

has adjustable seat and handlebars so that adults under 5 ft 2 in can use it as well.

Your youngster may be the sort who is not going to instantly beat his machine to death and would like to cover some ground. In which case consider a junior racer (suitable for ages eight to twelve):

(1) Peugeot C45 CXE Junior Sports. Lugless 18-in frame. Simplex derailleurs. Steel crankset 40 × 45 to 14–16–18–20–23 freewheel. Mafac centre-pull calliper brakes with hooded levers. Steel handlebars and gooseneck. Reflectorized rat-trap pedals. Alloy large flange hubs, 24-in tyres. Leather saddle. Colours: red or blue.

(2) Dawes Red Feather. Frame 18½ in, 70° × 72°. Huret 5-speed gears, steel crankset 40T to 14–24 freewheel, steel flange hubs, 24-in tyres. Weinmann alloy side-pull calliper brakes. Alloy gooseneck and mini-Maes pattern handlebars (all-rounder optional). Colours: gold or red, with contrasting mudguards.

Declining in popularity with children is the hi-riser bicycle, with 20-in or smaller wheels, small frame and wheelbase, extra high handlebars, banana seat, and an excess of flashy hardware. Highly manoeuvrable at low speeds, the hi-riser is otherwise unsafe and difficult to control. This is reflected in bicycle accident studies published in the *British Medical Journal*, which found that serious accidents with head injuries, broken bones, etc., involved these bikes out of all proportion to the number in use. Often it was a new, first bike (Christmas! Birthday!) or a first ride on a borrowed machine. Hi-risers are not much good for genuine cycling – and under no circumstances should they be a first bicycle.

The best hi-riser now on the market is the Raleigh Chopper II, which features a rear seat and chain stay design that pushes the centre of gravity forward to the bottom bracket and makes it difficult to lift the front wheel. The price of this bike (about £90) will of course also net a 10-speed, a safer bike with a much wider range of capabilities, and less likely to crack junior's skull.

Hi-risers are on the way out, but they have helped the birth of a new type of bicycle and sport – BMX. In America, this is off-road bicycle racing for kids, usually around a dirt course with features such as waterholes and jumps. BMX bicycles are light, extremely tough, and many even have suspension systems. BMX in Britain has not yet reached the stage of organized races with the riders kitted out with helmets, gloves, heavy boots and clothing. But BMX bikes are just great for general off-road use. Kids can mess about to their heart's content, and very importantly, do not have to be anywhere near motor vehicles. If you live near a park or out in the country I would rate a BMX bike very high for fun value, and just adequate for local utility use. It is not suitable as a first bike.

A good BMX bike should be light, obviously robust and sturdily built, and functional. Machines such as the Raleigh Boxer, Strika, and Grifter models have impressive looking features such as knobby tyres and reinforced handlebars, but are deadeningly heavy and little fun to ride. The Strika shock absorbers are inoperative fakes. At this writing authentic BMX bikes are a bit thin on the ground in Britain, but good brand names are Kawasaki, Yamaha, Dan Gurney Eagle, and Matthews.

LUDGATE HILL

3 The urban commuting bicycle

Road racing, cyclo-cross, and track bicycles each have distinctive characteristics appropriate to their intended use. So does the urban commuting bicycle. Many city streets are obstacle courses filled with bumps, potholes, uneven surfaces, 'temporary' steel plates which are slippery when wet, broken glass, and bits of sharp metal and other rubbish. In heavy traffic there is often not enough room for a cyclist to avoid an obstacle. A machine for these conditions must be tough. Theft is a constant problem in cities. An obviously expensive bicycle is more likely to be stolen, or stripped for parts. Finally, most regular commuters prefer a bike that requires a minimum of maintenance.

Several different types of bicycle are best capable of coping with urban conditions. Each has advantages and disadvantages according to your particular situation and needs.

The classic heavy-duty roadster offers a soft frame design which helps to iron out the worst of the bumps, enclosed hub gears which are well protected from wet and grit, robust $1\frac{1}{2}$-in tyres which have a fighting chance of surviving glass and other road litter, and an upright riding position which allows a good view of traffic conditions. However, at 50 pounds weight, the heavy-duty roadster is hard work to pedal, and is not suitable for long journeys or steep terrain. As far as security is concerned it is an odd-ball bike with a low black-market value and in theory would be less likely to be stolen.

The 3-speed sports roadster is much the same as the heavy-duty roadster except that it is lighter in weight, uses 26-in wheels with $1\frac{3}{8}$-in tyres, and is available in a wide range of frame sizes. It is still not much of a speed machine or hill climber. One performance improvement is to fit alloy 26 in $\times$ $1\frac{3}{8}$ in rims and high pressure tyres. An inexpensive way of improving hill climbing ability is to fit a larger rear sprocket of 20 or 22 teeth. This limits top speed to around 20 mph, but this is adequate for most traffic conditions.

The present deplorable state of Kingston Bridge

The bike is then also very suitable for off-road riding. Sports roadsters are not the most valuable of bicycles, but are easy to re-sell. Security is a problem.

Derailleur gear 5- and 10-speed bicycles are the obvious choice for long journeys and/or steep terrain. A longish wheelbase and fork trail, strong rims with thick spokes, and stout tyres, will maximize comfort and stability over rough surfaces.

There are a number of modifications to make a 10-speed more suitable for regular commuting. Fitting sealed bearing hubs, bottom bracket, and pedals will increase maintenance intervals. Spokes should be the minimum 14 gauge plain, cross four laced on small flange hubs, with steel rims or strong alloy rims such as Super Champion. Stout tyres such as the Michelin Sports should be kept inflated *hard*, to help absorb bumps. The addition of a puncture resisting sealant will increase tyre weight by 2 ounces but may spare you frequent tyre repairs.

Ten-speed bike security is a problem. For locking up on the street the only answer is a lock such as the Citadel (see Chapter 4 for details). Many people disguise high quality frames with a coat of dull looking, sloppy paint, and substitute low grade components (saddle, derailleurs, chainset). The resulting bike looks like an old banger but still goes fairly well. Some people booby-trap their bikes by slacking off the brakes or wheels, or removing the saddle. These are last ditch measures.

One way of obviating the security problem is with a folding

bicycle such as the Bickerton (see Chapter 2 for details). The bike
goes where you go. A Bickerton is light and fast, comfortable over
rough surfaces, and easy to take on a bus, train, or taxi if it rains
and you don't feel like getting wet. It is in many ways the ideal
urban bicycle, but for some people its quick handling
characteristics are a drawback in crowded traffic, where
predictability is important. Other people feel just the opposite, and
like being able to manoeuvre quickly in traffic. The Bickerton is a
specialized bicycle, and only personal investigation can tell if you
will enjoy riding it.

4 Buying and keeping a bike

New bikes

The best place to buy a new bicycle is a bike shop. You can
sometimes save money at a department or discount store, but you
are virtually guaranteed disproportionate headaches and problems.
In the first place, the quality of merchandise is almost always
inferior. Secondly, the sad fact is that not even the finest machines
are defect-free when they come from the manufacturer. Department
and discount stores do not employ trained bicycle mechanics, and so
the bikes they sell are often unassembled, or have been put together
by some cretin who has literally done more harm than good. It
takes a good bicycle mechanic to assemble a new bike without
damaging anything, check all the parts, and iron out the inevitable
defects. Even then, problems are not likely to be over. If a department
or discount store gives a guarantee – few do – they have no
mechanics to take care of after-sales problems. And if there is some
totally basic defect in a machine you buy, it takes weeks for a refund
or replacement.

A bike shop will assemble the machine. Although you must check
their work carefully, chances are they'll do the job right. If some
problem comes up later, they are available right away to fix it, and
so are replacement parts. You get a guarantee, which should be for
a minimum of a year, and is sometimes longer. And you will want
to deal with a bike shop anyway, for servicing, parts, accessories, and
advice.

The kind of bike shop makes a difference. Try to find one that
deals only in bicycles. The more local a shop you can deal with, the
better. Any bike shop must meet certain basic requirements in
quality of bikes and in service, but convenience means a lot. A
guarantee from a shop 50 miles away is useless for anything except a
major disaster. If there is a local shop and they don't have what you
want, talk it over with them. Perhaps they can order a bike for you.

If their 'brand' of bike is not the one you had in mind take a good look at what they offer. All other things being equal, as they may well be since many manufacturers use the same components, the convenience of a local shop is an excellent reason to switch 'brand'. Just make sure you get a fair value. Ask about servicing and parts. If their guarantee isn't good enough, explain the problem. Don't expect however, that they will be able to offer as good a deal as a high-volume super-powered bike shop. What you pay a little extra for is the fact that they are around the corner. Also, perhaps, the general feeling is friendlier.

At any rate, stay away from discount and department stores. I have not regaled you with horror stories about machines purchased from such sources, but they are legion, and cover everything from kids' tricycles to ultra-fancy racers. The tiny bit extra you spend in a bike shop buys an awful lot.

Taking delivery

Anticipate that any new bike will have something wrong with it. Dealing with a good bike shop minimizes this possibility but by no means eliminates it. When I picked up a new dream machine from one of New York's finest shops I was too bedazzled to give it anything but the most cursory inspection. As I accelerated away from the shop the rear hub and freewheel exploded in a blizzard of metal flakes and chips. Most problems you are likely to encounter are not apt to be so spectacular, but the point cannot be emphasized too strongly that a thorough inspection of any new bike is necessary. The best way to learn what to look for is to read the Maintenance and Repair sections of this book. Here are the main points to watch:

Check the frame for straightness. Stand behind or in front of the bicycle and see that the wheels are in line. Next, hold the bicycle by the saddle only and wheel it around the shop. If the frame or forks are bent, it will tend to veer to one side. Finally, if you do a test ride, at some point when you are clear of traffic hold the handlebars as lightly as possible, even riding hands off if you have the skill. The bicycle should go straight, in control, without pulling to one side. Reject any bicycle which fails these tests. A bicycle which will not track accurately is tiring and unsafe to ride.

🚲 Check quality of lug welds on frame. Sight down frame to check for bends.

🚲 Wheels should spin easily. When held off ground weight of valve stem should pull wheel around so valve is in six o'clock position. Wheel should be centred in fork arms or chain stays. If wheel can be moved from side to side and there is a clicking sound hub cones are out of adjustment. Check that rim is true by holding a pencil next to it and spinning the wheel. Brace the pencil on a fork arm or chain stay to keep it steady.

🚲 Pluck spokes. All should be evenly tight and give the same 'twang'.

🚲 Brake blocks should hit rims squarely and not drag when released.

🚲 Gears should work smoothly and with no slippage. Test first with wheels off ground and then on a ride.

🚲 Pedals and chainwheel should spin easily but without side-to-side play.

🚲 Ride the bike around the vicinity of the store for a few miles.

You may think that all this is a lot of trouble to go through. I have bought a fair number of new bikes for myself, family, or friends. There was something wrong with every one of them, and a few I rejected outright. You will save yourself a lot of grief if you invest some time at the outset on a careful inspection.

After you purchase a bike, check that all nuts, bolts, and screws are secure. Every last one. After riding 50 miles or so, repeat this operation. New bicycles 'bed in', and it is very common, for example, for the brake bolts to work loose. Cranks, particularly the cotterless type, are bound to need tightening. See the appropriate section under Maintenance for details.

Here is a list of bicycle shops noted for high-class machinery. It is of course not complete, and is just to give you a place to start.

Fred Baker
144 Cheltenham Road
Bristol 6

Condor Cycles
144–48 Gray's Inn Road
London WC1

Beta Bikes
275 West End Lane
London NW6 1QS

F. W. Evans Ltd
77–79 The Cut
London SE1

Norman Fay Cycles Ltd
109 South Eldon Street
South Shields
Tyne & Wear

Tommy Godwin
10–12 Silver Street
King's Heath
Birmingham 14

Hitchin's Bike Shop
117–119 Hamstel Road
Southend-on-Sea

W. F. Holdsworth Ltd
132 Lower Richmond Road
Putney
London SW15 1LN

Bob Jackson
148 Harehills Lane
Leeds LS8 5BD

John's Bikes
2 Cleveland Place East
Bath
Somerset

Ron Kitching
Hookstone Park
Harrogate
Yorkshire

Mercian Cycles Ltd
28 Stenson Road
Cavendish
Derby DE3 7JB

Major Nichols
48 Durban Road
Smethwick
Birmingham

Cliff Pratt Ltd
84 Spring Bank
Hull
Yorkshire

Harry Quinn Ltd
7–9 Walton Road
Liverpool 4

David Rattray & Co Ltd
261 Alexandra Parade
Glasgow G31 3AD

Roy Swinnerton
69–71 Victoria Road
Fenton, Stoke-on-Trent

Jack Taylor Cycles
Church Road
Stockton-on-Tees
Teesside TS18 2LY

Woodrup Cycles
345 Kirkstall Road
Leeds 4

You may be far from a suitable bike store. This one sells parts,
accessories, and custom bikes by post:

Freewheel
275 West End Lane
London NW6 1QS
(catalogue 45p, free with order)

Used bikes

Good used bikes are elusive, especially when you actually want one. But they are a good way to save money. Expect to pay about 75 per cent of list price for a machine in excellent as-new condition, and about 50 per cent of list price for one in average condition.

Sources of used bikes depend on where you live. A few bike shops sell used machines. Two excellent newsagent sources are *Exchange & Mart* and *Cycling* (161–66 Fleet Street, London EC4P 4AA). Most cities and counties have local classified publications listing all kinds of stuff – including bikes – for sale. Check also the classified ads in the regular papers. Sometimes families and people moving sell off furniture and household goods and this often includes a bicycle. Auctions are sometimes useful. A good bet in the spring are local bulletin boards at universities and colleges. Put up some cards yourself or take an ad in the student newspaper. Naturally, the more prosaic a bike you seek, the faster you will be likely to find it. But if you just put the word out something will turn up – eventually.

When buying a used machine you have to be particularly careful to avoid getting a lemon. Try to find out the history of the machine. It's best if you can talk to the owner. What does his attitude seem to be? Do you think he was interested in his bike and took care of it, or just left it out in the rain? Where did he ride it?

In inspecting the bike, cover all the points listed for a new bike. Pay particular attention to the frame. A certain number of nicks and scrapes are inevitable, but there should be no major dents or rust spots. Be suspicious of new paint. Wrinkled paint may indicate a bent frame.

It will be to your advantage to read carefully through the sections on Maintenance and Repair in this book. Often a used machine will need some work, or some component is not the one you need. You should know the cost and what is involved in replacing or repairing various parts. A £40 racer that needs £40 worth of work is no bargain. On the other hand, if you are looking for a touring bike and find a machine set up with close-ratio competition gears, it costs only about £5 to get a new wide-range gear freewheel.

A final word about used bikes related to the next problem: keeping your bike. I hope that this is not a self-fulfilling prophecy, but concurrent with the new popularity of the bicycle I expect that we shall see a growing market in stolen machines and parts. Doubtless this will not reach the giddy heights of the American black market, where newspapers publish articles about marketplaces for stolen machines and in some areas you can even order the type of bike you want. But in case the proposition ever seems even slightly attractive, I remind that to get a bike this way is a crime. Legally and morally. Simply put, you are helping to steal. Additionally, it is not some giant pound-greedy company's candy bar or rip-off piece of junk which you are stealing, but a possession somebody quite probably loves and cherishes.

Keeping your bike

As yet this is not a serious problem – at least not by American standards, where about 20 per cent of the bikes in use at any given moment will be stolen within a year. Here, in many towns you do not need to lock up your bike at all. But bicycle thefts – especially of quality machines – are steadily increasing. Precautions are a must.

Except in areas where you know everybody and everybody knows you never leave your bike unlocked. It is a temptation to impulse. While it is not serious when somebody tumbles out of the local and staggers off around the corner on your machine, it is inconvenient. I find that for on-again/off-again type riding a cable combination lock such as sold in bicycle and ski shops is the lightest and easiest to manage.

After deterring the impulsive, locking-up procedures are a function of situation. A well-lit street is a better bet than, say, a dark alley,

Carriage propelled by dogs; from France

but in either case security counts. For day and evening use in average neighbourhoods with ordinary bikes, I use a length of chain – real chain, purchased from an ironmonger's – and a quality padlock. For night-time and/or first-class machinery I use an American lock made of case-hardened steel throughout called the Citadel. In tests conducted by police departments and cycle clubs the Citadel has withstood attack by prybar, hammer, hacksaw, and bolt cutter, while competing locks have failed. There is no reported case of bicycle theft involving a Citadel, and in America the manufacturers guarantee to replace to a value of £90 any bicycle stolen while locked with a Citadel. The Citadel is available from cycle shops for £15, and by post from Freewheel, 275 West End Lane, London NW6 1QS. The Citadel is expensive, but at the time of writing is the only absolutely secure lock made. Consider your requirements carefully and think of how you will feel if one day you find your bike – gone.

When locking up on the street you must:

🚲 Lock your machine to serious immovable objects like lamp posts, parking signs, heavy fences, etc.

🚲 Run the chain through the frame and back wheel. Take the front wheel away with you, if you can, or run the chain through it too.

🚲 Be selective about when and where. Slum neighbourhoods are a bad bet at any time. Even if the bike is not stolen, kids may make bits and pieces disappear. Business and industrial districts are

OK during the day. Always pick a busy, well-illuminated spot.

🚲 Try to enlist help. The cashier for a cinema will usually keep an eye on your bike. Newsagents and other merchants will often help, particularly if you do business with them.

🚲 Keep a written record of your bike's particulars, including the serial number stamped on the frame – most often found on the underside of the bottom bracket, but sometimes on a stay or tube.

There is another problem, not at all extensive, but perhaps new for those of you who have led sheltered lives and now astride fancy machines are meeting the world, and that is direct assault. Britain has its share of tough neighbourhoods where a good bike is an easy candidate for liberation. And there is a bit of the irrational Clockwork Orange violence which necessarily accompanies a consumer society. Happily, it is not the jungle warfare prevalent in the United States with attacks from the bushes or from behind parked cars and where, in many areas, it is just not safe to ride day or night. Things are under better control in this country. But if you are in a bad neighbourhood, stay alert, as you should in any case anywhere, and move along smartly – at 20 to 30 mph you will leave most trouble behind before it happens.

5 Fitting and gears

Getting the most out of your bike requires careful fitting, e.g.
placement of handlebars, seat, and controls. The standard formulas
for this process are the result of considerable work and study by
genuine experts and will probably work the best. After you have
finished setting your bike up 'according to the book' the resulting
position may feel a bit odd. Give yourself at least 50 miles to get used
to the new arrangement before making alterations. You may find
the 'odd' position considerably more efficient and less fatiguing than
a 'comfortable' position. At the same time, no two people are
exactly alike, and some variation from the norm may be in order.
Just give the orthodox position a fair trial, and make alterations
gradually.

For how to make alterations in the position of seat, handlebars,
stem, and brake levers, look up Adjustment under the relevant
heading in the Maintenance and Repairs sections.

Frame

Frame size is measured from the seat lug to the centre of the
bottom bracket. There are two methods of calculating the proper
size:

Inside length of leg from crotch bone to floor, measured in
stocking feet, less 9 in, and
Height divided by 3.

Thus, a person with a 32-in inside leg measurement should have a
23-in frame, and somebody 6 ft tall would get a 24-in frame. Be sure
in any event that you can straddle the frame comfortably with your
feet flat on the ground. An undersized frame can be compensated
for to some degree through the use of an extra-long seat post and
stem, but an oversized frame will inevitably slam you in the crotch.

Most frames are the 72° parallel touring design, good for both long trips and local urban use, where the springiness of the frame softens bumpy streets. Additionally, there is no problem fitting mudguards. Racing road and track frames ordinarily use steeper seat tube angles of 73° or 74° to put the rider further forward and tighten up the bike. These frames are not usually intended for use with mudguards, although the ingenious may find a way.

Saddle

The position of the saddle determines the fitting of the rest of the bike. For most riders the correct fore-to-aft position is with the nose of the saddle $1\frac{3}{4}$ in to $2\frac{1}{2}$ in behind a vertical line through the crank hanger:

A more precise way of determining fore-to-aft position depends on rider height. A person 5 ft 6 in tall would normally have the nose of the saddle 1 in back of the bottom bracket, while for a person 6 ft 3 in tall the distance would increase to 3 in. Thus for someone 5 ft 10 in tall the usual position would be 2 in back. However, there are many variations. Touring riders often use a slightly rearward saddle position together with handlebars set on the high side. They are interested in comfort and steady power output over long distances. Sprint riders and traffic jammers who use brief bursts of sharp energy often use a more forward saddle position. This is the reason sprint frames come with a steeper seat tube angle. For around-town use, if you are a vigorous rider, you may like a more forward saddle position. For extended going and best overall efficiency, however, stick to the normal position.

The horizontal tilt of the saddle, i.e., height of the front relative to the rear, is crucial. There is, in your crotch, a nerve. Pinching it even just slightly over a long ride can disable you with numb crotch for weeks. Start with the nose and rear of the saddle dead level, and if you experience any discomfort, immediately lower the nose a degree or two. It can make all the difference. This is where a good quality seat post with micro-adjusting bolts is important.

I have never seen a serious racing or touring bike with a back-tilted saddle.

Most saddles are set too low. A rough rule of thumb is that while sitting on the bike with your heel on the pedal at its lowest point, your leg should be straight. This means that when riding with the ball of your foot on the pedal, your leg is almost but not quite fully extended at the bottom of the stroke.

A precise formula for the best saddle height has been worked out in a series of scientific tests. Measure inside length of leg from crotch bone to floor without shoes. Multiply this length (in inches) by 1.09. Example: 32 in × 1.09 equals 34.88, or $34\frac{7}{8}$ in. Set saddle so distance A (opposite page) from top of saddle to centre of pedal spindle in down position with crank parallel to seat tube is $34\frac{7}{8}$ in.

This formula has been put together by experts. They found that an alteration in saddle height of 4% of inside leg measurement from the 1.09 setting affected power output by approximately 5%. So once the saddle is set, give it a good long trial before making changes.

Handlebars

Let's settle one thing now: there are many reasons why dropped bars are more efficient and comfortable than flat bars. Here are a few:

(1) A much greater variety of positions is possible. Not only can you select the best position for conditions – like low down when headed into the wind – but being able to shift about and bring different groups of muscles into play greatly increases comfort, to say nothing of power.

(2) Because weight is supported by both the hands and seat, road shocks and bumps rock the body rather than jar it. With conventional flat bars the whole weight of the body rests on the saddle. With dropped bars, not only is weight supported by the arms, but because the body is forward, it tends to pivot at the hips going over bumps. As it happens this is also very desirable from an anatomical point of view: leaning forward stretches the spine, allowing the absorption of shocks, and increases breathing capacity. Conventional bars force the rider into a stiff-spined position where the invidizual vertebrae of the spine are pinched together. Further, because there is no pivoting give at the hips, each and every jolt and bump is transmitted directly up the spine, greatly increasing fatigue.

(3) The better distribution of weight allowed by dropped bars provides improved stability and steering characteristics.

Positioning of the handlebars is crucial. For conventional use they should be set so that the top bar is just level with the nose of the saddle. Sprint bikes have the bars a whole lot lower, and if you do a lot of traffic riding you may want to set yours down a bit. Mine are about $1\frac{1}{2}$ in lower than the saddle. Just remember that if you opt for short-term speed it will be at some cost to overall efficiency.

The stem should position the bars so that the distance between the nose of the saddle and the rear edge of the centre of the handlebars equals the distance from your elbow to your outstretched fingertips. Another way to determine this distance is to sit on the bike in your normal riding position while a friend holds it steady. Without changing position, remove one hand from handlebars and let arm dangle fully relaxed. Now rotate your arm in a large arc without stretching. If, as your hand comes back to the bar, it is ahead of or behind the other hand, the bars need to be moved. Stems come in increments of length, or you can buy an adjustable stem. This costs and weighs more.

The standard rake for the ends of drop bars is 10° from the horizontal:

Start with this setting, which makes the tops of the bars level and thus affords the greatest variety of riding positions, and make changes as you desire.

Brakes

Do not tape new bars until you have ridden the bike enough to fully fiddle with and set the position of the brake levers. Most levers are too low. Almost all braking is done from above:

and the levers need to be high enough so that you can stop quickly and without undue effort.

Toe clips

Use them! They virtually double your pedalling efficiency. They may be a little awkward at first, but soon you will be able to slip in and out of them without a thought (see Riding). Be sure to get the size which corresponds to your shoe size: small for ladies with small feet, medium up to size 8, and large size 9 and up. To avoid scratching up fancy shoes, tape the fronts of the clips with a little cloth tape.

Cleats

Cleats are metal or plastic strips fastened to the soles of bicycling shoes. Used in conjunction with toe clips they hold your foot to the pedal with a vengeance, and are quite unsafe for traffic riding unless you use very loosely set straps. But they are essential for racing and great for touring. To fit cleats properly, ride your bike for a few miles without toe clips so that the soles of your shoes take an impression from the pedals. Then simply position cleats so cleat tunnel is aligned exactly with the pedal marks. Then fit toe clips.

Gearing

Fitting also includes the selection of gearing. Understanding this subject requires some knowledge of basic riding technique. Some of the information I am going to give you now is rather technical. Just use it as you need it.

When I bought my first 10-speed I was surprised to find that the gears, instead of each having a separate range like on a car, overlapped considerably. One gear really wasn't much different from the other. The reason for this is that there is a rate of cadence – the speed with which the cranks are spun around – which is the most efficient. For most people this rate is from 65 to 85 strokes per minute. Racers run 120–130 and up. The idea behind a multitude of gears is to allow the rider to maintain the same cadence regardless of terrain.

In consequence, a racing bike will have close ratio gears, each one much the same as the next, while a touring bike will have wide-ratio gears, with much greater differences between each gear. The reason for this is that touring bikes frequently pack heavy loads up steep grades. They are also – rightly – usually the choice of the novice rider. Only expert riders in good condition can comfortably use close-ratio gears.

What determines ratio? The number of teeth on the front sprocket divided by the number of teeth on the back sprocket. Thus a 60 front and a 15 rear give a 4 to 1 ratio. For competition a typical set-up might be a rear cluster of 23, 21, 19, 17, 15 matched to front sprockets of 49 and 52. For touring it might be 28, 24, 20, 17, 14 rear and 40 to 50 front.

The Humber Tandem

To make everything a little simpler, gear ratios are expressed as a single number. The formula is:

$$\frac{\text{Number of teeth on front sprocket}}{\text{Number of teeth on back sprocket}} \times \text{wheel diameter} = \text{gear ratio}$$

A chart of commonly available gears is given on pages 100–1.

In general, 100 is the top range and is hard to push, 90 is more common, and 80 the usual speed gear. 60 and 70 are the most often used, 40 and 50 are for hills. Below 40 is for extremely steep terrain and heavy loads. Most people gear too high and pedal too slowly. This increases fatigue. It is much better to pedal briskly against relatively little resistance.

There are other factors besides range to consider in setting up gears. Ease of transition from one gear to another is important. If you have to shift both front and back sprockets every time, it is laborious. For example:

Rear		14	17	21	26	31
Front	52	100.2	82.3	66.9	54	45
Front	47	90.4	74.5	60.2	48.6	40.8

means that to run up through the gears consecutively requires continuous double shifts. On the other hand, a set up like:

Rear		14	15	17	19	21
Front	54	104	97.2	85.6	76.7	69.4
Front	38	73.2	68	60	54	49

means that you can run up through the gears using only one shift of the front derailleur. (Never use the small front to small rear or big front to big rear. I will explain why later.)

If you use wide gaps front and rear there is almost bound to be some duplication of gears:

Rear		14	17	21	26	31
Front	52	100.2	82.3	66.9	54	45
Front	42	81	66.7	54	43.5	36.4

and yet curiously enough, many good bikes are set up this way. It really depends on what you want the bike for, because in balancing the various factors of range, ease of shifting, and number of different gears, you are just going to have to make compromises. For novice riders I would suggest the following:

Hilly terrain
Competition – 45 × 52 front, 14, 16, 19, 20, 23 rear.
Touring – 36 × 52 front, 14, 16, 19, 23, 28 rear.

In Britain, which has quite steeply pitched hills, novices and heavily laden tourists may be better off with the recommendation of the Cyclists' Touring Club, 28 × 46 front, 15, 17, 19, 21, 23 rear, which gives closer ratios in a lower range, viz:

Rear		15	17	19	21	23	
Front	28	50.2	44.3	39.7	35.9	32.7	27-in wheel
Front	46	82·6	72·9	65·3	59·1	54	
				VS			
Rear		14	16	19	23	28	
Front	36	69.4	60.7	51	42.1	34.6	27-in wheel
Front	52	100.2	87.8	73.7	62	50	

Flat terrain
Competition – 49 × 52 front, 15, 17, 19, 21, 23 rear.
Touring – 40 × 54 front, 14, 16, 19, 23, 26 rear.

Compromise
Touring – 40 × 50 front, 14, 17, 20, 24, 28 rear.

I make these recommendations with some misgivings for there is one problem or another with all of them. There always is, but these are stock gearings with which you can do quite a bit. Each person of course has his own personal preferences, and you should work out gearing to suit your own needs. I, for example, don't care a fig about competition, and am mostly interested in traffic jamming and touring. On my all-time favourite bike (stolen by an addict) I had 46 × 60 front and 13 through 30 rear, which got me incredulous and pitying regard from bike-wise friends. It suited me perfectly. The 46 front running through the 30 rear gave me a 41 gear which got me up nearly everything. When in town I used only the 60 front and the three middle gears of the back sprocket, thus minimizing shifting. Down hills and long shallow gradients the super-heavy 60 front and 13 rear drove the bike along like a bomb. In short, it was ultra-wide range gearing also suitable for short sprints.

Opinions about gearing vary widely. An excellent series of articles by Frank Berto appeared in the March and April, 1975 (10-speeds), March, April, and May, 1977, and January, 1978 (15-speeds), and

For 27-in wheels

Number of teeth on chainwheel

No. teeth rear sprocket	24	26	28	30	32	34	36	38	40	42	44	45	46	47	48	49	50	51	52	53	54	55	56
12	54	58·3	62·9	67·5	71·8	76·4	81	85·3	89·9	94·5	98·8	101·2	103·4	105·6	108	110·2	112·3	114·7	117	119	121·5	123·7	126
13	49·7	54	58	62·1	66·4	70·5	74·5	78·8	82·9	87·2	91·3	93·4	95·3	97·5	99·6	101·5	103·7	105·8	108	110	112·1	114·2	116·1
14	46·2	49·9	54	57·8	61·6	65·3	69·4	73·2	76·9	81	84·8	86·7	88·6	90·4	92·3	94·5	96·4	98·3	100·2	102	104	106	108
15	43·2	46·7	50·2	54	57·5	61	64·8	68·3	71·8	75·6	79·1	81	82·6	84·5	86·4	88	89·9	91·8	93·6	95·3	97·2	99	100·8
16	40·5	43·7	47·2	50·5	54	57·2	60·7	64	67·5	70·7	74·2	75·9	77·5	79·1	81	82·6	84·2	85·9	87·8	89·4	91	92·1	94·5
17	38	41	44·3	47·5	50·8	54	57	60·2	63·4	66·7	69·6	71·3	72·9	74·5	76·1	77·7	79·4	81	82·6	84	85·6	87·2	88·9
18	35·9	38·9	41·8	44·8	47·8	50·8	54	57	59·9	62·9	65·8	67·5	68·8	70·5	71·8	73·4	74·8	76·4	78	79·4	81	82·3	84
19	34	36·7	39·7	42·4	45·4	48·1	51	54	56·7	59·7	62·4	63·7	65·3	66·7	68	69·4	71	72·4	73·7	75·4	76·7	78·1	79·3
20	32·4	35·1	37·8	40·5	43·2	45·9	48·6	51·3	54	56·7	59·4	60·7	62·1	63·4	64·8	66·1	67·5	68·8	70·2	71·5	72·9	74·2	75·6
21	30·8	33·2	35·9	38·3	41	43·5	46·2	48·6	51·3	54	56·4	57·8	59·1	60·2	61·6	62·9	64·3	65·3	66·9	68	69·4	70·5	72
22	29·4	31·9	34·3	36·7	39·1	41·6	44	46·4	48·9	51·3	54	55·1	56·4	57·5	58·9	59·9	61·3	62·4	63·8	65	66·2	67·5	68·6
23	28	30·5	32·7	35·1	37·5	39·7	42·1	44·5	46·7	49·1	51·6	52·6	54	55·1	56·2	57·5	58·6	59·7	61	62·1	63·2	64·5	65·6
24	27	29·2	31·3	33·7	35·9	38	40·5	42·7	44·8	47·2	49·4	50·5	51·6	52·6	54	55·1	56·2	57·2	58·5	59·4	60·7	61·8	63
25	25·9	28·1	30·2	32·4	34·6	36·7	38·9	41	43·2	45·4	47·5	48·6	49·7	50·8	51·8	52·9	54	55·1	56·2	57·2	58·3	59·4	60·4
26	24·8	27	28·9	31	33·2	35·1	37·3	39·4	41·3	43·5	45·6	46·7	47·5	48·6	49·7	50·7	51·8	52·9	54	54·8	56	57	58·1
27	23·8	25·9	27·8	30	31·9	33·7	35·9	37·8	40	41·8	43·7	44·8	45·9	47	47·8	48·8	49·9	50·7	51·8	52·9	54	54·8	55·9
28	22·9	24·8	27	28·9	30·8	32·7	34·6	36·4	38·3	40·5	42·4	43·2	44·3	45·1	46·2	47·2	48·1	49·1	50	51·1	52	53	54
29	22·1	24	25·9	27·8	29·7	31·6	33·5	35·4	37	38·9	40·8	41·8	42·6	43·7	44·5	45·4	46·4	47·2	48·3	49·1	50·2	51	52·1
30	21·6	23·2	25·1	27	28·6	30·5	32·4	34	35·9	37·8	39·4	40·5	41·3	42·1	43·2	44	44·8	45·9	46·8	47·5	48·6	49·4	50·2
31	20·8	22·4	24·3	25·9	27·8	29·4	31·3	32·9	34·8	36·4	38·1	39·1	40	40·8	41·6	42·6	43·5	44·3	45	45·9	47	47·8	48·6
32	20·2	21·9	23·5	25·1	27	28·6	30·2	31·9	33·7	35·4	37	37·8	38·6	39·4	40·5	41·3	42·1	42·9	43·7	44·5	45·4	46·2	47·2

Number of teeth on rear sprocket

Number of teeth on chainwheel

Number of teeth on rear sprocket	24	26	28	30	32	34	36	38	40	42	44	45	46	47	48	49	50	51	52	53	54	55	56
12	52	56·2	60·6	65	69·2	73·6	78	82·2	86·6	91	95·2	97·5	99·6	101·7	104	106	108·2	110·5	112·6	114·7	117	119·1	121·2
13	47·8	52	55·9	59·8	64	67·9	71·8	75·9	79·8	84	87·9	90	91·8	93·9	95·9	97·8	99·8	101·9	104	105·8	107·9	110	111·8
14	44·5	48·1	52	55·6	59·3	62·9	66·8	70·5	74·1	78	81·6	83·5	85·3	87·1	88·9	91	92·8	94·6	96·5	98·3	100·1	101·9	104
15	41·6	45	48·4	52	55·4	58·8	62·4	65·8	69·2	72·8	75·2	78	79·6	81·4	83·2	84·8	86·6	88·4	90	91·8	93·6	95·2	97
16	39	42·1	45·5	48·6	52	55·1	58·5	61·6	65	68·1	71·5	73·1	74·6	76·2	78	79·6	81·1	82·7	84·5	86·1	87·6	89·2	91
17	36·7	39·5	42·6	45·8	48·9	52	54·9	58	61·1	64·2	67·1	68·6	70·2	71·8	73·3	74·9	76·4	78	79·3	80·9	82·4	84	85·5
18	34·6	37·4	40·3	43·2	46	48·9	52	54·9	57·7	60·6	63·4	65	66·3	67·9	69·2	70·7	72	73·6	74·9	76·4	78	79·3	80·9
19	32·8	35·4	38·2	40·8	43·7	46·3	49·1	52	54·6	57·5	60·1	61·4	62·9	64·2	65·5	66·8	68·4	69·7	71	72·3	73·8	75·1	76·4
20	31·2	33·8	36·4	39	41·6	44·2	46·8	49·4	52	54·6	57·2	58·5	59·8	61·1	62·4	63·7	65	66·3	67·6	68·9	70·2	71·5	72·8
21	29·6	32	34·6	36·9	39·5	41·9	44·5	46·8	49·4	52	54·3	55·6	56·9	58	59·3	60·6	61·9	62·9	64·2	65·5	66·8	67·9	69·2
22	28·3	30·7	33	35·4	37·7	40	42·4	44·7	47·1	49·4	52	53·1	54·3	55·4	56·7	57·7	59	60·1	61·4	62·4	63·7	65	66
23	27	29·4	31·5	33·8	36·1	38·2	40·6	42·9	45	47·3	49·7	50·7	52	53	54·1	55·4	56·4	57·5	58·8	59·8	60·8	62·1	63·2
24	26	28·1	30·2	32·5	34·6	36·7	39	41·1	43·2	45·5	47·6	48·6	49·7	50·7	52	53	54·2	55·1	56·2	57·2	58·5	59·5	60·6
25	25	27	29·1	31·2	33·3	35·4	37·4	39·5	41·6	43·7	45·8	46·8	47·8	48·9	49·9	51	52	53	54·1	55·1	56·2	57·2	58·2
26	23·9	26	27·8	29·9	32	33·8	35·9	38	39·8	41·9	43·9	45	45·8	46·8	47·8	48·9	49·9	51	52	52·8	53·8	54·9	55·9
27	22·9	25	26·8	28·9	30·7	32·5	34·6	36·4	38·5	40·3	42·1	43·2	44·2	45·2	46	47·1	48·1	48·9	49·9	51	52	52·8	53·8
28	22·1	23·9	26	27·8	29·7	31·5	33·3	35·1	36·9	39	40·8	41·6	42·6	43·4	44·5	45·5	46·3	47·3	48·1	49·1	49·9	51	52
29	21·3	23·1	25	26·8	28·6	30·4	32·2	34·1	35·6	37·4	39·3	40·3	41·2	42·1	42·9	43·7	44·7	45·5	46·5	47·3	48·4	49·1	50·2
30	20·8	22·4	24·2	26	27·6	29·4	31·2	32·8	34·5	36·4	38	39	39·9	40·6	41·6	42·4	43·2	44·2	45	45·8	46·8	47·6	48·4
31	20	21·6	23·4	25	26·8	28·3	30·2	31·7	33·5	35·1	36·7	37·7	38·5	39·3	40	41·1	41·9	42·6	43·4	44·2	45·2	46	46·8
32	19·5	21·1	22·6	24·2	26	27·6	29·1	30·7	32·5	34·1	35·6	36·4	37·2	38	39	39·8	40·6	41·3	42·1	42·9	43·7	44·5	45·5

Number of teeth on rear sprocket

May, 1978 issues of the American magazine *Bicycling* (PO Box 10098, Palo Alto, CA 94303 USA).

If you do elect to muck about with gear ratios, you will have to take derailleur capacity into account. Besides shifting the chain from sprocket to sprocket, the rear derailleur also keeps the chain taut. A 14 to 30 rear and 36 × 54 front gives a variation in chain slack (between the 36 to 14 and 54 to 30) which exceeds the capacity of some derailleurs. Derailleur capacity is a function of design: competition units do not have to cover a wide range and can therefore be much lighter; touring units are heavier and sturdier. Generally, capacity is marked on the box as, for example, 13–24–36–53. The outer figures give the high gear, the inner, the lower. Some advertised figures are as follows:

Brand	Rear gear range	Front and rear
Simplex Prestige	13–28	37
Huret Allvit	13–28	28
Campagnolo Nuovo Record	13–30	32
Campagnolo Gran Turismo	13–36	43
Sun Tour GT	13–34	40

For wide range gearing the Campagnolo Gran Turismo is a whirlaway winner. It is sturdy, beautifully made and designed – and heavy.

You will have to decide for yourself which elements in the weight *v.* range balance are the most important. Here is the final titbit to take into account and round out an already confusing picture: you don't need the full range of the derailleur. You should not ever run the big front sprocket to the big rear, or the small front to the small rear, because it causes the chain to cut across at too severe an angle, causing excessive wear, usually rubbing of the derailleur gates, and reduced efficiency.

So . . . the important range is between the large front sprocket to the next largest back sprocket and the small front sprocket to the next to smallest rear sprocket. Since this is a more limited range with a little diddling you can use a competition derailleur with relatively wide-range gears. The advantage is lighter weight and improved performance.

This business of cross-angle strains on the chain bears on the subject of triple front chainwheels. These units are the choice of many experienced tourists for mountain country and packing heavy loads, as they give the most range. Because of cross-over problems however, you do not get that many extra gears. In addition, triple chainwheels are difficult to adjust and align, and the derailleur cages tend to get screwed up. Some manufacturers have simply stopped selling 15-speed bikes. Unless you really need the extra range I'd advise staying away from this combination.

A Danger Board

6 Riding

Anybody can ride a bicycle. You just get aboard and pedal. Heh!
Try following an experienced tourist on a 100-mile run or a
competition rider around the track. Physical condition of course
plays a part, but here technique counts more than anything else.
Fifty-year-old grandmothers can and do run rings around fit young
adults. Attention to the basics of technique will make riding easier
and more enjoyable, and give you greater freedom than if you had
not bothered with the subject at all.

Of course even basic technique varies somewhat with conditions.
And there is a lot more to riding than technique. The following
chapters on traffic jamming, and touring and racing, amplify
considerably the information you need in order to cycle safely and
comfortably.

Shifting

Take it easy when first learning to shift. Once you get the knack
you can make smooth split-second gear changes, but let your skill
develop gradually and avoid damaging 'clunk' sounding shifts.

3-Speeds: To shift up to a higher gear, ease pressure on pedals,
move selector to next gear, resume pressure. Extra-fast shifts may be
made by maintaining pedal pressure, moving the selector, and
then pausing momentarily when the shift is desired. If done too
hard, this may damage gears. Going down to 1st from 2nd or 3rd
and coming to a stop, back-pedal slightly. If not stopping, use same
procedure as for upshifts.

10-Speeds: Never, ever shift a 10-speed unless pedalling. To
see why, hang your bike up so that the rear wheel is off the ground,
rotate the cranks, and manipulate the gear shift levers so you can
see how they work. Shifting a 10-speed without pedalling may
result in a bent or broken chain or gear teeth. If you park your bike
in the street, always give the gears a visual check to make sure
passers-by have not fiddled with them. It happens often.

When going up or down through the gears, ease pedalling pressure during shift. The shift levers do not have stops for the different gears, and you have to learn where they are by feel. Do not let the derailleur cages rub the chain. Sometimes it is necessary to make a small adjustment in the front derailleur when using a wide range of rear sprockets in order to prevent this. Do not run the big front sprocket to the big rear sprocket, or the small front to the small rear. It causes the chain to cut across at too severe an angle, greatly increasing wear and reducing efficiency. Proper shifting should also take into account the demands of cadence (see below).

Pedalling

Ride with the ball of your foot on the pedal, not the heel or arch. The fundamental technique for easy cycling is called ankling. This is where the foot pivots at the ankle with each revolution of the crank. Start at the top of the stroke (12 o'clock) with the heel slightly lower than the toes. Push with the ball of the foot and simultaneously pivot at the ankle on the downstroke so that the foot levels out between 2 and 3 o'clock, and continue this motion so that at the bottom of the stroke the toes are lower than the heel:

With toe clips pull up on the upstroke as well. The main thing to strive for is smoothness and steady, even pressure. Practise this slowly, in a high gear, and away from traffic so you can concentrate on watching your feet.

Toe clips are a great boon. By allowing you to pull up on the pedals as well as push down, they virtually double pedalling efficiency. They are completely safe. Smooth-soled conventional shoes can always be slipped out even when tightly strapped down. If using bicycling shoes and cleats, keep the straps loose in traffic. The technique for getting underway is simple: start with loose straps. Straddle the bike, slip a foot into a pedal at the 1 o'clock position, and tighten the strap. Push off, using the downstroke of this crank to get you underway, and simultaneously reach down with the free foot, give the pedal a light tap to spin the toe clip around to the proper position, slip foot in, bring crank around to 12 o'clock position, and tighten strap. It sounds more complicated than it is. The key is the deft, light tap to the pedal to bring the toe clip around so you can slip your foot in. Practice will soon make it second nature. When coming to a stop, reach down and loosen one strap so you can get your foot back in easily when underway again. Do not worry about being trapped by toe clips. I have made zillions of emergency stops and have always been able to get my feet free. On the other hand, do not tempt fate by riding in heavy traffic with ultra-tight straps. And if you use sneakers or other soft-soled shoes (bad – not enough support), or cleated bicycling shoes, keep the straps loose when conditions warrant.

Cadence

This subject was mentioned in connection with gearing. Briefly, human beings pedal most efficiently at a certain number of strokes per minute. The optimum cadence varies with the physical condition and technique of the individual rider. Generally, novices run from 60 to 85 strokes per minute, experienced tourists approach 100, and racers run 120–30 and up.

Most people gear too high and pedal too slowly. They don't think they are getting anywhere or getting any exercise unless they are pushing against resistance. It is precisely this pushing which creates needless fatigue. It is much better to pedal rapidly against relatively little resistance. Especially when first starting with a bike, always try to pedal as rapidly as you can without going into orbit. Soon you will find your natural cadence, and should always try to maintain this as a uniform rate of pedalling. Allow this to be one of the primary functions of the gears, and always shift up or down as necessary to maintain an even cadence. Learn to shift just before you need the new gear. Do not let a hill slow down your cadence, for example, but shift just before you hit it, and as needed going up. The way you will be able to churn along will be absolutely amazing.

Bumps

When you come to bumps, pot-holes, cables, etc, put most of your weight on the pedals and handlebars. This allows the bike to pivot underneath you, reducing shock for both you and the bike. You know how motorcycle scramble riders stand up on the pegs? Like that.

Braking

Try to use your brakes as little as possible. This will help you to 'look ahead' and anticipate traffic conditions in advance. Be careful of braking too hard and skidding or pitching yourself over the handlebars. It is the front brake which does most of the work, and the more rapidly you decelerate, the more work it can do. This is because weight is transferred forward, increasing the coefficient of friction between the front tyre and the road surface. Simultaneously, weight on the back tyre is lessened slightly, decreasing the coefficient of friction and making it more liable to skid. The technique for a rapid or panic stop is thus one of keeping the body weight as far back as possible, progressively increasing pressure on the front brake, and holding pressure on the back brake to just below the point where the wheel will lock and skid. It is a question of feel and can only be learned by practice. Start with quick stops from low speeds and gradually increase velocity. After you feel reasonably adept, have a friend give you emergency stop signals at unexpected moments.

In slippery conditions or when banked hard over in turn favour the rear brake. The rear wheel does have a greater tendency to skid, but if it goes you may still be able to keep yourself upright, and at worst will land on your hip. A front-wheel skid will pile you on your face.

The police have strict orders to arrest any Bicyclist riding without a bell or whistle

In wet conditions frequently apply the brakes lightly to wipe water off the rims. Otherwise you may need four or five times the distance for stopping with dry brakes.

Going down long hills avoid overheating the brake shoes or wheel rims by pumping (on-off-on-off-on, etc.) the brakes. Always be able to stop.

Turning

If you can ride a bicycle then by definition you can turn it. But there are different methods and styles of turning.

Underway, a bicycle is in a constant state of imbalance. A tendency to lean one way will be corrected by the rider, the bike will move through centre of balance to a lean the opposite way, and the rider will correct again. Most turning consists simply of taking advantage of a lean in the desired direction. Instead of correcting, the rider allows the lean to continue and thus effects a turn. The *feeling* is that the rider has changed balance and the bike has followed to suit, and in that bicycle geometry is designed for a certain amount of self-steering, the feeling is accurate enough. The rider does in fact change balance. This type of turn has two faults: it is slow, and it puts rider and bicycle weight in one single line down to the point of tyre contact with the road.

In racing, and in traffic riding, it is often necessary to turn FAST! This can be done by hauling back on the handlebar end opposite to the direction in which you wish to go. The bike will move out from under you, you will start to fall, and then you will TURN. Can you see it? In the 'normal' turn you topple to one side gradually; in the 'haul handlebar' turn you snatch the bike out from underneath you, and immediately fall into a turn. It is very handy for avoiding unexpected obstacles such as broken glass. In effect, you go one way, the bike goes the other, and afterwards you catch up with each other. Like panic braking, this type of turn must be learned slowly, and with lots of room for manoeuvring.

Another type of turn consists of laying down the bike, while you remain relatively upright, i.e., the bike 'leans' more than you do. This is useful when the road surface is rough, because then a percentage of the rider weight pivots as the bike move up and down, lessening the load on the wheels. Better for the bike, better for you. It is also a quick turn, although not as fast as hauling handlebar.

Another type of turn consists of leaning the body more than the bike. I think – but cannot assure you – that this helps lessen the chances of a skid. At any rate, when I unexpectedly encounter a wet manhole cover or oil slick while turning I throw the bike *up* while keeping my own weight down. This, and the lay down turn, can be done by moving the whole bike underneath you while you pivot sideways at the hips, and can be accelerated by hauling on the handlebars as well.

Haul, lay down, and set up turns are esoteric in description but relatively simple in practice. For your own safety you should be able to execute a haul turn instantly and automatically whenever circumstances require.

7 Traffic jamming

Every rider must know how to ride on streets and highways shared
with motor vehicles, the same way if you walk you have to know
how to cross the street. Beyond this, for many people 99 per cent of
their riding is in traffic, and they might as well make it as safe and
enjoyable as possible. I have the worst misgivings about this chapter,
for on the one hand I want you to use a bicycle as much as possible,
but there is no way I can tell you that riding in traffic is safe. In
plain fact, it is dangerous. Bicycle industry pundits point to the fact
that cyclist casualty figures have declined since 1960, but statistics
from the Annual Traffic Census indicate a decrease of two-thirds in
annual mileage in the same period, so that the accident rate per mile
cycled is rising. With an increasing preponderance of skilled riders
and eventual segregation of motor vehicles from pedestrian and cycle
traffic, this trend will reverse, but those who have been frightened
away from cycling have ample justification for their fears. The other
side of the coin is that taking a bath is dangerous too. There are
some things one has or wants to do, accepting and attempting to
prepare for attendant dangers. Each person needs to make her/his
own evaluation of the amount and kind of traffic riding that suits
him/her. Although the basic principles are the same, there is a
considerable difference between mixing it up with heavy weekday
commuter traffic and cycling a few blocks to the park on Sunday.

This chapter contains a multitude of facts and suggestions, but
the most important thing I have to tell you about riding under any
conditions, *and especially in traffic*, concerns psychological attitude
and attentiveness. You must at all times be alert, and know
everything that is going on, from the size of the pebbles on the road
to the debris which might fall on you from a construction project to
the number and type of vehicles before and behind you – absolutely
everything. Traffic riding requires total concentration. There is no
place for woolgathering here, or idyllic pastoral pleasures. If you
don't pay attention, you may die.

Attentiveness has benefits. First of all, total engagement is refreshing. For example, I like physical changes but spend most of my time pushing a pencil. For me the change of pace represented by traffic jamming is at times exhilarating. It does, as they say, take your mind off your troubles. Secondly, once you gain a little experience you will hopefully still be alert, but relaxed. Is crossing the street a C. B. DeMille production for you? In a more relaxed state you will appreciate the benefits of attentiveness, and see more, notice more, feel more. Getting from one place to another will be a distinctly real experience, and something *you* do.

I would like to deal with two other drawbacks to traffic jamming which unfortunatcly have no redeeming features:

Air pollution*

The inhalation of exhaust fumes and other pollutants is a serious health hazard. The automobile contributes up to 85 per cent of all air pollution in urban areas. As a cyclist not only are you at nose level with the maximum concentration of the pollution, but you are breathing harder and faster (hyperventilation). Estimating the precise degree of possible or actual damage is difficult. One statistic is that the average urbanite inhales the equivalent in particles and poisons of two packs of cigarettes a day. Does this translate for the bike rider as four packs of cigarettes a day? Five? Six?

Cars emit lead, unburnt gas, nitrogen oxides, sulphur oxides, carbon monoxide, and small quantities of grit. The worst for the cyclist are lead and carbon monoxide.

According to Dr Derek Bryce-Smith, Professor of Chemistry at Reading University, there is a good chance that airborne lead is causing real physical damage to large numbers of children today. He has also suggested that a portion of mental illness may be due to otherwise undetectable brain damage from lead pollution. *Bicycle Buyers Guide* Number 3, 1978, reports that 'the effect of lead on human beings varies from person to person', and cites the work of Dr Oliver David, New York City, whose study of 600 Brooklyn children 'showed that those with the most lead in their blood and urine were more likely to have conduct problems, academic disabilities and be hyperactive than their less polluted fellows. This was despite the fact that *none of them had levels of lead in their bodies*

* Thanks to Francis Arnold for much of the information here.

which would be considered dangerous by current medical opinion.' (Italics mine – R.B.) Lead poisoning has been listed as a cause in the death of zoo animals. In London alone, five tons of lead pollute the air each day.

Carbon monoxide is the greatest immediate risk for the cyclist. It is a classic poison which interferes with the oxygen-carrying capacity of the blood. Long before it kills, this action results in decreased alertness, headaches, vague dizziness, and nausea. This dehabilitation adds to the hazard of traffic jamming.

The concentration in the air in many urban areas of both lead and carbon monoxide is already far above recommended levels. These levels are themselves suspect, for in the Soviet Union the permitted concentration of lead is 100 times lower than in the United States.

An interesting fact is that the chief source of airborne lead, tetraethyl lead in petrol, is completely unnecessary. Many cars in America, and all cars in Japan, run on lead-free petrol. The additive tetraethyl lead is simply a cheap way of boosting octane rating, and therefore profits.

You cannot draw any final conclusions from this sort of information and say, well, so and so many people are being injured. Mental illness, headaches, animal deaths, Soviet standards, two packs a day, and other titbits of information are not readily translatable into an accurate assessment of damage, and particularly not for the cyclist, who rides through the very worst of the pollution. But the simple fact is that I get sick with headache, eye pains, nausea, and general malaise when I ride on smoggy days, and particularly the days which have a yellowish tint.

I would advise against riding at all on high air pollution count days. Try to stay clear of smoke-factory lorries and buses, and pick roundabout routes that favour parks and less-travelled streets. Most gas masks will only filter out grit, but of course the sight of you using one would be wonderful guerrilla theatre.

The hazard of air pollution should not be minimized at all: the benefits you gain from the exercise of riding may well be offset by the damage caused by inhaling the chemicals, poisons, and other wondrous substances freely released into the air we breathe.*

* In correspondence with me, the National Society for Clean Air (NSCA) suggested that I revise this sentence to read: 'The hazard of air pollution should not be disregarded; but the benefits you will gain from the exercise of riding will certainly offset any damage you may think can be caused by

Harassment

Most often the problem with a driver of a motor vehicle is that she/he does not take sufficient notice of the cyclist, and unthinkingly drives inconsiderately or even dangerously. There are times, however, when motorists deliberately harass cyclists, passing too close at high speeds, forcing them into the kerb or off the road, or turning directly into their path and right of way. Many theories have been offered to explain this behaviour: chiefly, envy on the part of the moribund traffic-jammed motorist at the easy passage of the cyclist. From my own experience I would say that these people are unhappy and frustrated – perhaps justifiably – with their work or love lives or whatever, and – unjustifiably – are taking it out on the nearest defenceless object. Whatever the cause, there is no excuse for the inhumanity of flinging a ton or more of steel at unprotected skin and bone. If it happens to you there is little to do but move out of the way, but sometimes it is possible to communicate with the offender. Once, in London, while making a properly signalled and executed right turn from a two-way street into a one-way street, a following saloon cut around my left side and made the same turn, forcing me off the road. I remounted and caught up with the saloon farther down the street, halted it, and with polite fury informed the middle-aged gentleman driver that if he were younger he would have a bloody nose. Judging from his open-mouthed astonishment, it had never occurred to him that this was a possibility. I do not wish to recommend violence to you, but harassing drivers are bullies, meanies – and cowards who, if they encounter spirit and resistance will pick easier targets.

There are innumerable physical hazards to look out for while riding in traffic, but it is motor vehicles which are your main concern. Theory and law says that the bicycle is a vehicle which must be operated according to the rules of the road and which has the same privileges as other vehicles. Fact says otherwise. In many, many cases, the motorist is convinced that his/her vehicle gives her/him the complete right of way. Anything which obstructs

---

inhaling the various pollutants in the air.' They '. . . contend that some of the views expressed by Barry Commoner and Dr Bryce-Smith are alarmist and upsetting,' I can only refer to practical experience: on an early-morning sprint around the park sans motor vehicles the air is refreshing; add motor vehicles and there is a bad smell, and sometimes, dizziness.

her/his forward progress – like a slow-moving bicycle – just
shouldn't be there. He/she may be wrong, but it is essential for your
survival to understand how she/he thinks. As a cyclist you don't
really exist for him/her. As often as not she/he will cut you off, make
turns in front of you, or sit right on your tail when there is no room
to pass. It never even occurs to him/her to put on his brakes and give
you room to manoeuvre, as she/he would for another car. Many
motorists have never ridden a bicycle, and are unfamiliar with the
problems of the cyclist. The Department of the Environment gives
financial support to the National Cycling Proficiency Scheme, which
trains cyclists in riding skills and the Highway Code, but does
nothing for motorists. The Ministry of Transport's manual, *Driving*,
has only a few sparse words on cycles. For most motorists, cycles
are therefore not road-users of equal status, but a peripheral,
obstructive nuisance.

Accordingly, riding successfully in traffic requires a blend of
determination and knowing when to give in. For example, try never
to block overtaking cars. At the same time if it is unsafe for you to
let them pass, don't hesitate to take full possession of your lane so
that they *can't* pass. Both you and the other human have exactly the
same right to use the street or highway. Just because he/she has a
motor vehicle confers no additional rights or privileges, and in fact
the wasteful consumption of energy and vicious pollution of the
environment for which her/his vehicle is responsible is a serious
infringement of your rights. It is important that you understand and
believe this. You have nothing to apologize for. You are not
'blocking' or 'in the way'. At the same time you have to be practical.
A lot of people behind the wheel are authentic maniacs. No matter
how right you are, any confrontation with a motor vehicle will wind
up with you the loser.

There are enough aspects and tricks to traffic jamming so that I
am simply going to run them as a list. Before doing so, a brief
discussion about traffic regulations.

A cyclist must ride according to the Highway Code. If you
are not familiar with the basic rules of the road, the meaning of
various signs and lights (a selection is shown on the next page), and
the proper techniques for turns and roundabouts, then get a copy of
the Code from a post office or bookshop and study it. You can also
enrol in the National Cycling Proficiency Scheme which trains and
tests in the fundamentals of cycling and the Code. It takes only a few

Those with Red Circles — Mostly Prohibitive

Stop and Give Way

No Entry

Stop

No Right Turn

No Left Turn

No U Turns

No Cycling

GIVE WAY

Blue Circles with no Red Border - mostly Compulsory

Give Way to Traffic on Major Road

Ahead only

Turn Left (Right if Arrow is reversed)

Turn Left Ahead (Right if Arrow is reversed)

Keep Left (Right if Arrow is reversed)

Route for Cyclists (Compulsory)

Warning Signs mostly Triangular

1:10

Steep Hill Downwards

Level Crossing without Gate or Barrier Ahead

hours and is free. I recommend it as compulsory for children. Enquire at your police station or school.

This may all seem like a bit much to you. In my view, any user of the road whether on a lorry, bicycle, roller skates, or pogo stick should pass a test. Getting about on roads is a serious business which if it is to be done safely, and with consideration for the rights of others, requires that you know what is going on. Further, your equal status and rights are an important protection which can be maintained only by obeying the same rules as everybody else, and this is possible only if you know what the rules are.

In general, these are:

🚲 that you ride as well to the left as is consistent with safety;
🚲 obey traffic signs and lights;
🚲 give way to pedestrians at zebra crossings;
🚲 signal turns and stops. Left turn is left arm held straight out to the side, right turn ditto with the right arm, and stop a downward patting motion of the extended right arm.

I feel compelled to pass on to you the information that a cyclist can be prosecuted for endangerment of self or others, recklessness, dangerous riding, or riding under the influence of drugs or alcohol.

A knowledge of the rules is essential, but is only a bare beginning. Moreover, and especially as a relatively defenceless bicyclist, you should not rely on your 'rights' to protect you, but engage in a form of defensive riding which assumes that if there is some way for somebody to get you, they will. So . . .

🚲 Hands near or on brake levers at all times. If you need to stop as quickly as possible and are not going too fast, twist the front wheel as you apply the brakes. The bike will melt into the ground in a controlled crash as the wheel and forks buckle.

🚲 Be alert. There is plenty to watch for. Keep your eyes constantly moving. When looking behind don't twist your head, duck it down. Easier to do, quicker, and smoother. Do this constantly. You might have to swerve to avoid an obstacle or serious accident, and must know if you have the room or not.

🚲 Be definite. Save meandering for country lanes where you can see for a long way in both directions. Ride in a straight line. Signal all turns clearly. Make right turns from right lane and left turns from left lane, if on a wide street. If you are going to do something, do it. Being definite takes the form of a certain amount of aggressiveness. Don't get bulldozed into immobility – nobody is going to give you a break. Make and take your own breaks. As far as most other drivers are concerned you either don't exist or are some alien foreign object which they want behind them. Draw attention to yourself and be super-clear about your intentions. Colourful clothing and/or a bright hat are a good idea.

 Be defensive. Always assume the worst. You can't see around the stopped bus? *Assume* a pregnant lady who is the sole support of 21 children is going to come prancing out. There is a car waiting to cross your lane? *Assume* it will, because *it will*. In 4 out of 5 accidents involving bicycles and motor vehicles, the motor vehicle committed a traffic violation. Always ride within a margin of control which allows you to stop or escape should absolutely everything go wrong.

 Look for openings in traffic, driveways, streets, garages, etc, that you can duck into should the need arise. Try to plan where you would go should you and the bike part company. The natural tendency in a collision situation is to try desperately to stop. Many times your interest will be better served by launching yourself over an obstacle. Far better to hit the road at an angle than a car head-on.

 While not exceeding a speed which gives you control, try to

keep moving. Within reason, avoid using brakes. This will have the effect of making you figure out well in advance what traffic situations are going to occur. There is a car double-parked in the next block. Are you going to be able to swing out? Also, a lot of the danger from other vehicles in traffic comes from differences in velocity. If you are going slow, cars bunch up behind, crowd, become impatient, etc. A racing bike can easily keep up with and pass a lot of traffic. You may find it a bit unnerving to run neck and neck with cabs and lorries at first, but it is safer than offering a stationary target. Try to *integrate* yourself with the traffic.

🚲 To this end, always be in a gear low enough to give you power and acceleration. In heavy traffic an even cadence is difficult to maintain, but try to keep your feet churning away and avoid getting stuck in a 'dead' high gear. As a cyclist you have only a fraction of the power available to the motorist. To stay integrated with traffic requires that you be prepared to accelerate hard and quickly.

🚲 On the other hand, do not follow the car in front too closely. Car brakes are better than bike brakes. Most bike accidents consist of the bicycle running into something. Leave plenty of room up front. This is where motorists accustomed to running bumper-to-bumper will try to pressure you from behind, even though you are moving at the same speed as the car you are following. Maintain position and if they give you the horn give them the finger.

🚲 Be extra-cautious at intersections where you already have right of way. Cars coming from the opposite direction and turning right will frequently cut straight across your path. Even if the vehicle is seemingly waiting for you to pass, don't trust it, for at the last moment it will leap forward. Letting a motor vehicle precede you to clear the way is often a good tactic.

Another danger at intersections is cars coming up alongside from behind and then making a sudden left turn. One way to stop it is for you to be in the centre of the lane. However, if the intersection you are entering has a light which is going to change soon, then traffic from behind may be storming up at a breakneck pace. You'd better be out of the way.

🚲 In any city anywhere in the world taxi drivers are a hazard. All things are relative, and in London, for example, most cabbies are decent. In the US of A cabbies have the highest ulcer rate of any occupational group, as well they might considering their working conditions and how they drive. Abilities vary, but most are just no good. New York City cabbies are the bottom of the barrel.

The reason a cab driver is often a problem is that he is a professional. Driving in traffic every day, he soon knows exactly what is going on and becomes accustomed to moving ahead at every

THE CITY CYCLIST

opportunity. It is second nature, and does not even require hostile intent on his part. It is just something that he does. Every day. As long as you ride clearly and decisively a cabby will present you with few difficulties; but if you start to fumble and wonder what to do, then he will quickly become impatient, and shut you in behind a bus, or cut you off, or submit you to some other unpleasantry about which you can do nothing.

🚲 Very often you will be riding next to parked cars. Be especially careful of motorists opening doors in your path. Exhaust smoke and faces in rear-view mirrors are tips. Even if a motorist looks right at you and is seemingly waiting for you to pass, give her/him a wide berth. Believe it or not, you may not register on his/her consciousness, and she/he may open the door in your face.

🚲 The law requires you to ride to the left of the left lane as far as is consistent with safety. This is a very elastic and sometimes abused definition. Cyclists have been ticketed for causing an obstruction by riding too far to the right, and there have also been instances of opening car door/cyclist accidents where the cyclist was held at fault. Always allow enough manoeuvring room to avoid road litter and potholes. Pass parked cars with room to spare should a door open. If somebody objects to your 'obstructing', ignore them. If you get a ticket, it is a far better deal than a trip to the hospital.

When the road or street is too narrow for overtaking vehicles to pass you with enough room, then ride bang out in the centre of the lane. Do not let them pass, or if it is a two-way road or street, make them pass in the opposite lane. Vehicle drivers may hoot or shout, but this is far safer for you than letting them pass with only inches to spare. You are equally entitled to road space and safe passage.

🚲 On multi-lane roads or streets where there is a left-turn-only lane at an intersection, and you intend to go straight through, get into the right through-lane well before the intersection. Ditto if there is a bike lane. In fact, even if there is no left-turn-only lane, it is better to move out of the bike lane into the next lane right for going straight through an intersection. This helps minimize the chance of a left-turning vehicle cutting you off.

Lane changing in fast, thick traffic can take muscle. John Forester does it by eyeball to eyeball contact with a particular motorist while positioning himself with the clear intention of moving right.* If the motorist makes room Forester then changes lane. The method has a distinct advantage in that both hands stay on the brakes, where they belong in heavy traffic. However, if you have enough room in front to take one hand off the bars and stick it out in a jabbing, emphatic signal, the situation is then much clearer to other road users.

🚲 Keep an eye on the road surface. Watch out for broken glass, stones, potholes, etc. Plenty of bumps and potholes are big enough to destroy a bike – and you. Going over bumps, cables, etc, get off the saddle and keep your weight on the pedals and handlebars.

🚲 Quite a few things can dump a bike:
Oil slicks in the centre of traffic lanes at busy intersections and on sharp curves. When cars stop or turn hard, a little oil drops off. The resulting slick can send you off the road or sliding out into the middle of a busy intersection.
Newly wet streets. There is a light film of oil which until it is washed away mixes with the water to make a very slippery surface.
Wet manhole covers and steel plates can dump you in a hurry. I have seen this happen often. So can: wet cobblestones, wet autumn leaves, gravel and sand. Many storm sewers are just the right size to swallow up a bicycle wheel.

🚲 Ride with the traffic. Sometimes when there is no traffic coming the other way, it is better to ride in the opposite lane.

🚲 The velocity of traffic on free-way style streets which have no parking is usually too high to permit safe cycling. If you run in the centre of the lane, you block traffic. If you go to the side, cars whizz by you at high speeds with only inches to spare. Stick to streets with parked cars and look out for opening doors.

🚲 Cars and lorries pulling out. They do it unexpectedly and without signalling. Look out for driveways, building entrances, construction projects, cab ranks, and any other possible source of a vehicle. Remember, you don't exist for many drivers. They look right at you, the image is flashed on their brain, but they don't comprehend. They don't *see* you.
And perhaps some do. One time in New York City I had the

* Forester, John. *Effective Cycling*, Custom Cycle Fitments, 782 Allen Court, Palo Alto, CA 94303 USA. The best and most comprehensive book on cycling that I know of.

lights in my favour at an intersection with a police car waiting on the cross street. The eyes of the driver fixed steadily on me and he waited until I was just going through the intersection before pulling through a red light and right in front of me. Expect the unexpected.

🚲 Pedestrians are another unreliable bunch. They don't think 200 pounds of bike and rider coming towards them at 30 mph means anything, and will frequently jaywalk right in your path. Your odds are much better here than when mixing it up with a car, but even so any collision is going to hurt you, the pedestrian, and your bike. Use a horn, yell – and give them the right of way if you have to.

🚲 Kids. As much of a hazard to the cyclist as to the motorist. Any child has the potential to race out suddenly into the street.

🚲 Other cyclists. I don't know why, but many cyclists and especially children are erratic. Give them a wide berth.

🚲 Yellow glasses are good for city riding to keep the dirt out of your eyes.

🚲 Lights are a legal requirement at night. You must have a white front light, and a red rear light marked BS 3648 mounted on the centre line or offside of the bike not more than 20 in from the rear-most point, and between 15 in and 42 in off the ground. For around town use, generator lights have the advantage that they can be left on the bike when you park, and the disadvantage that they only work when the bike is in motion. Battery lights stay lit at all times, but unless you modify the mounting bracket with a screw or other locking device, you should not leave them with the bike. See under Accessories, and Touring, for other discussions about lights. I like a large, permanently-mounted rear reflector. Lights have a habit of failing.

All these endless cautions are depressing. It seems that riding in traffic involves girding yourself for battle and inducing a constant state of morbid apprehension for your life. This is true. The idea of mixing cars and bicycles together is crazy. Cars themselves are an atavistic idiocy responsible for millions of deaths and injuries. It is entirely logical to want to have nothing to do with them.

On the other hand you can get used to it. If you are an alert, defensive rider you are reasonably safe. In return for the risks there

are many benefits and it is up to you to decide how they balance. It isn't all bad by any means, but never deny the stark reality: in traffic there is a chance that you will be killed.

Accordingly, if you can avoid traffic, do so. In Great Britain it is illegal to ride on the footpaths. However, a cyclist is closer to a pedestrian than a car is to a cyclist. Mixing pedestrians and cyclists together on footpaths is not only much safer than mixing cars and cycles on roads, it is not even dangerous, as the accident statistics from Stevenage where the two have mixed for twenty years, bear out. A number of factors make this so, but the simplest is that the cyclist, like the pedestrian, is vulnerable and exposed, and has every interest in avoiding conflicts.

Riding on footpaths must be done with discretion – dashes through Sunday parks filled with strollers are inconsiderate – and you must give way to pedestrians, dismounting if necessary. But many footpaths are little used and offer a more sensible transit than running with the road traffic. Just remember, however rational your case, to ride on a footpath makes you liable to infringement of the law, an alternative you may prefer to risking your life.

8 Bang!

As William Sanders pointed out in a *Bike World* article (October 1973) it is all very well to preach defensive riding, but the cyclist should also know what to do should an accident actually occur. The problem is not so much knowing what to do, as being able to do it.

Most people react to an imminent crash with panic.

'AN AGED WOMAN ON HER BACK,
TWO BABES IN GUTTER PRONE.'

They may freeze into immobility and do nothing, or blindly clamp down on the brakes and lose directional stability. This can make a bad situation fatal. For example, if a car is about to hit you from the side and you death grip the brakes, locking up the rear wheel and sending the bike down in a slide, then when the car hits you are likely to be rolled up underneath it. If, on the other hand, at the moment of impact you try to get clear of the bike and make a dive for the hood of the car, you may slide along to the windscreen and perhaps even over the roof. Not fun, but the survival chances are much better than if you are underneath the car.

Panic induced muscular tension increases physical damage in a crash. The person who falls or is thrown and is able to stay loose and relaxed will suffer less injury than the person who tenses and tries to save him or herself.

The ability to exercise the best of a series of bad options, and stay physically relaxed in a situation offering damage, can only be learned through experience and practice. I have been an avid skiier since I was four, a high diver since I was seven, and when I suddenly find myself flying through the air upside down I am automatically loose, looking to tuck and roll when I hit.

If you do not know how to fall, try to have someone with training – fighting experts, skydivers, skiiers – give you pointers. I find that fast woods riding with an old trasho bike is useful. A few spills are inevitable, and as long as they are in loose dirt, usually little damage results.

Practise the braking and turning techniques discussed in the Riding chapter. Think of how to use them in various circumstances. If a car pulls up alongside you and then unexpectedly turns left, cutting you off, a sudden application of the brakes will simply pile you into the car. A rapid haul turn however, just might avoid an accident, and if you do hit, you will both be going more or less in the same direction. Suppose a car pulls out in front of you from a side road or driveway. There may be enough room for a haul turn so that you hit the car a glancing blow. If there is not enough room to turn, then brake as hard as possible without skidding, and just before hitting the car launch yourself clear of the bike. You may be able to sail right over the car. Stay loose and roll when you hit the pavement.

If you are hit from behind DO NOT BRAKE. Try to get away by steering to the side.

A MIDDAY HALT

9 Touring

'A merry heart goes all the way,
Your sad tires in a mile, a.'—*Shakespeare*

Touring is the real joy in biking. The only better way to see the
country is to walk or roller skate. A bike has advantages in mobility
and luggage-carrying however, and the aesthetic sacrifice is not too
great. Touring can be done in a tremendous variety of ways. You
can go for an afternoon's jaunt or spend a summer or more
travelling thousands of miles. You can go as a self-contained unit
with your own camping gear, or ultra-light and stay in inns, guest
houses, hostels and hotels. You can count the miles travelled, or
concentrate on the scenery (yeah!). Your journey can include transit
by auto, bus, train, boat, and plane, so that you can hop from one
interesting place to another. You can have a plan, or absolutely none
at all. Touring is a call to adventure, beauty, new sights and
experiences.

There's a lot to touring, and plenty for you to think about.
At the same time it can be kept simple. Any bike headed for the
sticks should have a tool kit, unless you don't mind pushing your

bike a few miles to a garage and/or the possibility of an overnight stay until it opens. Equipment makes a difference, but the main thing is to get out there. My greatest, happiest tour was on a battered 1935 BSA whose vital parts shed like water.

Part of the fun of touring is figuring it out and planning or not planning for yourself. Some people insist that the only way to tour is with a meticulous and detailed plan; others heave map and compass into the bushes and go wherever fancy takes them. For some the fun and relaxation comes as a result of planned and concentrated effort; for others it is through not thinking about anything. There is no 'right' way to tour. Each to his own. Accordingly, this chapter tries simply to give basic information about touring. It is not a step-by-step guide. It's up to you to decide where and when you want to go, and what sort of equipment you expect to need.

Great Britain

Where

One source of information is books, obtainable in bookshops or by post from Selpress Books, Suite 413, 4th Floor, 16 Berkeley Street, London W1X 6AP, or from The Cyclists' Touring Club, 69 Meadrow, Godalming, Surrey GU7 3HS. *Explore the Cotswolds by Bicycle*, by S. Ebel and D. Impey (50p), lists a number of detailed, relatively traffic-free tours, with historical background and notes on places and events of interest. Written with the cyclist in mind is *The Roadfaring Guide to South West England*, by R. Wellby (10p). *Bike & Hike* (£1.95) lists 60 UK tours. *Adventure Cycling in Britain*, by T. Hughes (£5.95) covers basic touring techniques and equipment, and lists specific tours varying from easy day rides to strenuous mountain 'rough-stuff'. Another book is *England by Bicycle*, by F. Alderson (£1.15). Full of really useful specific information is *Traveling by Bike*, by World Publications (£1.30).

The British Cycling Bureau,
Stanhope House, Stanhope Place, London W2 2HH

distributes leaflets on various aspects of cycling.

The British Tourist Authority,
239 Old Marylebone Road, London NW1

An Essex Farm — Near Epping

T. Warren

publishes *Inns of Britain, Egon Ronay's Pubs and Tourist Sights in Great Britain* (£1.75), and *Britain: 100 Historic Inns* (free). General information on touring, brochures, accommodation lists, etc., can be obtained from tourist authorities:

British Tourist Authority
Tourist Information Centre, 64 St James's St, London SW1, tel (01)-629 9191.

England

English Tourist Board and London Tourist Board, 4 Grosvenor Gdns, London SW1, tel (01)-730 3400.

East Anglian Tourist Board, 14 Museum St, Ipswich, Suffolk, tel (0473) 21411.

East Midlands Tourist Board, Bailgate, Lincoln, tel (05522) 31521.

English Lakes Counties Tourist Board, Ellerthwaite, Windermere, Westmorland, tel 4444.

Isle of Man Tourist Board, 13 Victoria St, Douglas, tel (0624) 4323.

Isle of Wight Tourist Board, 21 High St, Newport, tel (0983-81) 4343.

Northumbria Tourist Board, 8 Eldon Sq, Newcastle/Tyne, tel (0632) 28795.

North-West Tourist Board, 119 The Piazza, Piccadilly Plaza, Manchester 1, tel (061) 236 0393.

South-East England Tourist Board, 4–6 Monsoon Rd, Tunbridge Wells, Kent, tel (0892) 33066.

West Country Tourist Board, Trinity Ct, Southernhay East, Exeter, Devon, tel (0392) 76351.

West Midlands Tourist Board, 1 Shaw St, Worcester, tel (0905) 29511.

Yorkshire Tourist Board, 312 Tadcaster Rd, York, tel (0904) 67961.

Wales

Wales Tourist Board, Welcome Hse, High St, Llandaff, Cardiff, tel (0222) 567701.

Mid-Wales Tourism Council, 3 China St, Llanidloes, Mont, tel 664.

North-Wales Tourism Council, Civic Centre, Colwyn Bay, Denbighs, tel (0492) 55222.

South Wales Tourism Council, Darkgate, Carmarthen, tel 7557.

Scotland

Scottish Tourist Board, 23 Ravelston Terrace, Edinburgh 4, tel (031) 332 2433.

The Borders Tourist Association, 66 Woodmarket, Kelso, Rox, tel 2125.

Clyde Tourist Association, c/o Information Centre, George Sq, Glasgow, tel (041) 221 9600.

Grampian Tourist Association, 17 High St, Elgin, Moray, tel (0343) 3451.

Highlands and Islands Development Board, Bridge Hse, Bank St, Inverness, tel (0463) 34171.

South-West Scotland Tourist Association, Douglas Hse, Newton Stewart, Wigtowns, tel 546.

Northern Ireland

Northern Ireland Tourist Board, 48 High St, Belfast, tel (0232) 31221.

Probably the best way to get into touring is to join a society or organization. You get a variety of planning and insurance services, and riding with fellow members you receive a planned tour, the benefit of a group leader who will set a pace within your capacity, and lots of free friendly help and advice. First and foremost is:

Cyclists' Touring Club,
69 Meadrow, Godalming, Surrey GU7 3HS.

I recommend this organization to every cyclist, tourist or not. The largest and oldest (1878) national cycling association, it not only provides an extraordinary range of services, but also safeguards and

135

MAPS: READ IN CONJUNCTION WITH
BARTHOLOMEWS' ½ INCH TO
MILE NUMBERS 5 AND 6
OR ORDNANCE SURVEY 1 INCH
TO MILE NUMBERS 181 AND 182
OR O.S. 1:50,000 NUMBER 197

LIC...

A286

...LODSNO

A272

MIDHURST

A286

B2146

STH. HARTING

ELSTED

TREYFORD

DIDLING

Church

BEPTON

UP PARK Hot.

SOUTH DOWNS

COMPTON

UP MARDEN Church

B2146

Museum of Building

SINGLETON

A286

EAST DEAN

STOUGHTON

Bow Hill

CHARLTON

GOODWOOD

Race Course

Kingly Vale

WEST. STOKE

B2178

A285

A27

A27

FISHBOURNE PALACE

CHICHESTER

Cathedral

Theatre

BOSHAM

B2201

B2145

Chichester Harbour

IT IS RECOMMENDED THAT
ROUTE IS FOLLOWED CLOC...

CYCLISTS' TOURING CLUB
TOUR OF WEST SUSSEX
90 MILES LONG © 1974

Heywood Hill did it

miles

route on paved roads
route on rough track or path
other tracks
other roads

THE ENGLISH CHANNEL

champions the cyclist's rights at every level of government and municipal authority. Membership includes the Cyclists' Touring Club Handbook, a thick list of 3,000 recommended accommodation addresses, places to eat, cycle repairers, and CTC local information officers for Great Britain; a list of overseas touring correspondents; information about touring areas, equipment, and travel by air, rail, and sea, including ferries, tunnels, and bridges; a catalogue of the books and maps for Great Britain, the Continent, and Morocco available through the bookshop; and a complete exposition of club services. For the tourist, the most important of these is the Touring Department, which not only has available a large library of comprehensive, personally researched tours, complete with maps (see overleaf) but which will also plan and suggest tours for routes and areas you request, as well as advising on cycle and personal equipment, gears, maps, and travel books. In addition, the CTC London office,

CTC Travel Ltd,
13 Spring Street, London W2 3RA

will make bookings for all air, sea, and rail journeys abroad, and has information sheets on most European countries. In this connection, CTC is a founder member of the Alliance Internationale de Tourisme, linking touring clubs all over the world, and provides on request an AIT cycletouring card as introduction for requests for advice and assistance. There is an International Camping Carnet, and CTC members are allowed to take cycles via cross-channel hovercraft, which you normally cannot do from April to September. Membership includes subscription to the bi-monthly *Cycle Touring*, filled with news of interest to the cyclist, articles on touring and tours, equipment tests, letters, adverts, and useful information. Insurance services include free third-party liability anywhere in the world up to £50,000 and policies are available for personal accident, damage or theft to cycle, cameras, luggage; and inclusive, which takes in all the foregoing, cancellation and curtailment, and personal liability up to £250,000. Membership is worth it for the third party £50,000 cover alone, even for the cyclist who goes only to the station and back. The CTC also provides free legal aid in obtaining compensation for members in road accidents ranging from encounters with motor vehicles to dog bites to damages caused by bad road surfaces. The CTC will make representation to the appropriate local authority or to Parliament in regard to any justified complaint by members on such matters as dangerous road surfaces, traffic difficulties and unfair restrictions on the use of cycles; discourtesy and poor service in the conveyance of cycles by public transport; and misinformed or biased Press or public criticism of cyclists.

The CTC organizes any number of rallies, tours, and competitions on both national and regional levels, and district associations and sections organize local cycling tours and events and social occasions. Tours vary in difficulty, with accommodation at youth hostels, guest houses, and inexpensive hotels.

Another organization providing an accommodations handbook, touring and insurance services for members, and maps, is The British Cycling Federation, 70 Brompton Road, London SW3 1EX.

This is also the internationally recognized controlling body for cycle racing in Great Britain, and is affiliated to the Union Cycliste Internationale, the world governing body of the sport.

The Youth Hostel Associations:

Headquarters:
Trevelyan House, 8 St Stephen's Hill, St Albans, Hertfordshire

A CTC hotel.

Offices and shops:
29 John Adam Street, London WC2 6JE

35 Cannon Street, Birmingham B25 EE

36/38 Fountain Street, Manchester M2 2BE

Scottish Youth Hostels Association, 7 Glebe Crescent, Stirling, Stirlingshire, Scotland SK8 2AJ

Irish Youth Hostels Association, 39 Mountjoy Square, Dublin, Eire

Youth Hostel Association of Northern Ireland, Bryson House, Belfast BT2 7FE, Northern Ireland

The Youth Hostel Associations are a somewhat straitlaced but nevertheless very good outfit with over 4,000 hostels in forty-seven countries, many in beautiful and/or historic areas. Hostels are sometimes spartan, but always serviceable. You provide your own sleeping bag, and help a bit with the chores. Inexpensive, and you can cook your own food. The Association stores sell camping and touring equipment and have a tourist service, as well as running guided tours. An essential organization for the economy-minded.

So. Where you go depends on your own temperament, interests, physical condition, and equipment. If you favour back roads off the beaten track and camping, you are going to have to deal with equipment for both you and the bike; touring on better roads and sleeping in inns means less and lighter equipment. I would suggest that you make your initial rides about 20 miles or so, and work up to longer tours and overnight stays as you get used to it. Until you are quite experienced, do not target over 50 to 60 miles a day, and try to balance hard runs with days of relaxation and shorter jaunts. Excess zeal will turn you into a basket case. Start easy and finish strong.

Riding

I recommend taking the smallest, least travelled roads practically possible. These are B-class roads and smaller. Not only are they almost always more interesting, but the fewer cars there are around the more comfortable you will be. Motor vehicles in the country are a serious hazard for the cyclist. The speed differences between cycles and cars are much greater. On the dual-lane carriageways,

A club ride in the country

for example, the vehicles run at 70 mph plus, often bunched so
tightly together that the drivers' vision is limited by the vehicle they
are following, and hence they do not see the cyclist until the moment
of overtaking, when they no longer have the time to swing out
and give room. This danger is acute at night-time. Often there are
footpaths adjoining such roads, little-used and a sensible alternative,
but keep a keen eye out for broken glass and other litter. On the
two-way A and B class roads many vehicles move smartly, particularly
if the driver 'knows the road', and hare around tight corners at 40
to 60 mph. With an up to 50 mph difference in speed between the
motor vehicle and the cyclist, and limited space for manoeuvring,
a bad situation can develop faster than the many drivers who
over-rate themselves think is possible. You, the naked, exposed,
defenceless cyclist are utterly dependent on the abilities and
emotional maturity of drivers. Even acceding to the insanity which
states that rapid motoring is permissible when executed with requisite
skill, there is still the odd (these days?) exception, for whatever
reason simply incompetent.

The best bet for the cyclist are small roads which keep vehicle
speeds down to about 30 mph, at which rate there is almost always
enough room and time to prevent serious accidents. These roads

meander and take longer, but are usually more interesting. The point of cycling in the first place is to savour and enjoy, and so for reaching somewhere in a hurry use other transport, or take you and your cycle by rail or air.

An alternative to roads are bridlepaths (which the cyclist is legally entitled to use) and footpaths (which he is not). These honeycomb Britain and I have taken many long tours touching road for only a mile or so. The scenery is usually fantastic, and the riding often demanding. Most bikes will stand up to this sort of use well enough, although tubular tyres are pretty much out. An exception of sorts are the special cyclo-cross lugged tyres, but while these provide excellent traction the casings are not as strong as for wire-on tyres. As far as the legality of footpaths is concerned I again suggest common sense. A popular walking area filled with Sunday strollers is a poor choice and you should dismount and walk. But most times there is nobody around and you will have the outdoors to yourself.

Safe country road riding is largely a matter of common sense. Most of the rules for traffic riding apply here also.

🚲 Always carry indentification and notes on your medical particulars (allergy to certain drugs, etc.). Leave a motor vehicle operator's licence at home, as it can be endorsed with traffic offences committed on a bicycle.

🚲 The cardinal rule is 'what if?' Look and think ahead. Don't, for example, time your riding so that you and an overtaking car reach a curve at the same time. If a car – or worse yet a lorry – comes the other way there just isn't going to be enough room.

🚲 Bear in mind the tremendous relative velocity of cars. In traffic you can pretty much keep up, but in the country cars will have up to 70 mph over your 5 to 15. If you crest a hill, for example, and there is no oncoming traffic, move over into the opposite lane for a while. This avoids the hazard of overtaking cars who cannot see you over the crest.

🚲 Try to have a hole to duck into should everything go wrong. Where will you go if that tractor pulls out? If a car comes around the corner on your side of the road, are you going to try for the ditch or a tree? You may wreck a bike going off into a field, but this is a lot better than colliding with a car. Think about this as much as you can and try to make it an automatic process. This way, when an emergency arises, instead of freezing in panic you may be able to save your life.

🚲 Be particularly wary, when you have to speed up, of people doing odd things. Cannonballing down a hill you may be doing 30–50 mph, a fact that many motorists and pedestrians do not comprehend. They see a bicycle, and automatically class it as slow and unimportant, dismissing it from mind (as you can be sure they would not do for a large lorry), and step out or pull out on to the road, or pass, or whatever. This capacity for visual recognition with no subsequent cognitive comprehension may seem bizarre, but I assure you it is so. Never trust other road users – you cannot afford to do so.

🚲 Mind your brakes. After running through puddles or wet grass, dry off by applying them lightly as you ride. When running down steep hills, do not hold the brakes steady, which causes heat build-up and fade, but pump on and off. This also tells you if you have something in reserve – which you always should.

🚲 Run well to the left (or right, on the Continent) but leave yourself a little bit of room to manoeuvre. There are all sorts of broken pavement, sewers, and odd bits of litter which crop up unexpectedly at the road's edge.

🚲 On two-lane roads watch out for overtaking motorists coming towards you. They often do not see or just plain ignore a bicycle coming towards them. If you move out to the centre of your lane most motorists will return to their lane. Some will not and you must be prepared to stop on the shoulder of the road. You might care to have a few rotten tomatoes handy for such moments.

🚲 Beware the Hun in the Sun. At sunrise and sunset motorists with the sun in their eyes may not see you.

🚲 Rural farm traffic is a law unto itself. Many farmers operate machinery on local public roads as if they were in the middle of a field.

🚲 Watch for loose gravel, dirt, or sand, and especially at driveway and side road entrances.

🚲 Bridge gratings, cattle guards, railroad tracks, etc. can all swallow up a bicycle wheel and send you flying.

🚲 Dogs. Dogs and other creatures of the field and air are a menace to the cyclist. I was once attacked by a determined and large goose. Dogs are the main problem though, and you need to keep a constant lookout for old Towser.

This is not such a problem in England, and I have been advised that what I have to say next is offensive. I do not think so. I offer a variety of techniques for dealing with a threatening or attacking dog designed to resolve the situation without harm to either you or the dog. These failing, and assuming you are under meaningful attack and must defend yourself, I tell you how to kill a dog. If this is too stark, then skip this section.

There are many theories about why dogs attack two-wheeled vehicles. I think that the spokes make a noise which drives them nuts. There are also a number of dog owners who take a not-so-secret pleasure in having vicious, attack-prone animals, and others who should not even try to take responsibility for a cockroach. One couple expressed puzzlement to me after their dog bit my riding companion: every time the dog was disobedient they said, they beat it until their arms hurt. Why wouldn't it obey? With treatment like that, any dog will become vicious and irrational.

Understanding that old Poochie may not be directly at fault does not make being bitten more fun. Dogs are livestock, fully the responsibility of the owner and, excepting dogs crazed by disease, can be trained to leave cyclists bloody-well alone. I like dogs very much and accept that some adjustment to their particular natures and quirks is necessary if they are to be around. I do not accept being knocked off my bike by some giant hound. If the owner will not control the dog, I will, and with brute force if necessary.

Most dogs attack according to a pattern. They circle to the rear of the cyclist and come up from behind. So sometimes you can outrun a dog. Often this is not possible, but 99 times out of a 100 there is still no serious problem. Many cyclists become hysterical on the subject of dog defence, and recommend whips, car aerials, clubs, and other weapons that will really hurt a dog. This is not necessary. It really isn't the dog's fault. Nine times out of ten he is normally friendly. All you have to do is stop, dismount, and face him directly. That's all. Simply stop. Often he will come up wagging his tail. When you leave, walk away like all 'normal' (to the dog) people do, and the matter will be forgotten.

The tenth time, when a dog still threatens to attack: the main thing when dealing with a vicious dog is to have *confidence*. As a human being you are one of the largest mammals on earth and a formidable contender in a fight. Suppress your fears and radiate the notion that any dog that messes with you will regret it for the rest of his days, if he lives that long. It is only the rarest of dogs that will attack a human obviously prepared for self-defence. Speak to the dog in firm tones, keep your bike between you, and slowly walk away.

If the dog attacks: one defence is aerosol pepper sprays made for exactly this purpose. They have a range of about 10 feet and are light enough to clip to the handlebars or your belt. A water pistol loaded with a water-ammonia solution will also work, but is a good deal less convenient. If you have neither of these and can't or won't climb a tree get a stick or large rock. No? The bicycle pump. Try to ram it down his throat. In any event, don't cower or cover up, because the dog will only chew you to ribbons. *Attack*. Any small dog can simply be hoisted up by the legs and his brains dashed out. With a big dog you are fighting for your life. If you are weaponless try to tangle him up in your bike and then strangle him. Kicks to the genitals and which break ribs are effective. If you have got a pump or stick, hold it at both ends and offer it up to the dog horizontally. Often the dog will bite the stick/pump and hang on. Immediately lift the dog up and deliver a very solid kick to the genitals. Follow up with breaking the dog's ribs or crushing its head with a rock. If worst comes to worst, ram your entire arm down his throat. He will choke and die. Better your arm than your throat.

If you are bitten and the dog gets away, make every effort to find the dog and owner. If the dog cannot be quarantined you will have to get a long series of painful rabies shots. Ask around the area, check with local petrol stations, stores, etc. In any event, get immediate medical treatment, even for a light bite. Then notify the police or the dog owner of the incident. If the dog owner is uncooperative, just find a solicitor. The law is completely and absolutely on your side.

If you successfully fend off an attack, notify the dog owner or police. This is a very real responsibility because the next person might not be as well prepared as you. A little girl, for example, like the one who lived down the road from my parents' place; several summers ago she was pulled down and killed by three dogs.

The affluent may care to try an electronic sounder which emits a noise painful to dog ears. This is the Dog Chaser, about £25 from Spencer Aircraft, 8410 Dallas Avenue South, Seattle, Washington, 98108, USA. I do not know if it works or not.

Technique

Cadence (see Riding for basics) plays an extremely significant part in the technique of long-distance touring. In a short sprint you can drain your body's resources and strength, but on a long tour output must not exceed ability to continuously replenish fuel and oxygen. Which makes it sound simple: just take it easy and have something in reserve. Not quite.

If you are interested in covering a lot of ground (not everybody is) and in feeling comfortable, then you must strive for an exact balance between energy output and the body's ability to synthesize and store energy. There is a *pace* which works best. Go too fast and the result will be fatigue and possibly strained muscles that will dog you throughout the tour. But go too slow, and you will become sluggish and lethargic, and mistake this for genuine tiredness.

A rough indicator of pace is respiration and heart-beat. You simply cannot sustain for long periods effort which noticeably increases either. Thus, the exact pace you can maintain depends on your physical condition, not on your strength.

I particularly recommend that you take it easy at first, sticking to the lower gears and not pushing hard against the pedals. This will help you to find your own cadence and pace, and perhaps avoid excessive initial effort. Most people tend to lean into it hard the first day. The result is strained and sore muscles, and the next day they can hardly move. You'll go farther and faster if you take it easy at the start.

Riding position can make a tremendous difference. Going into the wind try to get low down. With a strong tail wind, straighten up and get a free push. In Europe many riders use home-made 'sails' resembling kites strapped to their backs. These are effective even with a quartering wind. Position determines the muscle groups in use: hands high on the bars eases the back, stomach, arms, and hands; down positions do exactly the opposite and are best for hill climbing.

Equipment

Bike

Choice of bike depends on the kind of touring you do. A 3-speed is good for durability and off-road riding, but heavy weight and an inefficient gear train make it a poor choice for distance work. For all-round use, the 10-speed is best by far. It can be set up to favour durability, and thus be usable off-road, or to favour performance, for fast road riding. Experienced tourists often prefer 15-speed bikes with ultra wide gear ranges, but for the tiro these bikes can be a mechanical headache. Tourists who mix transportation modes frequently, going by bus, train, plane, or car from one place to the next, may find a portable folding bike such as the Bickerton the most convenient.

Most 10-speed bikes can easily be altered for touring, and the discussions of luggage, lights, etc. below will suggest what bits and pieces are necessary for your needs. Available off-the-shelf touring bikes include the Dawes Galaxy, the British Eagle, and Falcon Olympic. The Falcon Black Diamond and Viscount Sport, with the addition of mudguards and luggage racks, are also suitable. Specifications for these bikes are given in Chapter 2. Whatever bike you use, be sure it is geared right for the terrain you will encounter (Chapter 5).

Most manufacturers of lightweights will build a touring model to order, and have stock 'bespoke' deluxe touring models with either Reynolds 531 plain or double-butted tubing throughout, and high-grade components. Prices range from £200 and up at most of the shops listed on pages 84–5. Firms with considerable experience are:

Beta Bikes
275 West End Lane
London NW6 1QS

F. W. Evans Ltd
77–79 The Cut
London SE1

Condor Cycles Ltd
144 Gray's Inn Road
London WC1

W. F. Holdsworth Ltd
132 Lower Richmond Road
Putney
London SW15 1LN

Major Nichols   Cliff Pratt Ltd   Jack Taylor Cycles
48 Durban Road   84 Spring Bank   Church Road
Smethwick,   Hull   Stockton-on-Tees
Birmingham   Yorkshire   Teesside TS18 2LY

An alternative to buying is renting. Two firms are:

Beta Bikes   Rent-a-Bike Ltd
275 West End Lane   Kensington Student Centre
London NW6 1QS   Kensington Church Street
                         London

One excellent form of sport/touring is along trails and bridlepaths
and cross-country. The going can get muddy and rough, and even on
smooth sections there are concealed rocks, limbs, and other debris.
Machines for this sort of use need heavy-duty tyres with the widest
and roughest tread possible, and should have a minimum of
equipment to rattle off or get damaged. Mudguards will be found to
be both a curse and a boon, protecting against water spray and
flying stones, but also jamming up tight with mud and litter. Riding
technique calls for sensitivity and control. On bumpy sections keep
the weight on the pedals. Not only easier on the bike, and you, but
aids balance. Be relaxed. To a certain extent let the bike find its
own way.

Machines made especially for this sort of riding are called
cyclo-cross. They feature extra clearance for the wheels, and lugged,
tubular tyres. Since they are competition bikes, the rims are typically
alloy and if used hard, sooner or later bend. Also, as they are 5- or
10-speeds, the derailleurs constantly need soaking and cleaning.
All worth it if you are particularly keen on the sport, but my own
choice for an off-road bike is a stock 3-speed with an extra large rear
sprocket, cut down alloy mudguards, cage pedals, and knobby
speedway tyres. It cannot be jumped and bashed like a BMX racer,
but it is also still perfectly usable as a road bike.

An association devoted to off-road riding is:

The Rough-Stuff Fellowship, H. G. Robson,
23 Spring Terrace, North Shields, Tyne & Wear.

Tyres
The development of narrow profile, high-pressure clincher tyres
precludes the use of tubulars by all but a handful of affluent
fanatics. For poor roads and/or very heavy loads use a $1\frac{1}{4}$-in

heavyweight tyre, or at the ultimate, a 650-B $1\frac{3}{4}$-in tyre. For more performance, use a lighter, $1\frac{1}{4}$-in high-pressure gumwall, and if you really want to blast along, then use a $1\frac{1}{8}$-in high-pressure (90 lb/sq in) tyre. Remember: the narrower and harder, the faster, and the more punctures.

Tool kit

What you need depends on how far you go and how you maintain your bike. I keep basic tool kits for each type of bike (3-speed or 10-speed, wire-on or tubular tyres), and expand the tool kit with extra tools and parts when necessary. At the minimum, have:

Tyre repair kit including levers and spare valve
Dog bone or 4-in adjustable spanner
Screwdriver
Chain tool and spare links
Any special Allen spanners required for your bike.

For longer journeys add:
A few assorted nuts, bolts, and screws
Brake and shift cables
Spokes and nipples
Brake pads
Do-all spanner to fit hub cones, brake locknuts, etc., *or* hub cone spanners and assorted small spanners as necessary
Spare tube
Spoke spanner
Wire cutters
Freewheel remover
Cotterless crank extractor
Lubricants, including grease
Any special gizmo you might need.

Sounds like a lot, but it can all be packed into a compact bundle. On group rides cut down on the number of spare parts per rider, and share one set of tools. Your lighting system as a matter of course should carry spare bulbs. Include a bit of wire and tape for longer runs.

For mending yourself, a basic first-aid kit. I generally also carry: a multi-purpose pocketknife, compass, waterproofed matches, button thread for clothing repairs, game snares, or fishing line, and when appropriate, a snake-bite kit.

A WELL-KNOWN SPOT ON
THE GODSTONE ROAD.

The Rose & Crown Riddlesdown

Lights

A requirement at night. Most tourists prefer generator lights as they are consistently bright and less expensive than battery lights. However, some people do not care to pedal against the resistance of a wheel or hub generator, and wiring tends to snag and break at inconvenient moments. Unless fitted with a storage battery adding 14–16 ounces weight, generator lights go out when the bike stops.

Battery lights are simple, can be used off the bike for map reading or roadside repairs, and left off the bike altogether on a fast daytime run. They are best for off-road riding, as they do not dim if you go slowly, and there are no wires to snag.

What is best for you depends on how you ride. Generator lights are about the only sensible answer for strong lights and extended night runs. However, if you are riding when the days are long, and need lights only for an hour or so at a time, then lightweight battery lights will do. In either case, have a spare light in case the main system fails.

I strongly suggest using a warning flasher unit such as the Belt Beacon (see Accessories). Another good item is the Matex flashlight, which straps on the arm or leg and shows a white light to the front, red light to the rear. It will also do as a camp light or for roadside repairs.

Mudguards

These are pretty much a requirement for British and Continental touring. The plastic models are light and easily removed when not needed, but eventually warp and allow water to spray. The alloy and stainless steel models are sturdier and heavier, and offer mounting points for lights and other nick-nacks. They have an annoying characteristic of transmitting sound, but this can be prevented by using undercoating paint, available at motorists' accessories shops.

Bicycle shoes and cleats

Used in conjunction with toe clips these are essential for any long-distance travelling, unless you plan to be on and off the bike frequently. Pack shoes for walking as bicycle shoes are very unsuitable for this.

Baggage

Loading a touring bike is an art. There are two cardinal principles: load low and load evenly. Piling gear up in a high stack or all in one place creates tremendous instability for the bike. Bicycle carriers are designed to distribute loads properly. There are three basic kinds: handlebar bags, saddlebags, and panniers. People travelling light can get by with a saddlebag. These fasten to the seat and seat post and can hold a lot of gear. The next addition would be a handlebar bag. This makes for good fore and aft weight distribution, and is handy for food, cameras, and other things you often need. Get one with a transparent map case and that opens forward for easy accessibility. Campers will want rear panniers hung on special frames alongside the wheel. Panniers both front and rear are just too much baggage. Front panniers also stiffen steering and do not have the carrying capacity of rear panniers.

Panniers come in one of two basic designs: single bag, which allows maximum cramming in of gear, and multi-compartment bag, which separates gear for easy access. Most panniers made today are quick on or off the bike, and some can be converted into backpacks.

Good brand names are Karrimore, Carradice, and Eclipse. Recommending one over another would not be fair as different models suit different uses. You really need to go to a bike shop and inspect the merchandise personally. One mail-order firm is:

Freewheel
275 West End Lane, London NW6 1QS.

There are also many American firms manufacturing really first-class equipment, and if you are very serious about touring you may want to write for their catalogues:

Bellwether
1161 Mission Street
San Francisco, CA 94103

Bikecology
1515 Wilshire Boulevard
PO Box 1880
Santa Monica, CA 90406

Cannondale
35 Pulaski Street
Stamford, CT 06902

Eclipse
PO Box 372 B-7
Ann Arbor, MICH 48107

Gerry
5450 N Valley Highway
Denver, CO 80216

Kangaroo Baggs
306 E Cota
Santa Barbara, CA 93101

Kirtland
Box 4059 FN
Boulder, CO 80306

Recreation Equipment
1525 11th Avenue
Seattle, WA 98122

Touring Cyclist Shop
PO Box 4009
Boulder, CO 80306

Frostline Kits (D.I.Y.)
Dept BY077
Frostline Circle
Denver, CO 80241

Handlebar bags should be used in conjunction with a rack which prevents the bag from fouling the wheel, brake mechanism, or brake levers. Rear panniers require a stout rack which will not sway under load. Karrimore's is a proven performer.

When you load, put heavy gear at the bottom of the bags, light bulky stuff like sleeping bags at the top. Give yourself a few local shakedown trial runs. The extra weight takes getting used to, and nothing is quite so irritating as rebuilding a luggage rack in the middle of a tour. After the rack bolts and screws have bedded in, use a locking material such as Loctite to hold them firmly in place.

On the Wrong Road

Maps A compass is not only useful in conjunction with a map, but can itself guide you in the general direction you want to go without strict routing. Sometimes it is fun to dispose of maps altogether. Just go where fancy takes you, and ask directions on the way. You get to meet people, and often they can suggest really interesting routes, scenic attractions, swimming places, and the like. But have a map in reserve.

As well as keeping you on a desired route, maps have the vital function of keeping you off main arterial roads and out of industrial areas. Petrol station maps are inadequate. Excellent are the Ordnance Survey maps, a catalogue of which is available from:

Director-General
Ordnance Survey, Romsey Road, Maybush, Southampton so9 4DH.

The maps are obtainable in many bookshops, and from Ordnance Survey agents, a list of which is obtainable from:

(for England and Wales)
Cook, Hammond & Kell Ltd
22–24 Caxton Street, London sw1 ;

(for Scotland)
Thomas Nelson & Sons
18 Dalkeith Road, Edinburgh eh16 5bs.

The 1:25,000 scale maps are extremely detailed, showing individual buildings, walls, tiny streams, and the like, and give an endless amount of information about the area covered. They are wonderful for detailed exploring, but for overall route planning $\frac{1}{2}$-in or 1-in scale maps are better. These still show virtually all roads, footpaths, villages, rivers, and other stuff like youth hostels, inns, National Trust properties, windmills, public rights of way and more. There are also a number of tourist maps made up especially for popular and scenic areas, and archaeological and historical maps.

   Bartholomew's $\frac{1}{2}$-in series, probably the most useful size, is obtainable in bookstores or from:

John Bartholomew
12 Duncan Street, Edinburgh eh9 1ta.

Both Ordnance and Bartholomew's maps are available from the Cyclists' Touring Club at a reduced price for members.

Clothing
Shorts are pretty much universal garb. Morning chill evaporates after two or three miles. Wash and wear is a must for long jaunts. A nylon windcheater is very useful, as are cycling jerseys with big pockets for stashing gear. A poncho will serve also as a groundsheet and/or a tent, but most people use cycling capes, which have an annoying habit of flapping about, and do not really protect the legs. The alternative, a proper rainsuit, means that one gets drenched from within by perspiration. Best is outerware made from Gore-Tex (see p 156). Sweaters, suits, morning dress, according to climate and the preferences of the cyclist, but I suggest minimizing your load wherever possible. See also Accessories.

Camping
Membership in The Camping Club of Great Britain and Ireland Ltd, 11 Lower Grosvenor Place, London sw1 includes an International

Camping Carnet, insurance services, a handbook on camping, and a guide to 1,500 sites in Great Britain and Ireland. Another organization is:

Cycling Section
Association of Cycling and Lightweight Campers, 30 Napier Road, Wembley, Middlesex;

and site lists are also available from:

British Tourist Authority
239 Old Marylebone Road, London NW1.

Camping gear

Personal preferences and abilities can completely determine choices here. Some people need a tent and a prepared campsite with running water. Others insist on portable stoves, radios, etc. There are many good books on camping equipment and woods lore, and if you are unfamiliar with this craft you should get one. There is space here for only the most generalized suggestions.

(1) Sleeping bag. Tents and stoves, etc., can always be improvised with fair success, but only the most skilled can keep warm in a bad bag. A poor bag weighs more, and if you freeze and can't sleep, this will give you ample time to brood on the economic and practical merits of having got something that would do the job in the first place. Get the best bag you can afford. Also, although your bike has carrying capacity and most of your touring is apt to be in warm weather, I suggest you keep other possibilities such as camping, or tours in the autumn (fantastic!) in mind.

The best bags, pound-for-pound, are of down. Down has the greatest range (temperatures at which the bag will work), resiliency (bag packs small), recovery (gets body back when unpacked), wicking properties (carries moisture away from body), and moral character. Down bags run from £30 to £60 and the less expensive, lighter (filled with $1\frac{1}{2}$–$2\frac{1}{2}$ pounds of down) models are OK for warm weather. I suggest a multi-layered and/or openable bag that will also take a flannel insert. This gives optimum range and comfort.

An interesting new insulative material is poly foam, used in Ocaté bags. These are only fractionally heavier ($4\frac{1}{2}$ pounds overall) than lightweight down bags ($3\frac{1}{2}$ pounds), and the manufacturer claims a degree range down to $-5°$, about that of a middleweight down bag (4–$4\frac{1}{2}$ pounds). The advantage is that it will keep you warm, wet or dry.

The least expensive bags contain synthetic fillers such as 'Dacron 88' and 'Astrofill'. These run from £6 to £15, weigh about 6 pounds and are OK for warm weather and low altitudes.

Still another new interesting material is Gore-Tex, a fabric which breathes from within, but is impervious to wet from without. It is used for rain clothing and sleeping bag shells, and is highly effective. Products are available from

Early Winters Ltd
110 Prefontaine Place South
Seattle, WA 98104
USA

Pak Foam Products
390 Pine Street
Pawtucket, RI 02862
USA

Marmot Mountain Works
331-B South Street
Grand Junction, CO 81501
USA

Sojourn Designs
57th & Valmont
Boulder, CO 80302
USA

and information is available direct from the manufacturer,

W. L. Gore & Associates
PO Box 1220
Elkton, MD 21921 USA

(2) A ground sheet such as a triple-purpose (raincape, tent) poncho.

The remaining equipment listed here can always be improvised. The trouble with this is that garnering boughs for a bed or building fires is rather wasteful and ecologically unsound. There are enough campers now so that the total destruction can be devastating. In many areas you are not allowed to do these things. So, drag that it may be, it is both practical and considerate to be as self-sufficient as possible.

(3) Sleeping mattress or pad. Air mattresses (avoid plastic ones) are comfortable but bulky. Pads such as ensolite are fine.

(4) Tents come in all shapes, sizes and grades. Conditions and personal preference dictate choice. Tents are good for protection against bugs, rain, and to ensure privacy. For myself I see no point in hieing to the Great Outdoors and then sleeping in a dark hole. Polyethylene fly sheets can be rigged into a decent shelter with only a little effort and are extremely cheap and light. A poncho is just as good. In tents, the Gerry 'Pioneer' is well thought of by everybody. This makes up as a one-man tent with floor and mosquito netting, or as a two-man tent without a floor.

Gerry
5450 North Valley Highway, Denver, co 80216 USA

For a two-man tent the Itisa Senior is rugged but heavy:

Blacks of Greenock Ltd
22 Gray's Inn Road, London wc1
and
53 Rathbone Place, London w1

(5) Cooking stove and utensils. The little alcohol and paraffin models can be wonderfully compact, but require that you carry fuel which, owing to weight, you will have to replenish often. The gas cylinder models are a bit cumbersome, but are quick to light.

I prefer a steel pot, a steel fry pan that will serve as a lid for the pot (and simultaneously keep its own contents warm), and a steel cup than can also go on the fire. Avoid aluminium, as it is toxic. Four skewers can be used to form a grid for a pot (you can build fires sometimes, and they are much cosier than stoves), as a grill, to skewer food, or as tent pegs.

(6) Food. Dried lightweight foods are extremely convenient and quite palatable. I suggest carrying enough for emergencies only, however, and trying for fresh food along the route. Stock up on breakfast and supper at about 4 o'clock. Mixtures of dried fruit, grains, dried milk, yeast, etc, are nourishing, tasty, and easy to carry.

Nearly every city or town has a camping equipment store. The Youth Hostel Association stores always offer good value. If you have a bit more money to burn, and would really prefer the lightest possible equipment, then your best bet may be an alpine outfitter such as:

Robert Lawrie Ltd
54 Seymour Street, London W1

Camping equipment can be hired from:

Crystal Palace Camping   and   Eaton's Outdoor Centre
5 Church Road   100 Haydons Road
London SE19   London SW19

Getting there

Other forms of locomotion complement bicycles very well.

Cars

A 10-speed with the wheels off will fit in the boot of many economy cars and certainly on the back seat. For carrying several bikes you can buy or make a car carrier. There are two types, rear end and top. The rear end version holds two bikes and is easy to load. It is hard to get at the boot however, and the bikes get a lot of road grit and scratch each other. Top-mounted carriers hold four to five bikes, and require each to be strapped down. But machines are kept clean, separate, and out of harm's way.

A line of rear- and top-mounted carriers is manufactured by Saba, with capacities from one to four bikes. They also have a Universal Rack which adapts to a regular car top rack, available at bicycle shops.

Or you can make your own. *Bicycle Camping and Touring* (Tolby Publishing Co, Box 428, New Canaan, CONN 06840 USA; $4.95) has plans, and so does:

Bicycle Institute of America
122 East 42nd Street, New York, NY 10017, USA (free)

When loading, alternate direction for three or more bikes. Seat on one cross-bar, handlebars on the other. Careful of brake and shift cables. Lash down with toe straps or elastic luggage straps at contact points, and especially the handlebars, since these hold the bike upright. Guying, i.e. running straps from the side of the car to high points on the bike (as with a sailing mast) is a *good idea*.

Mixing up a tour with public transport, or even just complementing a trip with a bicycle, is a great way to travel. You have the benefits of mobility and covering a lot of ground, but at the same time a bike lets you examine interesting areas in detail. Preparation of your bike for travel depends on the kind of carrier you will use.

Airlines
These handle bikes well and some provide special bike boxes. Remove the rear derailleur if you have one, and loosen stem and twist handlebars parallel with front wheel. They may ask you to remove or reverse the pedals. I myself would protect the frame and chain-wheel with a broken-up cardboard box. Deflate the tyres to half pressure. Airlines sometimes let bikes on free, and sometimes charge.

Railways
Really perfect for speeding you on to a particular area, or for skipping over uninteresting sections on a long tour. Load the bike into the luggage van yourself, and use elastic straps to hold it firm. Thanks to the efforts of the Cyclists' Touring Club, the one half adult fare charge for a bicycle has been rescinded on all but the Inter City 125 trains, and even these may be free by the time this book goes into print. If not, you can fox the charge by popping your bike into a box (obtainable from a cycle shop); it then goes as personal luggage, for free.

A special note: do not ever ship a bicycle by itself by British Rail unless it is insured against any possible disaster. I had a bike shipped to me which was mangled into a worthless pile of junk – frame, forks, and even the cranksets bent beyond repair – and did not get a penny compensation. Insure – and be prepared for the worst.

The Continent

Cycle touring is a particularly satisfying way of travelling around the Continent, allowing you to explore and savour to a degree not otherwise possible. People are exceptionally friendly and helpful to cyclists. You really 'get into' the country. And for uninteresting or arduous sections of the journey, you simply take a train, boat, or plane.

There is no end of information available. Selpress Books, Suite 413, 4th Floor, 16 Berkeley Street, London W1x 6AP, and The Cyclists' Touring Club, 69 Meadrow, Godalming, Surrey GU7 3HS offer: *Cycle Touring in Europe*, by P. Knottley (£3.00), containing many

AWHEEL IN FRANCE

useful tips on camping by a veteran tourist; *Bicycle Touring in Europe*, by K. & G. Hawkins (£1.25), with solid information on technique and places to go, including nine complete, mapped tours; and *International Bicycle Touring* (£1.65, from Selpress only), another useful compendium of specific information. There are cycling clubs, associations, federations, and organizations to which you can write for information. Those marked * are specifically concerned with touring; others sometimes operate touring services, and will usually assist with information:

Albania

Federata Sportive Shgiptare-Bruga, Abdi Toptani, 3, Tirana.

Austria

Österreichischer Radsport Kommission, Prinz Eugenstrasse 12, Vienna IV.

*Österreichischer Automobil, Motorrad und Touring Club, Schubertring 3, Vienna I.

Belgium

*Touring Club Royal de Belgique, Rue de la Loi 44, Brussels.

*Royale Ligue Vélocipédique Belge, 49 Avenue du Globe, 1190 Brussels.

Ligue Vélocipédique Belge, 8 Place des Martyrs, Brussels.

Bulgaria

Fédération Bulgare de Cyclisme, Boulevard Tolboukhine 18, Sofia.

*Automobil and Touring Club, Rue Sv Sofia 6, Sofia.

Czechoslovakia

*Ustredni Automotoklub, CSSR, Opletalova 29, Prague 1.

Ceskoslovenska Sekce Cyklistiky, Na Porici 12, Prague 1.

Denmark

Danmarks Cykle Union, Gronneraenge 21, 2920 Charlottenlund, Copenhagen.

Danmarks Professionelt Cykle Forbund, Grambyvei 56, 2610 Rodovre.

*Dansk Cyklist Forbund, Avedøre Tvaervej 15, 2650 Hvidovre.

East Germany

Deutscher Radsport Verband, Kochhannstrasse 1, 1034 Berlin.

Finland

Suomen Pyorailyliitto, Yrjonkato 21b, Helsinki.

*Suomi Touring Club, Unioninkatu 45H, Helsinki 17.

France
*Touring Club de France (TCF), 65 Avenue de la Grande-Armée, Paris 16.
*Fédération Française de Cyclotourisme (FFCT), 66 Rue René Boulanger, Paris 10.

Germany
*Allgemeiner Deutscher Automobil-Club (ADAC), Königinstrasse 9–11a, Munich 22.

Greece
*Automobil et Touring Club de Grèce, 6 rue Amerikis, Athens.
Hellenic Amateur Athletic Association, 4 rue Kapsali, Athens.

Hungary
Magyar Kerekparos Szoveteg Millenaris Sporttelep, Szabo Jozsef u3, Budapest XIV.

Iceland
*Felag Islenzkra Bifreidaegenda (FIB), Eiriksgata 5, Reykjavik.

Irish Republic
Irish Cycling Federation, 72 Prospect Avenue, Glasnevin, Dublin 9.

Italy
Federazione Ciclistica Italiana, Palazzo delle Federazione Viale Tiziano 70, Rome.
*Touring Club Italiano (TCI), Corso Italia 10, Milan.

Luxembourg
Fédération du Sport Cycliste Luxembourgeois, Case Postale 145, Luxembourg City.

Netherlands
*Koninklijke Nederlandse Toeristenbond (ANWB),
Wassenaarseweg 220, The Hague.
Koninklijke Nederlandse Wielren Unie, 15 Nieuwe Uitleg, The
Hague.
*Stichting Fiets, Europaplein 2, Amsterdam.
*Netherlands Cycletouring Union (NRTU), Ambachtsherenlaan
487, Zoetermeer, Alphen-a-d-Rijn.

Northern Ireland
Northern Ireland Cycling Federation, S. Martin, 13 Premier Drive,
Belfast 15.

Norway
Norges Cykleforbund, Youngstorget, 1 Oslo.
*Norges Automobil-Forbund (NAF), Bertrand Narvesens Vei 2,
Etterstad, Oslo 6.

Poland
Polska Zwiazek Kolarska, 1 Plac Xelaznej Bramy, Warsaw.
*Polskie Towarzystwo Turystyczno-Krajoznawcze (PTTK),
Senatorska II, Warsaw 40.

Portugal
Federação Portuguesa de Ciclismo, Rua Barros Queiroz 29–1,
Lisbon.
*Automovel Club de Portugal (ACP), Rua Rosa Araujo 24 & 26,
Lisbon.

Romania
Federatia Romina de Ciclismo, Vasile Conta, Bucharest 16.
*Association des Automobilistes (AAR), Stradan Beloianis 27,
Bucharest 1.

Russia
Fédération Cycliste USSR, Skatertnyi Pereoulok 4, Moscow 69.

Spain
Federación Española de Ciclismo, Alfonso XII 36, 1st Dacha,
Madrid 14.
*Real Automobil Club de España (RACE), General Sanjurjo 10,
Madrid 3.

Sweden
Svenska Cykelforbundet, Stora Nygatan 41–43, Stockholm C.
*Svenska Turistföreningen (STF), Stureplan 2, Stockholm 7.

Switzerland (German-speaking Cantons)
  Schweiz Radfahrer-u-Motofahrer-Bund, Schaffhauserstrasse 272, Zurich 57.

Switzerland (French-speaking Cantons)
  Union Cycliste Suisse, 4 rue du Vieux-Collège, 1211 Geneva 3.
*Touring Club Suisse (TCS), rue Pierre-Fatio 9, Geneva.

Turkey
*Turkiye Turing ve Otomobil Kurumu, Sisli Meydani 364, Istanbul.

West Germany
  Bund Deutscher Radfahrer, Westanlage 56, BP 263, Giessen-Lahn (Hessen).

Yugoslavia
  Fédération Yougoslave de Cyclisme, Hilendarska 6, Belgrade.
*Auto-Moto Savez Jugoslavije, Ruzveltova 18, Belgrade.

Many national tourist offices have developed information especially for the cyclist, with pre-planned tours, information on roads, places to rent bicycles, cycling areas, and other relevant data.

The best source of information is the Cyclists' Touring Club. They have information sheets, pre-planned tours, maps, and insurance and travel services which make them unbeatable value for the tourist. They also conduct tours. So do the Youth Hostel Associations, and membership includes a number of useful guides and handbooks. The British Cycling Federation does not conduct tours, but does offer insurance services and some 50-odd pre-planned tours. The

International Bicycle Touring Society
846 Prospect Street, La Jolla, California 92037 USA

also runs tours in Europe. These tend to be at an easy pace, with a following 'sag wagon' car for carrying all but members' personal clothing, and accommodation in inexpensive hotels and meals in restaurants. Higher in cost than hostelling of course, but pre-selection of hotels keeps expenses moderate.

And then there are always the traditional aids to travel – the Michelin Guides and various sight-seeing tomes. One of the nicest things about cycle touring is that you are not obliged to make a plan and stick to a schedule. Even in crowded holiday areas you should not have much difficulty in finding accommodation if you just veer off the beaten track – which a bike makes easy.

Africa

Bicycles are a common form of transport for Africans, but their machines are of course extremely stout and sturdy, as often there is simply no road at all. In Morocco, for example, south of the Atlas Mountains and into the Sahara Desert, the roads are dirt tracks resembling streambeds. Most of the locals simply cycle over the desert itself. However, in Northern Morocco the roads are quite negotiable, and there are not many cars. I should imagine that similar varied conditions prevail throughout Africa.

Parts are a problem, and in many areas so is thievery. Cyclists in Africa have been trapped in disease quarantine areas. There are all kinds of wars, revolutions, famines, and other excitements to interest the tourist. Life is less than cheap. Still, I would say the prospects for cycle touring were good. A lot depends on your own attitudes and how you get on with people. In any case, few enough people have cycled in Africa so that there is little annotated information. If you go it will be as something of a pioneer. The magazines *Bike World* and *Bicycling!* carry articles on African touring from time to time. The Cyclists' Touring Club has correspondents in Africa, and if you are seriously interested you might try corresponding with Walter Stolle, c/o PO Box 728, Lagos, Nigeria, who has cycled extensively throughout Africa.

Asia and the Pacific

A chronicle of cycling conditions in Asia is to be found in *Sting in the Tail*, Peter Duker's account of his around-the-world ride (Pelham, 52 Bedford Square, London WC1, £2.60). Duker battled sandstorms and government officials, crashed, ran endless gauntlets of rock-throwing men and boys, was clouted viciously by three men who tore limbs off a tree and attacked him, and in general had a hard time. By his own account Duker seems a unique enough individual so that his experience is not necessarily the norm, but it would be foolish not to anticipate some difficulties. Both the Cyclists' Touring Club and the Youth Hostels have information on Asia.

Organizations which may be able to supply information are:

Japanese Cycling Federation
Kishi Memorial Hall, 25 Kannami-Cho-Shipuyaku, Tokyo

New Zealand Amateur Cycling Association
COP Box 30459, Lower Hutt

Philippine Cycling Association
Rizal Memorial Track-Football Stadium
Dakota Street, Manila

Australia

Duker's ride covers this area, and you should be able to get information from:

Amateur Cyclists' Association of Australia
W. S. Young, 34 Wardell Road, Earlswood, Sydney, New South Wales

Australian Cycling Council
153 The Ringway, Cronulla, 2230, Sydney, New South Wales

as well as the Cyclists' Touring Club and the Youth Hostels.

United States

Bicycle touring is a fine way to see the United States. Unless you are extraordinarily perverse you will not find ghetto areas such as New York's Lower East Side or Harlem attractive, and so do not need to worry overmuch about personal safety. Most of your riding will probably be in the countryside where you are relatively safe. But be warned: the level of violence in many urban areas is considerably greater – shockingly so – than most people from civilized countries are prepared for. Americans no longer say in parting, 'Have a nice day', but 'Have a safe day'.

Another problem is that American drivers have not fully caught on to the bicycle boom. The idea that motor vehicles take precedence over any other road-users is much more prevalent than in Britain, and the problem of motorists not really noticing or thinking about cyclists is much worse. Most American cars are large, softly sprung, and do not handle well. Roads are wider and straighter. Accordingly, American drivers have not developed the same level of skill and expertise as their British counterparts, who have to cope with narrow, twisting roads. In terms of road safety cycling in America is, overall, more dangerous than here.

These nasty things said, I am sure that if you go touring the States, you will have an excellent time. Although it is more dangerous than Great Britain, it is not so unsafe as to be inadvisable. And Americans are warm, open, friendly people.

One source of detailed information is books. *Bicycle Camping and Touring* (Dell, $4.95) has a lot of solid information on techniques and equipment. *The Best of Bicycling* (Pocket Books, $1.95) has all sorts of wonderful stories about short- and long-distance touring and a potpourri of technical information. *North American Bicycle Atlas* (American Youth Hostels, $2.25) gives detailed, mapped tours throughout the USA. So does *The American Biking*

Atlas and Touring Guide (Workman, $5.95). Good reading is *Bike Tripping* by Tom Cuthbertson (Ten Speed Press, $3.95). Full of really useful specific information is *Traveling by Bike* (World Publications, PO Box 366, Mountain View, CA 94040, USA, $1.95).

Once again the bicycling organizations are especially useful. Tours are run by

American Youth Hostels
20 West 17th Street, New York NY 10011

whose hostels are sometimes spartan but always serviceable, with fees up to $2.00, and the

International Bicycle Touring Society
846 Prospect Street, La Jolla, California 92037

which is an easy-going outfit for adults only. Tours are volunteer-organized and fairly luxurious. A trailer follows each tour and carries baggage and repair parts. Overnight stays at inns and motels at about $5 to $10.

Information about routes can be got from the:

League of American Wheelmen
119 South Bothwell, Palatine, ILL 60067

whose nation-wide members will give you information about local conditions to aid in planning a tour. The

Bicycle Institute of America
122 East 42nd Street, New York, NY 10017

is a trade organization which gives out a lot of free information on all aspects of cycling. If you send

Clifford L. Franz
36 Grand Boulevard, San Mateo, CA 94401

your favourite local tour, mapped, and tell him where you want to go, he will provide you with recommended mapped routes together with information on campgrounds and/or motels and an assortment of checklists.

Of petrol station maps I have found Esso's to be the most detailed, but even these do not meet the needs of the cyclist. The best source is the US Geological Service, who publish contour maps for each state. If you know the exact area you'll be in, they also have local maps down to 1 : 24,000, a scale which shows walls, footpaths, tiny streams, etc. These are too detailed for any but the most local use, but are extremely interesting. Many map stores carry the USGS maps, or you can order them direct (for local maps ask first for free state index map) :

East of Mississippi
US Geologic Survey
Washington District Section
1200 South Eads Street
Arlington, VA 22202

West of Mississippi
US Geologic Survey
District Section
Federal Center
Denver, CO 80225

If you plan a tour which includes travel by rail, be chary of baggage handlers. The make-work contingent has rigged it so that a baggage handler must load the bike aboard the train – badly. Stories of bikes mangled into oblivion by these clods are legion. Insist on personally supervising loading or don't travel by rail at all. Hang the bike from the ceiling or side of the luggage van if possible, and in any case see that it is lashed down securely and that no heavy objects can fall on it.

Take your own bike over with you. British bikes are expensive in America. Japanese bikes in America are good value, but frames tend to be less flexible. And incidentally, if you buy a bike here and remove it from the country within three months you get a refund on purchase tax. Between the price difference and the tax refund, if you sell your bike in the States at the finish of your tour you should at least break even. But a more important reason for taking your own bike is that it allows you to sort it out before going, and not waste vacation time hanging about a bike shop making adjustments and screwing on bits and pieces.

You may wish to purchase Stateside regardless, or need repairs. Bicycle shops now litter the landscape but, just in case, here are a few of the better known:

Thomas Avenia
131 East 119th Street
New York, NY 10035

The Bicycle Exchange
3 Bow Street
Cambridge, MASS 02138

Thomas Avenia
10205 Rio Hondo Parkway
El Monte, California

*Bikecology
1515 Wilshire Boulevard
PO Box 1880
Santa Monica, CA 90406

The American Star Machine

*Bike Warehouse
215 Main Street
New Middletown, OH 44442

*Big Wheel Ltd
Dept K
310 Holly Street
Denver, CO 80220

Bud's Bike Shop
217 West First Street
Claremont, CA 91711

Cupertino Bike Shop
2098 Sunset Drive
Pacific Grove, CA 93950

*Cycle Goods Corporation
17701 Leeman Drive
Minnetonka, MN 55343

*Cyclo-Pedia
311 N Mitchell
Cadillac, MICH 49601

Fulton Street Cyclery
3038 Fulton Street
San Francisco, CA 94118

John's Custom Bike Center
741 East Dixie Drive
West Carrolton, Ohio

Lifecycle
1005 Massachusetts Avenue
Cambridge, MASS 02139

Hans Ohrt Lightweight Bikes
9544 Santa Monica Boulevard
Beverly Hills, CA 90210

*Palo Alto Bicycle Shop
171 University Avenue
PO Box 1276
Palo Alto, CA 94302

Pleasant Valley Shop
PO Box 293
Livingston, NJ 07039

The Spoke
1301 Pennsylvania
Boulder, CO 80302

Stuyvesant Distributors
10 East 13th Street
New York, NY 10003

Turin Bicycle Co-op
2112 North Clark Street
Chicago, ILL 60614

Velo-Sport Cyclery
1650 Grove Street
Berkeley, California

Starred firms also do business by post.

Twenty per cent of the bicycles in use in the United States are stolen every year. You must have a serious lock, and the only two worth considering are the Citadel, and the Kryptonite KBL4, each about $30 at bicycle shops.

First-rate cycle touring and camping equipment is available in the States. Some manufacturers are listed in the section on baggage in this chapter. Camping equipment may also be had by post from:

L. L. Bean
Freeport, ME 04032
(Catalogue free)

Colorado Outdoor Sports
PO Box 5544
Denver, CO 80217

Early Winters Ltd
110 Prefontaine Place South
Seattle, WA 98104

Gerry
5450 North Valley Highway
Denver, CO 80306

Herter's
Route 1
Waseca, MA 56093
(Catalogue $1.00)

Recreational Co-op
1525 11th Street
Seattle, WA 98122

Sierra Designs
4th and Addison Streets
Berkeley, CA 94710

Canada

The Canadian Bicycle Book (D. C. Heath Ltd, Toronto; $3.95) is mostly an introduction to cycling but has some touring information. Organizations are:

Canadian Cycling Association
3737 rue Monselet, Montreal Nord, PQ
also at
333 River Road, Vanier, Ontario

Canadian Youth Hostels Association
268 First Avenue, Ottawa, Ontario

Mexico

Federacion Mexicana de Ciclismo
Confederation Sportive Mexicaine
Avenue Juarez Num 64–311, Mexico City 1

The Cyclists' Touring Club has correspondents in Mexico.

South America

Organizations are:

Federacion Ciclista Argentina
Ave Pte Figueroa, Alcoeta 4600, Buenos Aires, Argentina

Brazilian Confederation of Sports
Rue da Quitanda 3, 2nd Andar, Case Postale 1078, Rio de Janeiro,
Brazil

The Cyclists' Touring Club and Youth Hostels may have
information. I'm headed that way myself with a boat and bicycles
and will be happy to let you know how it goes, but this won't be for
a while yet.

10 Racing

For me cycling as a sport is personal, a way of being with myself, and while an interest in going fast has necessarily involved me with competition machinery, the only race I have ever seen was by accident, and I did not see the finish. Information here has been gleaned from books and talking to people.

Selpress Books, Suite 413, 4th Floor, 16 Berkeley Street, London WIX 6AP, offer over half a dozen books on the subject, including *All About Bicycle Racing* and *Bicycle Track Racing*, both of which are very good, and also the classic *Cycling*, published by the C.O.N.I., Central Sports School, Rome. John Forester's *Effective Cycling* (Custom Cycle Fitments, 782 Allen Court, Palo Alto, CA 94303, USA) contains much information of value to the racer. Other books include *Cycling*, edited by David Saunders (Wolfe Publications Ltd; 30p; available from Foyles, 119 Charing Cross Road, London WC2), *Cycle Racing* by Bowden and Mathews (Maurice Temple Smith Ltd, 42 Russell Square, London WC1), and *The Book of the Bicycle* by Roger St Pierre (Ward Lock Ltd, 116 Baker Street, London WIM 2BB; £1.50). The flavour of the sport is contained in books such as *Continental Cycle Racing by* N. G. Henderson (history and results of major continental tours and one-day classics) and *Cycling Crazy* by Charles Messenger (a British team manager's reminiscences of three decades of racing), both published by Pelham Books, London at £1.75 each. A marvellous chronicle of the 1976 Tour de France is *The Great Bike Race*, by G. Nicholson (Hodder and Stoughton, London; £4.95), a good read even if your interest in racing is slight. The psyche of the racer and the all-out effort that attends serious competition is suggested in a novel, *The Yellow Jersey* by Ralph Hurne (Weidenfeld and Nicolson, London; £2.25). The periodicals *Cycling* (161–66 Fleet Street, London EC4 – weekly) and *International Cycle Sport* (Kennedy Brothers Publishing Ltd, St John Street, Silsden, near Keighley, Yorks – monthly) offer comprehensive coverage of the sport.

To race, you will have to belong to one or even two organizations, depending on the type of event(s) in which you compete. There are basically four types of events: time trial, road race, track, and cyclo-cross. Here are the addresses of the national organizations:

Maurice Cumberworth, General Secretary
British Professional Cycle Racing Association
Hebden Travel Lodge, Mill Lane, Hebden, Yorkshire
Pro racing under BCF rules.

British Cycling Federation
70 Brompton Road, London SW3 1EN
International, affiliated to Union Cycliste International

R. J. Richards, General Secretary
British Cyclo Cross Association, 5 Copstone Drive, Dorridge, Solihull, Warwickshire

E. G. Kings, Secretary
Road Time Trials Association, 210 Devonshire Hill Lane, London N17 7NR

Irish Cycling Federation
155 Shanliss Road, Shantry, Dublin 9 Eire
Also known as the CRE, supervises organized cycle racing in Irish Republic. Many races are held under the National Cycling Association, which is not internationally recognized.

J. E. Fletcher, Secretary
Northern Ireland Cycling Federation
144 Princes Way, Portadown, County Armagh, Northern Ireland
Ulster sport, but the NCA operates here also.

The appropriate national organization above will supply you with the name and address of a local club for you to join. Time-trialists need only be a member of a club affiliated to the Road Time Trials Council, but competitors in other events must also take out membership with the British Cycling Federation.

You compete according to age, sex, and ability, so if you are a beginner do not worry about being trounced first time out – most of the riders will be fairly evenly matched. Some of the greatest bike riders in the world are little shrimps. The less weight to lug around the better. Big people are not excluded either – on downhills

Crawley: going down

they generally have the edge. What counts in the end is heart.
Bike racing is an extremely rigorous sport. In skiing, running,
football, and most other sports, when you are finished you drop.
On a bike a lot of your weight is supported by the machine and
only a small amount of energy is required to maintain balance.
It is quite possible to run your body to the finish and beyond,
so that when you stop you are unable to stand on your feet. Any
serious racer has to keep fit with a year round physical conditioning
programme.

The three basic types of races are road, track, and cyclo-cross.

Road

Time trial
This is the premier type of event in Britain, in which
each rider is timed separately over 10, 25, 30, 50 and 100 mile
courses, or rides as far as possible in 12 or 24 hours. Riders are
dispatched at regular intervals and must ride alone. The season is
February to October, with a predominance of 10 and 25 mile events
to start, then the 50 and 100 mile and 12 and 24 hour events at the
height of summer, and ending with hill climbs. An advantage is that
anybody can participate, racing themselves against a record.
British courses are easier than those on the Continent.

Massed start
Everybody starts together, first human over the finish line wins.
The course can be 10 miles, or 2,600, as in the Tour de France.

Most single day events are between 50 and 100 miles for amateurs, and 80 to 180 for professionals. Races lasting two days or more are called stage races.

In road racing riders are pitted against each other, and the resulting shenanigans are sometimes incredible. Intelligence, strategy, trickiness, and psychology play an equal role with riding ability and strength. Teams work together to launch a strong teammate ahead of the pack to victory, and block opposition riders. In big races like the Tour de France bicycles collide and pedals jam into spokes. Bikes are of a conventional design, with freewheels and brakes.

A type of road race popular in America is the criterium. It is usually held on a closed circuit measuring less than two miles around, with sharp and narrow corners, over distances ranging from 25 to 62 miles. Very precise riding is needed to cope with the corners, and the dense pack of riders created by the narrowness of the streets or road. Criterium bikes tend to have very stiff frames for quick handling, and a high bottom bracket so that pedalling can continue through the corners.

Cyclo-cross

Cross-country races from point to point or around a course, from 1 to 16 miles in length, run either as a time trial or with a massed start. These are typically through steep climbs and descents, mud, thick woods, streams, and hurdles. Some sections are negotiated on foot. It a a rough sport, physically very demanding, with plenty of spills.

Track

The machine common to a wide variety of track events is the greyhound of bikes: an ultra-light frame with a short wheelbase; a fierce position with the saddle high and handlebars low; a single fixed wheel gear, with no brakes; and tyres bonded to the rims with shellac, to withstand the stresses of violent track manoeuvres. There are no quick-release hubs, gears, pumps, cables, etc, making these among the most lovely and functional of bikes.

There are many different kinds of track events. Here are a few:

Sprint
Usually a 1000-metre course with only the last 200 metres timed. Involves all kinds of trick tactics and scheming. There are times when racers hold their bikes stock still while jockeying for position. *Behind* the leader and in his slipstream until the final sprint is the favoured winning position.

Pursuit
Two riders or teams start on opposite sides of the track and try to catch each other.

Time trials
Against the clock, as in road racing.

Devil take the hindmost
Last man over the line every 2 or 3 laps is out.

Paced racing
Motorcycles are used as pace-setters for the riders, who stay as close as possible to the pacer's rear wheel so as to minimize wind resistance. Speeds up to 60 mph.

Madison
Two-man teams run in relays. Events run from 50 kilometres or one hour to six-day races. Each team member runs one or two laps and then hands over to a teammate, literally throwing him by the seat of his pants or by a hand-sling. A very spectacular form of racing.

Speedway
Run on dirt track ovals with stripped-down bikes using low gearing
and studded track tyres, this is a grass-roots sport as yet unrecognized
by any 'official' organization. Fast action, with lots of broadside
skids and spills. About 100 clubs in Great Britain under

Cycle Speedway Council
W. F. Gill, Secretary
67 St Francis Way
Chadwell St Mary
Grays, Essex RM16 4RB

The finish

11 Accessories

Most accessories are unnecessary. Whenever possible try to peel
weight off your bike. Streamers and decorative nick-nacks are out,
unless they are of such incredibly redeeming character as to make
them worth carrying at any cost. I had a Bombay taxi driver's horn
like that once, a great gleaming diesel-like trumpet, but it went when
the Golden Flash was stolen.

Pump
A necessity for tubular tyres, an excellent idea for clinchers.
What use is a tyre repair kit if you don't have a pump?
Pumps left on a locked bike tend to be pinched. A pocket-size pump
will do for an emergency.

Toe clips
These nearly double pedalling efficiency and with smooth-soled
shoes the feet can be slipped out easily in an emergency.

Bicycle shoes and cleats
Bike shoes are cut for ankling and have a steel shank for even
foot-pressure on the pedal. Cleats will give you tremendous get up
and go and are a must for long tours and racing, but not advisable in
traffic.

Lights
These present a whole series of problems. There are two basic
types of lighting systems: battery and generator. Generator types
take power off the wheel or hub, thus increasing pedalling
resistance. There is more hardware, wires can snag and break,
and the system is permanently attached to the bike. Underway
the lights are bright and strong, but when you stop they go out.

   Battery lights stay on when you stop, but gradually fade. They
can be got on and off the bike easily. This means you can eliminate
dead weight when you want to. Battery lights are useful for map
reading and roadside repairs. They are easily stolen off a parked

bike. They can be misplaced and difficult to find just before a ride.

Either a generator or battery light is capable of failing at any time. A second back-up light of some sort is essential.

The choice of main system type is up to you and the conditions you encounter. If you ride a lot at night and/or frequently lock up on the street and/or just want lights on the bike there, when you need them, then a generator system is probably best. You can complement it with a voltage regulator and battery charger unit which will keep the lights on when you stop and add 14 ounces weight to the bike, or a battery light (5 to 16 ounces).

If you have a performance bike which cannot be lumbered with additional weight when not needed and/or ride mostly in the daytime, battery lights will probably be the most convenient. You will want still another back-up light.

Lights are not so much that you see, as you are seen. This is where the back-up light can serve a vital function. The French Matex light has a white front and red rear, weighs only 5 ounces and straps to an arm or leg. Because it is moved about it is very visible. Every rider should have, at the minimum, the Matex light.

A still more eye-catching device is the Belt Beacon. This is an amber high intensity light which flashes on and off at between 40 and 60 times a minute. It can be attached to the belt or to the bike.

Lucas candle
lamp

Anybody riding regularly at night would be well advised to use one or even two (front and back) Belt Beacons (obtainable by post from Freewheel, 275 West End Lane, London NW6 1QS.) It may all seem like a bit much – main light system, Belt Beacon, and Matex or other spare light. The problem at night is to survive. Bicycle lights are diminutive. In cities and towns they are easily lost in the welter of traffic lights, street lights, and neon signs. In the country the car coming up from behind may be doing 70 mph to your 10 mph. That's an 88 foot per second speed differential, and if the visible range of your rear lights is 300 feet or less, it is under the distance required for a car to stop (315 feet). In short, if the driver blinks his eyes, or turns for a casual quick glance at a passenger, you can be wiped out.

The Belt Beacon is visible for at least 600 feet in cities and towns, and for far greater distances in the country. The rapid blinking action draws immediate attention. And that is what you want.

Another safety light which I have not yet tested is the Mighty Lite, which uses a fluorescent tube to cast a green-tinted light in a 25-ft circle around the cyclist. Power by generator. Sounds weird but might be good. Write Maxon Co, 20630 Harper Ave, Harper Woods, Mich 48225, USA for details.

Whatever type of system you use, carry spare bulbs. Room to store these can often be found inside the lamp, or you can wrap them in a bit of plastic and stuff them in the ends of the handlebars.

Reflectors
There are three types: rear (usually mounted on the mudguard), pedal, and wheel. Wheel reflectors are not very useful, as they are visible only when the cyclist is already broadside on to the motorist. Pedal and rear reflectors are more effective, but should be regarded only as additional precautions. What makes a cyclist visible at night are good lights. If you use panniers dress them up with a reflecting tape like Scotchlite. It adds virtually no weight but does a lot for visibility. Reflecting tape is also good for your helmet, the back of your jacket, and the backs of your gloves, so that turn signals are more clearly indicated.

Electric turn signals
These are silly. A blinking turn signal is useful only on a vehicle wide enough and with sufficient other lights so that the blinker is clearly on one side of the vehicle. Bike turn signals are too close

together for a motorist to tell from
a distance what is going on.

Helmet

In most fatal bicycle accidents the
injury is to the head. Even a drop
of two feet on to a hard surface is
enough to fracture the skull. Wear
a helmet whenever you cycle. It's
inconvenient. So is not being able
to think or talk because your head has
been pounded into jelly.

The Bell

The classic cycling helmet consists of padded leather strips with
spaces in between. It is better than nothing but far from good
enough. The best protection is provided by a hard-shell helmet with
a shock-absorbing liner or suspension system, and of these the best
is the American Bell.

This has an outer shell made of high-impact Lexan, an inner shell
of beaded polystyrene, and nine velcro-backed foam pads which
come in varying thicknesses to enable a perfect fit. A number of
air-ventilation holes, combined with the air gap between skull and
inner shell created by the foam pads, ensure maximum air
circulation and cooling. This is an important feature, as the biggest
drawback of a hard-shell helmet is that in warm weather it can be
stifling hot, especially on long hill climbs. The Bell (about £15) can
be ordered from the manufacturer, Bell Helmets Inc, 15301
Shoemaker Ave, Norwalk, CA 90650, USA, and also from the mail
order firms

Bikecology
1515 Wilshire Boulevard
PO Box 1880
Santa Monica, CA 90406
USA

Palo Alto Bicycle Shop
171 University Avenue
PO Box 1276
Palo Alto, CA 94302
USA

Quite a few people strongly object to using a helmet while cycling.
They want freedom, simplicity, and contact with fresh air. Or they
find a helmet inconvenient. In most cycling accidents it is only the
cyclist who is injured or killed. So the wearing of a helmet is largely
a matter of personal choice, in which the pleasure of 'freedom' must
be weighed against personal obligations and responsibilities, and
also of course, the prospect of death or disablement.

Calculating that prospect is not simple. The Department of Transport reckons that a given journey by bicycle is ten times more likely to include an accident than that same journey by motor vehicle. However, factors such as rider age and type of road can greatly affect accident potential. Under-20-year-olds have the greatest number of accidents but cycle the fewest miles, and cyclists (and motorists) on minor rural roads are in far less danger than their urban counterparts.* There is a statistical case, if one wants to make it, for saying that children, urban cyclists, and racing cyclists are well advised to wear helmets, while adult touring cyclists are at little enough risk so that a helmet is optional.

Statistics have none of the enduring imperishability of a tree or stone kerb with which your head has come into contact. They do not bleed, talk peculiarly, or spend six months in a hospital. Some of the people that this has happened to as a result of a cycling accident were among the most experienced racing or touring cyclists in the business. All too often the accident was in no way their fault. I go for what is real to me, and wear a helmet. I advise you to do the same.

As for the inconvenience of a helmet, I refer to a billboard poster showing a man in a wheelchair. The caption reads: 'I didn't wear a seatbelt because it was inconvenient.' Wear a helmet. Always.

Gloves
Cycling gloves are fingerless, with ventilated mesh backs and padded leather palms. The padding can help a lot to prevent numb hands from pinched nerves, and affords some protection in the event of a spill.

Handlebar tapes
Standard tapes of cloth or plastic are quite thin. If your hands numb easily you may want to use something thicker. 'The Tape' is vinyl backed and suede finished and feels very nice. Eight washable colours, about £1.75 a set at cycle shops. Not as good but still miles better than cloth or plastic is Andrew Hague Handlebar Tape, also suede finished.

Obtainable from Bikecology, 1515 Wilshire Boulevard, PO Box 1880, Santa Monica, CA 90406, USA, is: Bailey III cushioned tape, with a soft centre and tapered edges, in eight colours and about £2 a set; Cyclegrip tape, also soft-centre and tapered edge, but made of real leather giving really excellent feel, in tan or black and about

* Hudson, Mike, *The Bicycle Planning Book*, Open Books Publishing Ltd, London, 1978.

£3.50 a set; and, for ultimate thickness, contoured foam handlebar sheaths by Pro Tour or Grab On, about £5 a set.

The
HYDROMAC
(R. g)
UNIVERSAL
SMOCK
for LADIES
(as Illustrated).

" Klossie used it as her only waterproof on our cycling trip to Venice and back, just concluded ; and it kept her by far drier and more cosy than any waterproof she has ever had before."

Raingear

If it rains long enough, and hard enough, one way or another you will get wet. The classic cycling cape drapes over the shoulders, back and handlebars, allowing air to circulate up from underneath. Also circulated is road spray from your own tyres, and from passing vehicles. A proper rainsuit of jacket and pants protects against wet from without, but eventually you become drenched in your own sweat. An alternative are rainsuits made from Gore-Tex, a new material which is waterproof, but with the ability to breathe. A list of suppliers is given in the Camping section of Chapter 9.

Super Link

This is a master link made for derailleur gear chains which eliminates the need for a chain tool. It is strong, well made, and will last through several chains. About £4 at bike shops, or by post from Freewheel, 275 West End Lane, London NW6 1QS.

Bullseye pulleys

People interested in tuning a bike up for maximum performance might consider these sealed bearing chain roller wheels for derailleur units. They reduce friction by one-sixth. About £12 at bike shops.

Chains

Another performance option is the Shimano Uni-Glide chain. Used in conjunction with a Shimano freewheel, this chain gives noticeably smoother shifting for derailleur gear bikes. Obtainable from bike shops.

Junior pedalling attachment

This device fits on to the rear seat tube of a tandem bike, and consists of a bottom bracket and chainwheel which drive a freewheel fitted to the main bottom bracket below. It allows very small children to ride the back seat of the tandem and contribute to the pedalling when they feel so inclined. It is more interesting than sitting around doing nothing, and the position is safer. Obtainable from Andrew Hague Cycle Engineering, 1 Kipling Grove, Anstey Lane, Leicester LE4 OPF, for £15 plus postage.

Saddle bag clamp

Many racing saddles do not have the necessary loops for attaching a saddle or tool bag. This gizmo solves the problem and is quick release as well. From Andrew Hague, address above, for £1 plus postage.

Tool bag

Small and compact, these will hold a tyre repair kit, chain tool and chainlinks, and a few tools. Almost in the carrier class is the Bike Pocket tyre bag also fitting under the saddle, but able to hold two tubular tyres, tools, lamps, and other gear. Good for fast day rides. About $14 from Synergy Works, 255 4th Street, Oakland, CA 94607, USA.

Carrier

The best sort of carrier depends on your needs. A cloth slingbag or rucksack can go with you on and off the bike and is handy while shopping. So are the quick-release front baskets, and rear panniers.

For around-town use, the lightweight alloy racks fitting over the rear wheel and clamping to the back seat stays are quite adequate. For heavier going a steel rack designed for use with panniers is much better. See the baggage section in Chapter 9 for more information.

Child carriers

The only kind worth considering put the child behind the rider and have full leg shields to prevent feet from tangling in spokes.

In this latter respect there is no recommendable British product. Obtainable from Troxel Manufacturing Co, Moscow, Tenn 38057, USA, is their Model No. 1, made of polypropylene with a ventilated back, fitted pad, and full wrap-around, lace-on wheel guard. It also features quick-release mounting knobs. About £10.

Rear-view mirrors

Bicycle mounted rear-view mirrors wiggle about too much to be reliable. Wrist mounted mirrors such as the See-Bak and eyeglasses mounting mirrors such as the Golden View Mirror are useful accessories once you learn how to use them, and providing that you always take what you see with a grain of salt. The field of view of these mirrors is very small and limited to possibly warning you of

oncoming traffic. To check and see if the way is clear for you to pull out farther on to the road, duck your head and look directly.

Nail pullers or flint catchers
These are small half loops of wire that ride along just above the tyre and brush off shards of broken glass, pebbles, etc. For tubulars and narrow profile wire-ons.

Mudguards
A requirement for tourists and people living in rain forests. If you want to go like the clappers and don't mind getting dirty once in a while, leave them off. Plastic mudguards are light, and easy to get on and off (weekend racers, note), but eventually warp and fail. Stainless steel and aluminium are more durable, and offer a mounting point for lights and other gear, but are slightly heavier and make a noise. This last can be cured with a coat of undersealing paint (motor accessory shops).

Locks See Chapter 4.

Horns and bells
Yelling is quick, reliable, and the most expressive. Little bells and horns are forever failing or being stolen. Freon horns are wonderfully loud – excessively so.

Water bottle
On longer tours and races it is quite easy to become dehydrated. This raises body temperature. It is a good idea to carry your own supply of liquid and a bit of high energy food.

Spoke guard
This is a thin plate designed to prevent the rear derailleur from catching in the spokes of the rear wheel. With a properly adjusted derailleur it should never happen, but should the derailleur malfunction or break (as has happened to me) then down you go, and with the back of the bike twisted into spaghetti.

Chain guard – These are designed to help prevent the soiling of clothes by dirty chains, and are probably worthwhile on a commuting bike. I find them a needless amount of extra weight and trouble on a racing bike.

Kickstand
Adds a lot of weight for very little useful function. There is almost always something against which a bike can be leaned.

Odometer or velometer
Tells how far you have gone. Not important.

Speedometer
Tyre drive models are generally inaccurate and increase drag. Electronic models are expensive (about £50) but also include a pedal rpm counter. This can be useful when trying to determine maximum power points in various gears. A club could share one unit among several members.

12 Veteran and vintage

If you have a little spare space, antique cycles are a dandy item to collect and restore. Early models were largely a blacksmith's creation, and bringing them 'up to snuff' is well within the capacity of a competent handyman. The last part of the nineteenth century was the heyday of innovation and experimentation in cycles, and many wacky and wonderful machines were produced. Some are illustrated in this book. Because they are unique they can command high prices, and even a plain Ordinary (penny-farthing) in good nick can fetch £300 to £400. By about 1910 cycle designs had fairly well settled down, and machines from this date onwards can be had for a more reasonable sum. From my own point of view this is fortunate, as I collect (when I can) on the basis of aesthetic appeal, and on this count find the machines of the Twenties, Thirties, and even Forties very attractive.

The best source for old bikes is Grandfather's attic. Most machines already on the market are wildly expensive. The thing to do is find some old wreck mouldering in a field or root around in the old junk shed of friendly Uncle Fred the bicycle-dealer who unexpectedly kicked the bucket two decades ago. Often what you find is a disheartening pile of rust, but it is surprising what some elbow grease and rust remover can do. And, listen, if you do know of such a wreck or old shed and aren't interested . . . drop me a line, hm?

There are any number of books on old cycles, and a nice inexpensive one is *Discovering Old Bicycles* by T. E. Crowley (Shire Publications Ltd, 12B Temple Square, Aylesbury, Bucks; 35p). A real winner is *King of the Road* by Andrew Ritchie (Wildwood House, 1 Wardour St, London w1v 3he; £2.95). Another colourful one is *The Story of the Bicycle* by John Woodforde (Routledge & Kegan Paul, 39 Store St, London WC1; £1.50). There are a number of clubs but some have restricted membership. One which does not is: Southern Veteran Cycle Club, Iain Cowan, Woodbine Cottage, 8 Shrubbery Road, Gravesend, Kent

Others are

National Association of Veteran
  Cycle Clubs
Ray Heeley
124 Southfields Avenue
Stanground, Peterborough

Benson Veteran Cycle Club
C. N. Passey
61 The Bungalow
Brook Street
Benson, Oxfordshire

Boston Veteran Cycle Club
P. Bates
15 Rosebery Avenue
Boston, Lincolnshire

Bygone Bikes Yorkshire Club
J. W. Auty
85 Priory Road
Featherstone
Pontefract, Yorkshire

Long Sutton and District
  Veteran Cycle Club
P. Shirtcliffe
Hillcrest
Crowhall
Denver
Downham Market, Norfolk

Peterborough Vintage
  Cycle Club
Ms Young
48 Newark Avenue
Peterborough

Roadfarers Veteran
  Cycle Club
A. C. Mundy
22 High Street
Caister, Peterborough

Gibbons Pentacycle, or 'Hen-and-Chickens'

Enthusiasts headed for the United States
may want to get in touch with:

Antique Bicycle Club of America
Roland C. Geist
260 West 260th Street
New York NY

Veteran Wheelmen's Association
Franklin Institute
Philadelphia PA

The Wheelmen
Robert McNair
32 Dartmouth Circle
Swarthmore PA 19801

The Wheelmen Antique Bicycle Club
214 Maywinn Road
Defiance OH

The Wheelmen Newsletter (has ads)
Keith Larzelere
PO Box 38
Petersburg MICH 49270

Book Two

1 Maintenance and repair

Maintenance programme

The subject of maintenance and repair of bicycles is usually clouded with negative feelings. It is regarded as something in the 'must be done' category and approached as a chore. Bicycle repair books are fond of saying that any cretin can understand how to fix his machine, or that the book itself has the answer to any problem that might conceivably come up. Both approaches underestimate the reader's intelligence and compartmentalize maintenance and repair, keeping it separate from 'riding'. This is a basic mistake. The extent to which you get involved in working on your bike should be a direct function of how you ride. One follows the other like night and day. The awareness that riding a bike precipitates usually includes an awareness and interest in the bike itself. How the bike responds is very much a function of maintenance. Ideally, you are going to work on your own bike because you want a together, tight machine under you, i.e. you will do it because *you want to*.

As with all things, you get back in proportion to what you put in. It is essentially a question of fineness. It is the nature of bikes that they are at their best when well-lubricated and carefully adjusted. A sensitivity to this sort of refinement does not happen the instant you mount a bike. Give it time. As you ride you will become increasingly aware of your bike's mechanical characteristics. A well set-up bike fits you like a suit of clothes, and you will soon develop an 'ear' for the sound of bearings and a 'feel' for other parts, such as the brakes. The development of this sensitivity – the result of personal and direct participation – is part of the reason for owning a bike in the first place. Eventually, you will find that increased riding pleasure is not just a reward for doing your own maintenance, the mechanical sensitivity itself becomes part of the riding pleasure.

As I say, this is all something that you should grow into. The idea of having a bike is to have fun. A fair amount of latitude is possible in servicing bikes and you have hopefully chosen a machine suited to your level of interest. So you can minimize or maximize maintenance as per your own inclinations. But bear in mind that most machines, and certainly bicycles, need a certain amount of lubrication and adjustment if they are to function at all. Without it, they rust away, and because the parts are unlubricated and out of kilter, they slowly chew themselves to bits when ridden. I have seen 'old dependables' that have been left out in the rain for years and have never seen an oil can or a mechanic. They make it for years – and then snap a chain in the middle of a tour or a brake cable at the start of a long hill. Or eventually the rust destroys them. There is no need for this. A properly maintained bike will easily last a lifetime and more. For reasons of simple economy and safety, if you can't be bothered to do routine maintenance then take your machine to a bike shop for servicing at least twice a year.

An excellent reason for doing your own work is that you are apt to do a quicker and better job than the shop. By and large, bicycle mechanics are not well paid, and are thin on the ground. A familiar sign to be found on bike shop doors is: 'Sorry, no more repairs this month.' For want of what is only a ten-minute repair job, your bike can be out of commission for days or even weeks. And no matter if the shop is good or bad, you cannot expect the mechanic to have a total interest in getting the job done exactly right. Once you learn the drill you will almost always do a better job. Further, if you suffer a breakdown late at night or far out in the sticks, you will be able to deal with it.

Another important reason for doing your own work is that it makes preventive maintenance almost automatic. Preventive maintenance is replacing parts before they wear out and break, usually at an inopportune time and miles from any bike shop. If you are paying attention to the various parts of your bike and keeping it in tune, this is pretty much going to happen as a matter of course. In turn, breakdowns and repairs will also be fairly well obviated.

I think this approach is the easiest and the most efficient. I have studied every repair manual I could find. Most stress fixing something *after* it has broken. Even though I know how to fix bicycles, most of them lose me right away. Either they are filled with long passages of incomprehensible jargon, or they have computer-programming style directions ('If A, go to page 28 C; if not A, go to B, page 34, then to page 28 D') designed to reduce you to a mindless automaton.

Here is my approach: each major component system of the bicycle such as brakes, wheels, gears, etc. is broken down into four areas –

how it works; routine adjustments; replacing parts; trouble-shooting.

The idea is to give you a basic understanding of what is happening – and make you a mechanic! How it works for each section is required reading. It does no good for you to diddle with this or adjust that if you have no idea of how it works. And if something is broken, it is impossible for you to fix unless you know how it works in the first place.

It will help a lot if as you read, you look at and feel the corresponding parts on your bike.

I don't cover everything. One wheel is pretty much the same as another. I have tried to include representative types of equipment currently in use but there are bound to be exceptions. If this happens to you, try to find the item in this book which most closely resembles the part you are servicing or fixing. Pay particular attention to *function* and then analyse your own part the same way. This should get you through most things.

There are also some tasks which are just not worth doing. Delving into the innards of a coaster brake multi-speed hub is one of these. It takes a long, long time and isn't fun at all. Some people may resent these omissions. They want to do everything for themselves. Well, the point of diminishing returns is reached with attempts to service the coaster brake 3-speed hubs. Even most bike shops refuse to overhaul these units and simply replace them – it's actually cheaper this way. If you insist on doing this sort of work, detailed instructions are available from the bicycle manufacturer or from the hub manufacturer.

Tools

You can get by with amazingly little in the way of tools. However, for some kinds of work there are a few you will just have to get. Also, what you need depends on what kind of bike you have.

Before going into particulars a word on tool quality: do yourself a favour and buy good ones. Cheap shops, supermarkets, and even hardware stores carry cheap bargains like 10p screwdrivers and 40p spanners. These are a false economy, for they are made of inferior metals that will break or bend under stress, or they are made badly enough so that they don't even work. You do not need many tools, and the total investment should be between £8 and £12. In the long run it is worth it. I have had the same 8-in adjustable end spanner for 26 years.

For both 3- and 10-speed bikes:
Hardware shop
8-in or 6-in adjustable end spanner.
Pliers. Hammer.
$\frac{1}{4}$-in. tip, 4 – 5-in shank screwdriver.
$\frac{1}{8}$-in. tip, 2 – 3-in shank screwdriver.
Wire clippers.
6-in file, mill bastard.
Bike shop
Mafac tool kit – contains tyre irons, spanners, other gear, including tyre patching kit.
All-purpose tool like Raleigh give-away.
Thin hub spanners, 13 × 14 and 15 × 16.
Spoke key.
Pedal wingnut spanner (for pedals with outside dustcap only).
Tyre gauge: for Schrader valve if you have wire on tyres; for Presta valve if you have tubulars.
Tyre patch kit.
10-speed bikes:
Bike shop
chain rivet remover; freewheel remover, there are two basic types:

Look at your freewheel and see if it is splined or not on the interior to
see what kind you need.

Set of metric Allen spanners.

If you have a Campagnolo derailleur, a special Campagnolo
combination Allen and socket spanner.

If you have cotterless cranks you will need a special crank-removing
tool as per your brand of crank.

Other useful tools:
set of spanners, vice-grip pliers, channel lock pliers, small portable
vice.

As you can see from studying the list, many of the tools are for
specialized jobs so you do not have to acquire them all at once.
Absolutely essential, and especially for trips, is the Mafac toolkit,
a screwdriver, and an all-purpose combination tool like the Raleigh
give-away.

If you have difficulty obtaining tools from local shops, or would
just like to read over an amusing tool catalogue, write to The Third
Hand, 3945 High St, Eugene, ORE 97405, USA.

You will need some means of holding the bike steady. One
method is to simply turn the bike upside down. With downswept
handlebars use a narrow cardboard or wood box with slots cut in
the side to support the handlebars and keep the brake cables from
being bent against the ground. A nail driven into a doorjamb with
a rope to hang the bike by will also suffice. Best of all is a proper
work stand. These are rather expensive (£15 and up) but perhaps
you could share one with friends. Bikecology (1515 Wilshire Blvd,
PO Box 1880, Santa Monica, CA 90406, USA) sells a folding stand
that is easy to store and carry about.

Lubrication

This is a general discussion of lubrication. For details look under
the part in question, e.g. brakes, gears, hubs, etc.

There are a number of different types and forms of lubricants. Oil is the old standby. Be sure to use a good grade, such as motorist's SAE 30, or Sturmey-Archer cycle oil. Do not use household oils as these have a vegetable gum base which ultimately creates a hard residue.

Grease is used for bearings. Ordinary grease from a motorist's shop will work well enough. Lithium greases such as Filtrate and Cycle Pro are less likely to be washed away by water. Also good in this respect is Bardahl Multi-purpose grease. Best of all is Phil Wood Waterproof Bicycle Grease. The very, very expensive Campagnolo Special Grease is a load of old cod. For the ultimate in slipperiness add a small quantity of Moly-Slip to your grease and oil. This contains molybdenum disulphide, a sub-microscopic substance that fills in microscopic irregularities on metal surfaces, reducing friction and wear.

Your bicycle has upwards of 200 ball bearings held in place by cups and cones:

dust cover

locknut

spindle (axle)

bearings

cone

cup

The cone remains stationary while the cup, and whatever part is attached to it – in this example it would be a wheel – rides on the ball bearings and spins around.

The distance between the cone and the cup is adjustable and must not be too tight or too loose. Sometimes the ball bearings are held in a clip called a *race*. Typically, this is positioned so that the open side through which the balls stick is against the cup. You will find bearings at the headset, bottom bracket, wheels, and pedals:

These bearings are usually disassembled, cleaned thoroughly in paraffin or other solvent, packed with grease and reassembled, every six months. See under relevant section for disassembly technique. Some bearings are both greased and oiled, and in particular, 2- and 3-speed hubs and hubs on ultra-fancy racing bikes. You can tell these by the fact that the hub has a small oil cap or clip:

These need oil once a month: multi-speed internal gear hubs a tablespoonful, regular hubs about $\frac{1}{2}$ teaspoonful, and coaster brake hubs 2 tablespoonfuls. Some bottom brackets are set up to use oil. A teaspoonful once a month. Use oil wherever you find oil caps or clips. Too little is better than too much. If oil leaks out of the sides of the bearings and dribbles all over your crankset or wheels, you are using too much.

I prefer the use of a dry lubricant for the chain, freewheel, derailleur, brake pivots, cables, and any other parts which do not use grease:

Dry lubricants usually come in spray form and contain an exotic and sometimes secret blend of ingredients. Often included is molybdenum disulphide. Dry lubricants can be used as a substitute for oil. They are not as long lasting, but ease of application makes more frequent servicing relatively painless. The important thing is that the lubricants are dry. The trouble with oil is that it attracts dirt which then mixes with the oil and forms a gooey abrasive mess, greatly increasing mechanical wear. Everything gets dirty, including you. In the case of the chain, for example, this means that once a month you have to remove it, soak it clean in paraffin or other solvent, dry it, oil it, and then reinstall it. It's time consuming and messy. If you use a dry lubricant you need do this job only once every two or three months. You must lubricate more often – bi-weekly in normal service, weekly in hard service – but with a spray this job takes only a few seconds. The same rationale applies for the freewheel and derailleur. The spray is particularly useful for the brake pivots and all cables. Oil has a tendency to leak out on to the brake levers and handlebars, and brake shoes. Once a month is sufficient.

At this writing the best dry lubricant is LPS, which comes in three grades of thickness (LPS-1, -2, -3) and also as a paste which can be used as a grease for cables. I have not yet tested the suitability of the paste as a bearing grease.

Note : Dry lubricants will usually dissolve ordinary greases and oils. Do not mix the two types!

Another dry lubricant is paraffin wax, available in grocery stores. It is extremely good for prolonging chain life. Clean your chain in the conventional manner with paraffin or other solvent. Melt the wax in a coffee can over the stove. Dump the chain in and then hang to dry so that drippings fall back into can. Use oil or spray for the brake pivot points, freewheel and derailleur. The wax will not work well on these parts because it cools and hardens too quickly on contact with the metal to penetrate effectively. It is excellent for brake cables, however. Just run the cable through a block of wax a few times until it is well impregnated. Save and re-use the old wax. Wax, like spray, does not attract dirt.

Note : New bikes fresh from the dealer and bikes that have been standing around for a long time may be dry as a bone. *Oil Evaporates !* Be sure to lubricate such machines before using.

General words

There are a number of things to keep in mind when servicing bikes:

(1) Do not use a great deal of force when assembling or disassembling parts. Bicycle components are frequently made of alloys for light weight. These are not as strong as steel and it is not hard to strip threads or otherwise damage parts. Always be sure that things fit. Be careful and delicate. Snug down bolts, nuts, and screws firmly, not with all your might.

(2) Most parts tighten *clockwise* and come apart turning *anti-clockwise*. This is called a right-hand thread. A left-hand thread tightens *anti-clockwise*, and loosens *clockwise*. Left-hand threads are not used often.

(3) When fitting together threaded parts, hold them as perfectly aligned as you can, and turn one backwards (loosen) until you hear and feel a slight click. Then reverse and tighten. If this is new to you, practise on a nut and bolt until you have the feel of it perfectly.

(4) If you get stuck with a rust-frozen bolt or nut, soak it in penetrating oil, give it a few light taps to help the oil work in, and then try to undo it again with a tool that fits exactly. If this fails, try a cold chisel and hammer:

Go at this carefully since if you slip you may gouge a chunk out of your bicycle. If this fails, hacksaw or file the nut or bolt off. How did it get this rusty in the first place?

(5) When assembling or disassembling try to be neat and organized. Lay parts out in the order which they came apart or go together. Put tiny parts in boxes or jars.

(6) There are a number of little nuts and bolts on your bike for cable clamps, racks, brake lever mounts, gear shift lever mounts, and the like. These tend to get loose and need tightening about once a month.

(7) The left side of the bike is as if you and the bike both point forward.

(8) Solvents: Paraffin and paint thinner are good. Petrol is very dangerous. Another way of cleaning greasy parts is with a de-greaser such as Spray Away or Gunk.

(9) Finish: a good quality car wax will preserve your paint job and make it easier to keep clean. Wipe the bike down once a week and after major journeys. Do not wax wheel rims where brake shoes contact.

(10) Wire cable is used for brake and gear controls. If you need to trim a new cable to size, do so with wire snips for a clean cut. Pliers will fray the cable end so that it will not pass through the cable housing. After snipping, solder the cable end to prevent fraying, or alternatively, dip it in epoxy glue. File away excess solder or glue.

Ordinary cables and housings work very well, but when replacement time comes, consider using Aztec cables (from Freewheel, 275 West End Lane, London NW6 1QS). These are extra strong teflon-coated cables, perform excellently, and do not require lubrication.

(11) Sealed bearing hubs, bottom brackets, and pedals are not covered in this manual. By definition, such units are maintenance free. When servicing or repair is needed, usually special tools and techniques are required for each particular make of unit, and often the work is done by the factory.

(12) Never put a bike into storage after a wet ride. Wait until the weather clears and take a short spin for a mile or two. This will force out any water left in the bearings, cables, and so forth. Otherwise even a 'sealed bearing' unit can freeze up solid with rust.

Parts of a bicycle

1 quick release hub
2 rear brake
3 seat stay
4 seat post
5 saddle
6 seat tube
7 top tube
8 front changer
9 stem

10 expanderbolt
11 handle bars
12 headset
13 brake lever
14 head tube
15 front brake
16 front fork
17 chrome fork tips
18 quick release hub

19 rim
20 front hub
21 fork rake
22 down tube
23 chain guard and chainwheels
24 bottom bracket
25 crank
26 pedal
27 chain stay

28 chain
29 guide wheels of the rear changer
30 rear changer (derailleur)
31 rear sprockets (freewheel)
32 lugs
33 gear change levers
34 cotter pin

2 The brakes

General

Bicycle brakes come in three basic types: hub coaster pedal-operated, disc hand-operated, and calliper hand-operated. The coaster brake is inferior on several counts. Under conditions requiring a quick stop it tends to lock the rear wheel, causing the bike to skid rather than slow down.* It has poor heat dissipating qualities and can burn out on a long downhill. It is difficult to service. It is for the rear wheel only, thus cutting braking efficiency below 50% since it is at the front wheel that the greatest braking power can be attained. In fact, on dry pavement it is difficult if not impossible to lock up a front wheel. This is because braking throws the weight forward, increasing traction. If you have a bike which has only a coaster brake, equip it with a calliper brake for the front wheel. Only children without the necessary strength to operate calliper brakes should have a coaster brake, and they should not ride in any situation requiring quick stops or sustained braking.

If something goes wrong with your coaster brake, simply remove the entire rear wheel and take it to a bicycle shop for overhaul or replacement. It is complicated to fix, and infinitely more trouble than it is worth.

Disc brakes are heavy, but offer good stopping power under both wet and dry conditions. They are a logical choice for tandems and tricycles, but are a bit finicky to adjust and service.

Calliper brakes offer a good balance between weight and stopping power. Modern brake shoes give an at least reasonable performance under wet conditions, and very good performance under dry conditions. They are relatively simple to service.

Calliper and disc systems are roughly identical in operation and principle. All of the operations on brake levers and cables described in the section on calliper brakes below apply equally well to disc brakes. I therefore carry calliper brakes right the way through the chapter, with a section on adjustment and maintenance of disc brakes at the end.

---

* A screeching, tyre-smoking stop is not the quickest. When the wheel is locked, the rubber literally melts into the road, providing a *liquid* point of contact between the tyre and road surface, and greatly increasing stopping distance. The quickest stops are done by slowing the wheel to the point just before locking. Skidding also means a loss of directional control and often results in a fall.

How calliper brakes work

Calliper brake systems all work on the same basic principle. There is a hollow, flexible tube called a cable housing between the brake lever mount and the cable hanger:

The cable housing is flexible so that the handlebars can turn back and forth. Through the cable housing passes a cable which is attached to the brake lever at one end:

and to the brake mechanism at the other. This is in turn attached to the bicycle frame and functions like a pair of complicated ice tongs with double pivot joints. When the brake lever is operated, it pulls the cable through the cable housing and pinches together the arms (called *yokes*) of the brake mechanism, causing the two rubber brake shoes attached to the yokes to press against the wheel rim and stop the wheel:

When the lever is released, a spring forces the yoke arms away from the wheel rim:

this in turn returns the brake lever to an off position, and keeps continuous tension on the entire brake assembly. This is the basic centre-pull mechanism.

A variation is the cantilever brake:

in which the brake yokes are bolted directly on to the fork or seat stays.

The side-pull brake uses only one pivot point, with the cable housing attached directly to one yoke, and the cable to the other. The effect is the same:

All calliper brake systems have an adjusting screw (called a *barrel adjuster*) for changing the relationship of the cable housing length to the length of the brake cable. On the side-pull brake this is almost always found on the yoke to which the cable housing is attached (A), while on the centre-pull brake it is usually at the brake lever (B) or the cable hanger (C):

Properly adjusted brake shoes are so close to the wheel rim that the tyre will not slide between them when removing the wheel. Accordingly, better-grade brake systems have a means for creating a little extra slack in the brake cable. This is usually a small button which allows the brake lever to open more:

These are the basics of any calliper brake system: a brake lever, a brake cable and housing with adjuster barrel, a cable hanger for centre-pull systems, and the brake mechanism, including yokes, springs, and brake shoes. Better systems include either a button or cam to provide extra slack in the cable when removing the wheel or servicing the brakes.

Centre-pull

lever

mount

cable housing

barrel adjuster

yokes

cable

pivot bolt

cable anchor bolt

brake shoes

Side-pull

Lubrication

Try to avoid the use of oil. At the brake levers, it oozes out over everything and gets your hands dirty every time you ride. At the brake mechanism, it dribbles down to the brake shoes, cutting braking power. A better product is a spray such as WD-40 or LPS-1, dry film lubricants which displace water and do not attract dirt. Use a little plastic nozzle which comes with the can for pin-point accuracy, and spray pivot bolts, all exposed cable (use a piece of paper or cardboard as a backstop to prevent the spray from going all over the bike), yoke cable anchor points, brake lever pivots, and inside the cable housings. Machines used once or twice a week need lubrication every two months, those in daily use, monthly. More often on tours.

Routine adjustments

Whatever kind of calliper brake system you have, there are two basic kinds of adjustments: (1) seeing that the brake shoe hits the wheel rim properly, and (2) keeping slack out of the cable between the brake lever and mechanism, so that the lever travels the shortest possible distance when putting on the brakes.

First check to see that the wheel is true by spinning it and seeing that the rim, not the tyre, stays about the same distance from the brake shoe all the way around. If play is greater than approximately $\frac{1}{8}$ in (3mm) the wheel should be trued (see pp 280–81) before any brake adjustments are attempted. Check also that the wheel is reasonably centred between the fork arms, and that the rim is free of major dents and abrasions. If off-centre, take the bike to a shop to have the forks checked, and if the rim is badly banged up, get a new one.

Calliper brakes

Brake shoes

These need to be aligned so that the shoe hits the rim squarely:

wrong   wrong   right

Brake shoes are held on either by a conventional bolt:

A

or an eyebolt:

In either case, loosen nut A, adjust brake shoe to meet rim, and
tighten. One method is to loosen nut A just a little bit and gently
tap the shoe into the proper position with the spanner handle.
With conventional bolts you'll find that the brake shoe twists to the
right when you tighten the nut back down. A good trick is to set it
slightly anti-clockwise so that the final tightening brings it
perfectly into position. Do not use too much force. Brake bolt screws
strip easily.

Eyebolt-type shoes are easy to adjust so that the face of the shoe
is flush with the rim. Achieving this effect with a conventional-bolt
brake shoe sometimes requires bending the yoke. Remove the brake
shoe altogether and fit an adjustable end spanner snugly over the
end of the yoke:

If the yoke needs to be bent outward, simply pull on the handle of
the spanner. *Go Slow* – if you break or mangle the yoke you will
probably have to get a whole new (expensive) brake mechanism.
If the yoke needs to be bent inward, provide a pivot point by
wedging another spanner, screwdriver handle, or other object
between the yoke and tyre, and push on the spanner handle:

If you don't have a suitable spanner,
use a screwdriver:

Do not be especially keen to start bending things. New brake shoes,
for example, will frequently wear into correct alignment with a few
days' use:

new   broken-in

Use soft rubber racing-type brake shoes (usually coloured red) rather than the hard rubber (usually black) kind typically supplied with side-pull brakes. The soft shoes wear out faster but work a lot better and cost only a few pence each. You can buy the shoes separately from the metal holder and bolt. The holder is open at one end. Slide the old shoe out and the new one in:

If the old brake shoe will not come out easily and you do not have access to a vice to grip the holder securely while you tap out the shoe, forget it and buy a new set of holders and shoes. Be sure to install the new units so that the closed end faces forward (the direction the bike goes), or else the shoes will slide out when the brakes are applied.

Some people consider it good practice to toe-in the fronts of the brake shoes. This is done by twisting the yoke with a spanner or screwdriver so that the front of the shoe hits the rim $\frac{1}{32}$ in before the back. Under hard braking however, the whole shoe is flush to the rim. If you have squealing brakes this may cure the problem. Do not toe-in modern soft-composition shoes such as Mathauser's, as this can cause severe grabbing and snatching – hard braking when you do not want it.

Cables

Once the brake shoes have been properly aligned, they should be placed as close to the rim as possible without rubbing when the wheel is spun, $\frac{1}{8}$ in or less. This is done, for both side- and centre-pull brakes, with the barrel adjuster and locknut, and the cable anchor nut and bolt:

cable anchor bolt

barrel adjuster

The idea is to screw in the barrel adjuster, take up as much slack as possible at the anchor nut, and then use the barrel adjuster to take up slack every few days. The cable is always stretching. When the barrel adjuster reaches the limit of its travel, the process is repeated. There are a number of different methods for doing this job, depending on the number and type of tools that you have. A very handy gadget is called a 'third hand' and is a spring-like affair for compressing brake shoes together. Bike shops have them. The reason

for this tool, or substitute, is that if you just loosen the anchor cable nut the spring tension of the brake yoke arms will pull the cable through and you will have a hard time getting it back in. With or without a third hand, undo locknut and screw adjuster barrel all the way in:

Check and see that the brake release button or cam is set for normal operation (not on all bikes). If you have a 'third hand', mount it. Or use a C-clamp. Or even string. If you have none of these things, squeeze the brake yoke arms together with your hand. With the other hand, pull the cable at the brake mechanism out so the brake lever is fully home, as it would be if the brakes were not on. Make sure the cable housing has not caught on the outside lip of the barrel adjuster. Now look at the amount of slack in the cable. For centre-pull brakes this is the distance between the yoke cable and the cable anchor A:

And for side-pull systems, it is the amount of new cable protruding beneath the yoke A:

Estimate the amount of slack to be taken up with a ruler, tool handle, or finger. Disengage the yoke cable from the cable anchor (centre-pulls) or the cable end from the yoke (side-pulls). Eliminate this step if you have a 'third hand' or similar device. Use two spanners to slacken the cable anchor nut. Avoid twisting the cable. Pass the cable the required distance through the hole in the cable anchor bolt:

If it is sticky, use a pair of pliers to pull it. Tighten cable anchor nut. If no 'third hand', hold brake yoke arms together again and slip yoke cable back over cable anchor, or cable back into yoke. If you have the feature, now is the time to use the brake button or cam to give you that little bit of extra slack you need. Release the second or third hand, as the case may be. Only one or two turns of the barrel adjuster should bring the brake shoes as close as possible to the wheel rim without actually touching when the wheel is spun. If you have got it right (it usually takes a couple of tries), use wire cutters to snip off the excess cable for a neat job. Frayed cable ends have a habit of snagging fingers and clothing.

Pivot bolt adjustment
Side-pull brakes:

Side-pull

Make sure nut A is tight. Turn in locknut C one half-turn while holding acorn adjusting nut B still with another spanner. Turn both B and C in flush against brake yoke arm. Back B off one half-turn, hold in place, and lock locknut C against it.
Centre-pull brakes: see pp 239–41.

Roller lever brakes

As with calliper brakes, roller lever brake shoes must be aligned to hit the inside of the rim squarely. This is done by means of a metal guide (A) clamped to the fork blade or chainstay (see diagram).

B

A

Loosen bolt B, and move guide as necessary so
that when the brakes are applied, the shoes hit
the inside of the rim.

B

If there is too much slack in the system
take it up at a connecting bolt by
loosening bolt B, sliding the rods
together, and then resecuring bolt B.

Another way is to take up the slack with the adjusting bolt:

by first undoing locknut B, and then tightening nut A.

Replacing and disassembling parts

Brake shoes : see above.

Cables

The frequency with which you will need to replace brake (and other) cables depends on how you use your bike. Machines consistently left out in the rain, or used hard every day, are going to need them sooner than well-cared-for or average-use machines. There is no hard and fast rule. Any obvious defect, such as a frayed cable:

is immediate grounds for replacement, as is stickiness in the motion of the cable through the cable housing (see Trouble-shooting). It is generally good practice to replace both brake cables at the same time. They are cheap, and if one has run its course, it is likely that the other has too. The inconvenience of a broken cable is not worth the gain of a month's extra use. If you have purchased a used bike, I would replace cables all around unless you know they are relatively new and obviously in good condition. Good condition means they are clean, have no kinks or frayed spots, and pass easily through the cable housings.

Unless you can specify the brand and model of brake, take your bike or old cable to the shop. Cables come in different shapes, lengths, and thicknesses. It is very irritating to discover in the middle of things that you have the wrong part.

I recommend using the left hand brake lever for the rear brake. This follows standard practice, and since the rear brake is generally more favoured for routine braking, leaves the right hand free for cross-traffic signals.

For any calliper brake system, first screw home the barrel adjuster:

Centre-pulls: push together brake yoke arms (use 'third hand' or similar device if available) and slip yoke cable off brake anchor. Undo cable anchor bolt and nut and slide same off cable:

Side-pulls: One kind of side-pull brake uses a cable anchor bolt and nut at the yoke. Slacken it off and pull out the cable the same way as with a centre-pull. Another type of unit has a ball or nipple on the cable which slips into a slot on the brake yoke arm. You will have to replace both the cable and cable housing as a single unit. Compress brake yoke arms and release ball or nipple from yoke:

Centre-pulls and Side-pulls

Front brakes: Slide the cable housing off the cable. If yours has ferrules:

keep track of where they go.

Rear brakes: Leave the housing attached to the frame and pull the cable out of the housing. If you have a one-piece cable and housing (nipples on both ends of the cable), loosen the clamps on the frame and draw the unit through. Examine the cable housings to see if they need replacement. Are they kinked or broken?

Are the ends free from burrs?

wrong   right

You can eliminate a burr by

(1) Snipping off the cable housing end with a strong pair of wire cutters (pliers are not good enough);

(2) clamping the cable housing end in a vice and filing it down; or

(3) by using a tool called a taper ream, which you insert in the cable housing end and twist until the burr is gone.

If you use wire cutters be sure to get the cutting edges in between the coils of the housing or else you will mash the ends flat:

wrong   right

Use this opportunity to lubricate the inside of the cable housing.

Fully depress brake lever. Side-pulls: move cable until it is aligned with the slot on the side of the brake handle and then slide it out sideways:

On centre-pulls the process is exactly the same, or the slot may be parallel to the cable, as on the Weinmann:

When installing the new cable, save any cutting for last. Cutting invariably frays the cable end and makes it hard to slide through the housing and cable anchor bolt. Installation is the reverse of removal, and for clarification look at the illustrations for that section.

One-nipple cable: Slip cable through brake lever mount and attach to brake lever. Front brakes: including ferrules where used, slip housing on cable. Rear brakes: slide cable into housing. Twist the cable or housing as you do this to avoid catching the cable:

and be sure to do it in the right direction or the cable will unravel. Push free cable end through cable hanger (centre-pulls), or through barrel adjuster at yoke (side-pulls), and then through cable anchor bolt hole. To adjust see pp 223–6.

Two-nipple cable (one-piece housing and cable) : Attach to brake lever. For rear brakes, slide housing through clamps on frame. Front and rear, pass cable end through barrel adjuster on brake yoke arm and fix to opposite brake yoke arm by slipping ball or nipple into slot. Take up slack with barrel adjuster. Rear brakes, tighten housing clamps on frame, and take care that they are set so clothing will not snag on the screws when riding.

Handles
Outside bolt type:

To adjust, slacken A and move. To remove, take off bolt B. May have to be slid back off handlebar in which case grip must be removed. If your brake lever mount has a slot in the bottom:

or if the cable ball or nipple will pass through the hole in the mount,
then create enough slack by screwing home the barrel adjuster and
clamping together the brake shoes, and disconnect the cable from
the lever. If this is not possible, then disconnect the cable anchor
bolt at the brake mechanism and take the cable out altogether.

Inside bolt type:

Disconnect yoke cable from cable anchor. Fully depress brake lever
and use screwdriver or socket spanner on bolt A. If you are replacing
the brake lever, you may need to take out the brake cable (see
above). On some systems such as Weinmann the cable end will
pass directly through the hole B in the brake mount.

Brake mechanism
First disconnect brake cable.

Side-pull systems:
To remove entire brake from bike, undo nut A. Disassembly:
should be done only to replace a specific part if it won't work.

Side-pull

Start with brake mechanism on bike. Undo the brake spring by
prising it off with a screwdriver. Careful of fingers. Separate nut B
from nut C, and take them both off the pivot bolt. Then the rest of
the stuff. Keep the parts lined up in the order in which you remove
them. If you are replacing the pivot bolt, undo nut A and take off
bolt. Reverse procedure for reassembly.

Centre-pull systems:
To remove unit from bike, undo nut A, remove washers and seating
pads, and then brake mechanism (see overleaf). Disassembly:
there's no good reason for this. Any badly busted-up parts needing
replacement probably cannot be obtained, and you will need a new
mechanism. You insist? See pp 239–41.

Trouble-shooting

Before using this section please read How it works and Adjustments. You have to know how it works in the first place in order to figure out what's wrong. Brake problems come in three broad categories. In each category there are three possible areas in which the trouble may be: brake lever, cable or rods, or mechanism. The first thing is to find in which of these the problem originates, and this is done by isolating and actuating each unit separately.

Category 1 – No, or very weak, brakes.
🚲 Is rim oily?
🚲 Are shoes hitting rim?
🚲 Will brake mechanism compress when you squeeze it with your hand? If no, go to Category 3, sticky brakes, below. If yes,
🚲 Does lever move freely? Yes? Broken cable. Replace.
🚲 Lever will not move. Disconnect cable at brake mechanism end. Will cable housing slide off cable? No? Cable is frozen inside housing. Get it off somehow and replace. If cable and housing separate easily then,
🚲 Lever is frozen. First see if your unit has an adjustable bolt (A)

for the lever and if so give it a try. No? A major bash may have pinched together the sides of the brake lever mount housing. Examine it carefully and bend out dented parts with a big screwdriver:

Or the lever itself may be bent. Bend it back. If the bend has been severe, replace the lever or unit. Metal which has been bent a lot may look perfectly OK but is fatigued and weak, and may well snap under the pressure of an emergency stop.

Category 2 – Brakes work, but unevenly or make noises.
🚲 Juddering. Can be caused by a loose brake mechanism, uneven rims, or sometimes by a very loose headset. To fix the brake mechanism:

Side-pulls: Make sure nut A is tight. Undo locknut C from acorn adjusting nut B and screw both in flush against brake yoke arm. Back off B one half turn and lock in place with locknut C (see p 234).

Centre-pulls: Tighten up nut A on the mounting bolt.

Squealing. Brake shoes may be old and hard. Sometimes rubber from shoes has streaked rim. Clean with a strong solvent like benzene or cleaning fluid in a WELL VENTILATED AREA. Squealing brakes can sometimes be fixed by toeing in the brake shoes (see p 223), and sometimes this problem just can't be eliminated.

Category 3 – Sticky or dragging brakes.

This is the most common problem. First determine if it is the lever, cable, or mechanism which is at fault.

If it is the lever, see Frozen lever, above.

If it is the cable, replace it (see above).

Brake mechanism.

Side pulls :

First make sure everything is there and properly hooked up. This sounds simple-minded, but there is a reason for each of the parts and the mechanism won't work without them. Is the spring complete and attached to both yoke arms? Make sure nut A is tight. Undo locknut C from acorn adjusting nut B and screw both flush against yoke arm. Back B off one half turn and lock with C. Check that pivot bolt D is straight and replace if necessary. Lubricate.

If one shoe drags against rim: loosen the mounting nut A, hold brake yokes in correct position, and re-tighten. No soap? Examine brake seating pad F. If it has a slot for the spring you will have to try bending the spring. There are two ways to do this. One is to prise the spring arm off the brake yoke which is dragging and bend it outward using pliers or similar tool. The second is to take a big screwdriver and poise the end against point G or H, whichever is *opposite* the dragging shoe, and give it a sharp bash with a hammer. This second method is quicker, but of course a little riskier.

Still no soap? Check to see that the brake yokes are not rubbing against each other. If so, bend them apart with a screwdriver:

or slide in a piece of fine emery cloth (like sandpaper) and file it down.

   If this is not the problem and you have tried everything else a complete disassembly (see p 234) is necessary. Study each part to see if it obviously needs replacing (like a washer bent out of shape). It may be that the yokes cannot rotate on the pivot bolt. File down and polish the bolt, or enlarge the holes in the yokes (with a taper ream, or emery cloth wrapped around a nail). If none of these things work get a new brake mechanism.

Centre-pulls:

Is cable adjusted correctly?

Are all parts there? Is spring intact and properly mounted?

Is mounting nut A tight? (See previous page.)

If one shoe is dragging against rim, slack off A, centre brake mechanism, and retighten A.

If both shoes stick try lubricating the pivot bolts B while wiggling the yokes back and forth. No? You will have to get into the pivot bolts.

First disconnect the spring. Study the bolts to see if they are type 1, where the pivot bolt screws into the brake arm bridge H; type 2, where the pivot bolt screws into a post which comes off the brake arm bridge and on which the yoke rotates; or type 3, where the pivot bolt simply goes through the brake arm bridge and the yoke rotates on a bushing.

Type 1

Type 1 : First try slacking off the locknut R and undoing the pivot bolt P one quarter to one half turn. On some models the locknut R is on the other side of the brake arm bridge H. If yoke will now pivot, retighten locknut R. If not, remove pivot bolt P altogether. Keep track of all the washers. Is the pivot bolt P straight? Look for dirt or scarred surfaces on the pivot bolt P and inside the yoke. Clean and

Type 2

polish. If yoke will not turn freely on pivot bolt, enlarge yoke hole with a taper file or ream, drill, or emery cloth wrapped around a nail. Or sand down the pivot bolt. Lubricate and reassemble.
Type 2: Undo spring and remove pivot bolt P. Remove yoke and keep track of washers. Check for grit and clean. Is post R scarred? Polish with fine sandpaper or steel wool until yoke will rotate freely on it. Lubricate and reassemble.

Type 3: Undo nut A and remove pivot bolt P. Keep track of bushings and washers. Is pivot bolt straight? Is bushing B in good condition? Check for grit and clean. If yoke still sticks, try polishing pivot bolt with steel wool. Lubricate and reassemble.

Disc brakes

How it works
The operation of a disc brake is very similar to that of a calliper brake. Actuating the brake lever causes a cable to pull a cam-mounted brake arm which then compresses two brake shoes or pads against opposite sides of a revolving metal disc attached to the wheel.

Lubrication
Only a tiny bit of LPS spray inside the brake arm mounting point 23. Avoid at all costs oil or LPS on the disc or pads 28 and 32 (overleaf).

Adjustment

Unlike the calliper system, the cable adjuster bolt 17 and cable anchor bolt 24 are not used to adjust pad clearances, only to keep slack out of the brake levers.

To adjust pad clearances: Remove bracket cover 2 by undoing screws 1. Undo locknut 6 and slacken setting bolt 5. Use pliers to turn brake adjuster 15 clockwise until pads meet disc and wheel will not turn. Reverse brake adjuster anti-clockwise $\frac{1}{2}$ turn. Turn in setting bolt 5 until it touches holder 16 lightly and secure in place with locknut 6.

Check that the pads and disc are parallel (see opposite page).

If not, again slack off setting bolt 5. Slack off adjusting bolts 3, 3A, and 4. Diddle with these adjusting bolts until pad A is parallel with disc. Tighten each adjusting bolt an even number of turns until pads almost touch disc. You've done it. Turn in setting bolt 5 and lock into position. Replace cover.

Replacing parts

Cables: Procedure is exactly the same as for a calliper brake so refer to that section for instructions.

Setting bolt

Adjust bolt A

Adjuster

Adjust bolt B

Pad B
Disc
Pad A

Pad lock nut

(a)
(b)
Parallel

Hub for disc brake

Pads: Remove rear wheel. With a 6 mm Allen key undo through bolts 34 and remove holder 33. Take off locknut 40 and undo screw 31. Remove pad 32 and replace.

Next, undo screw 30 *carefully*, as there is a spring lurking underneath it. Remove pad 28 and replace. After tightening down screw 30, back it off $\frac{1}{2}$ turn. Restore holder 33 to mate and make sure bolts 34 are done up firmly. Follow procedure for adjustment above.

Trouble-shooting
Brakes slip or are weak: Grease or oil on discs and pads. Clean disc with solvent, rub pad surfaces with No. 60 emery paper.
Brakes don't work: Pull up on brake arm lever 23. If it moves and the pads are hitting the disc it is a cable or brake problem. Turn to calliper brakes, trouble-shooting, for instructions.

If it is the unit itself that is frozen up, try removing the pads and dunking the whole unit in solvent. No? Your guess is as good as mine. If you can't see what is wrong, take it to your friendly bicycle dealer and see if he wants to play with it.

3 Staying aboard

THE ARAB CRADLE
SPRING ON AN ADJUSTABLE
TILT-ROD.

Saddle

There are two important factors in bicycle saddle design: supporting weight, and reducing friction between the legs. The mattress saddle used on bikes with level handlebars has to support all of the weight of the rider, and is therefore usually wide, and equipped with coil springs:

Mattress

Bikes with dropped handlebars support part of the rider's weight on the bars, and can use a long, narrow seat which minimizes friction between the legs:

Racing

Adjustments

Springiness in the narrow racing saddle should be kept to a comfortable minimum as it adversely affects pedalling power.

If yours is too tight or loose, adjust it by turning nut A:

C thataway

A

B

D

To remove the saddle from the seat post, or to adjust its position backward, forward, or to tilt it, loosen nuts *B* and *C*. This applies also to mattress saddles. Some seat posts have micro-adjusting bolts or Allen screws:

Loosen bolt or screw on end to be raised, tighten bolt or screw on end to be lowered. Loosen both an identical number of turns to slide saddle forward or backward. For proper saddle position refer to Fitting, pp 92–4.

To raise or lower the saddle, loosen the binder bolt D.

Be sure to use a spanner which fits the nut exactly. It has to be tight, and the wrong tool can tear up the nut.

Only leather saddles need special care. A new leather saddle should be thoroughly saturated with neatsfoot oil from *underneath*.

Then, depending on how much you ride and how much you sweat, the saddle should be cleaned periodically with saddle soap and lightly dressed with neatsfoot oil. The idea is to keep the leather clean, nourished, and comfortably pliable. Once a year should be enough. You can avoid this bother by using a plastic saddle, but in warm weather you will slide about in your own sweat.

Trouble-shooting

Seat tilts or swivels unnecessarily. Tighten binding bolt nuts B and C (see opposite page).

If the seat bottoms harshly on bumps and you have a mattress type saddle – too bad. If you have a racing saddle, tighten nut A.

The seat post sinks slowly into the frame while you ride. This can be a real stinker. First see if the seat post is the correct diameter by checking that the lips of the seat tube do not meet at the binder bolt:

right   wrong

If the post is the right size and is greasy, try cleaning it and the inside of the seat tube thoroughly. On no account try the use of shims or abrasive material like emery paper between the seat tube and the seat post. The chances are excellent that some of the material will fall down the seat tube and get into the bottom bracket, where it will make mincemeat of your crankset bearings (thought seats were simple, hah?). The only sure-fire solution is to install a thin bolt through the seat post and seat tube at point P:

To do this you need a drill, hand or electric, a bolt, nut, and washer, and a drill bit. *Do all drilling with the bike upside down so that shavings do not fall down the seat tube into the bottom bracket.* If you are having a shop do the job make sure that they do this. Position seat at desired height. Make an initial dent with a centre punch or with a hammer and sharp nail at point P. Then put a couple of drops of oil on the end of the drill bit and drill through. Go slowly to avoid heat build-up. Use single-speed electric drills in short bursts. You will want more than one saddle-height position. To do this, loosen the binder bolt and rotate the seat post one-eighth of a turn at the same time that you raise or lower it a little bit. Now use the already existing holes in the seat tube as a guide for drilling a new set of holes in the seat post. Repeat 3 or 4 times. The idea is to be able to make fine adjustments in saddle height without weakening the seat post. At the finish, the job should look like this:

right

wrong

Be sure to clean up all shavings and filings so that they do not fall down into the bottom bracket.

If your seat post is the micro-adjusting type the holes will have to be in a straight line.

Handlebars

Adjustments

To change handlebar position loosen binder bolt A on stem and reset bars:

A

Height adjustments are made with the *stem* (next section).

Taping

I prefer non-adhesive tapes. Adhesive tapes gum everything up with a sticky residue which ultimately leaks out all over everything. Plastic tape is cheap and easy to clean. Cloth tape feels good but gets dirty quickly and is hard to clean. The Tape, suede finished and vinyl backed, and washable, is probably the best all around tape. See Accessories for more information.

Be sure that the brakes are in the position you want. Start about 2 in from the stem. Use a small piece of scotch tape to hold down the end of the tape where you start. Work directly from the roll to minimize confusion, and maintain a continuous light tension as you apply the tape. First take a couple of turns at the starting point and then start down the bar, overlapping $\frac{1}{2}$ to $\frac{1}{3}$ of the tape. At the bends you will have to overlap more on the inside than the outside. For a neat job, loosen the brake lever mount (see p 233), tape underneath, and retighten:

When you reach the end of the bar leave an extra 2–3 in of tape. Fold this over and push it inside the handlebar:

Finish off with a bar plug (bike shops) to hold tape securely. In a pinch this can be a cork or similar object. Use something – if you spill, an open bar end can make a hole in you.

Trouble-shooting

 Bar spins around on stem: tighten binder bolt A:

If binder bolt spins uselessly, remove it and see if the little protrusion on it has been worn off, or if the corresponding slot on the stem into which it fits has been damaged. If the problem is the bolt, get a new one. If it is the stem, get a proper bolt with a hex nut that you can grip with a spanner. At a pinch, you can use pliers or vice-grips to hold the round part of the old bolt.

If the binder bolt is in working order, check and see that the lips of the stem do not meet:

right

wrong

If they do, new bars (expensive) or a shim (cheap). Shimming: find a small piece of flat metal slightly longer than the width of the stem lips. Something that won't rust, like aluminium, is preferable (hardware stores, machine shop litter, junk lying around), but part of a tin can or a finishing nail will do. Remove binder bolt. Using a screwdriver, prise apart the lips of the stem:

Slip the shim into the gap between the handlebar and the stem, and reinstall binder bolt.

🚲 Bent bars: steel ones are hard to bend, alloy a lot easier. Lay the bike on its side. If the ends of the handlebars have been bent in, place your foot on the end resting on the ground (watch out for the brake lever) and pull up on the other end. If the ends have been bent out, lean your weight on the upright bar:

Stem
How it works

The stem is a tube which holds the handlebar in position, and fits down inside the headset. The tube is split at the end, and down its length runs a bolt, called an expander bolt, which is attached to a wedge nut:

A

When the expander bolt is tightened, it draws the wedge nut into the tube, and this in turn forces apart the split sides of the stem, pressing them against the sides of the headset and holding everything in place.

Adjust or remove

Undo expander bolt two turns. Using a wooden block or piece of cardboard held against the expander bolt to protect the finish, tap it with a hammer or heavy object:

Repeat as necessary to get stem loose. Adjust height or remove. If you remove altogether and reassemble, take note: some wedge nuts have a dog guide which must fit into a corresponding slot on the stem:

Keep at least 2½ in of the stem tube in the headset.

Retighten expander bolt so that when you stand in front of the bike with the wheel clasped between your legs you can twist the handlebar and stem in the headset. This way, if you take a spill the bars will give instead of bending or breaking.

Trouble-shooting

🚲 Stem is loose and expander bolt comes out freely: wedge nut has come off. Take out stem, turn bike upside down, and shake wedge nut out. Reassemble.

🚲 Stem is frozen in place and expander bolt spins uselessly: threads on wedge nut have stripped (1), or expander bolt has snapped (2).

(1) Separate expander bolt from wedge nut by grasping it with pliers or vice-grips and maintaining a continuous upward pressure while twisting it. If it is obstinate, help it along by wedging a screwdriver between the expander bolt head and the stem:

Once the expander bolt is free of wedge nut leave it inside the stem.

(2) Remove top-half of snapped expander bolt. Find a rod or bolt which will fit inside stem and touch wedge nut while still protruding an inch or two above the stem.

(1) and (2): Use a hammer to tap lightly the expander bolt or rod, working the end inside the stem around the edges of the wedge nut:

Work firmly but gently; too hard a blow will jam the whole thing. When stem comes loose, turn bike upside down and shake out wedge nut.

🚲 Stem tube cracked. Replace it.

Headset

How it works

The headset connects the front forks to the head tube of the bicycle frame and, through the stem, to the handlebars. The fork is held solidly to the bicycle but allowed to turn freely by using ball bearing sets at the top and bottom of the head tube. Starting at the bottom, the crown of the fork has a fork crown bearing race (A), then come the ball bearings (B), and next is the bottom set race (C), screwed or force-fitted into the head tube.

C
B
A

To keep the forks inside the head tube and evenly positioned, a second set of races is used at the top of the head tube. There is a top set race, screwed or force-fitted into the head tube, more ball bearings, and what actually keeps the forks in position is the top race, which is threaded on to the fork tube:

top race

top set race

This is capped by a washer, the cable hanger and/or other accessory mounts, if used, and a locknut to keep the top threaded race exactly in place:

Routine adjustments

Forks should turn freely but without excessive up and down play. A simple test for looseness is to lock the front brake and rock the bike forward and backward. A clicking noise from the headset indicates loose bearings. To adjust, loosen locknut A (above).

Sometimes this locknut is designed with notches. Loosen with a hammer and centre punch or screwdriver:

If you are using big spanners or pliers, be careful not to bend nuts or races.

Now turn down the threaded top race B handtight against the bearings, and then back it off one quarter turn.

Snug down locknut A, being careful to keep threaded top race B in position. Check play again.

Lubrication and disassembly

The headset should be dismantled, cleaned, and regreased about once a year. Remove stem (p 254) and front wheel (p 267).
Lay bike down on side with newspaper or white rag under the headset. This is to catch falling ball bearings. There are many different headsets, and no way for me to tell you how many are in yours. So don't lose any.

Undo and remove the locknut, washer, cable clamp (if you have one), and anything else necessary to get to the threaded top race. Secure the fork to the frame. You can do this with rubber bands, elastic carrier straps, shoelaces, etc. but the simplest way is to hold it with your hand. Be sure to do something, or what you do next will cause the fork to fall out along with a rain of ball bearings. Next: undo the threaded top race A:

You will have loose ball bearings and are to follow instructions for (1), or bearings in a clip in which case follow (2).

(1) A few may stick to the threaded race, a few may fall on the newspaper, and most will probably stay in the top set race.

Get them all together, count them, and put bearings and race into a box or jar. Next: make sure head tube is positioned over newspaper or rag. Slowly draw out fork tube. Ball bearings will fall out. Gather and count them, including any that are still stuck to the bottom set race, the fork tube, or whatever, and put them in a jar.

(2) Clipped bearings: Lucky you. Remove clip, noting carefully which side goes down against the top set race, and put in a jar or box. Now draw out fork tube and lift out clip for bottom race.

Further disassembly for routine lubrication is not necessary. (1) & (2) Soak and clean thoroughly all parts in solvent. Use a rag to clean out the top and bottom set races, and the fork crown race. Ball bearings should be smooth and unpitted. Clipped bearings should be securely in place. Races should be evenly coloured all the way around where the balls run. Place them on a glass surface to see if they are bent or warped. Replace any defective parts.

Reassembly: pack fresh grease in the top and bottom set races. Just fill the grooves; excessive grease will attract dirt.

(1) Push ball bearings into grease on bottom set race. Grease will hold them in place.

(2) Put some grease inside the clip. Slip it down over the fork tube to rest on the fork crown race.

(1) & (2) Carefully insert fork tube into head tube. Keeping it snug against the bearings, check that it turns freely. Hang on to fork so that it does not fall back out.

(1) Stick ball bearings into grease of top set race.

(2) Grease and slip on clipped bearings.

(1) & (2) Screw down top threaded race. These threads are fine, so do it carefully (see General words, p 207, for best technique). Set it hand tight, and then back it off one quarter turn. Pile on washer, cable anchor mount, etc. and locknut. Be careful to keep threaded top race in position when tightening locknut. Check for play.

Complete disassembly
If the bike has been in a smash-up or if rust has got to the bearings, it may be necessary to do a complete disassembly.

Take fork and ball bearings out as for lubrication. Remove crown fork race from fork. If it is stuck, prise it up *gently* with a screwdriver, working around the edges a little at a time. Be careful – it is easy to bend:

Remove top and bottom set races. You may possibly have threaded set races, in which case simply unscrew them. For force set races, insert a large screwdriver, piece of pipe, or stiff rod into the head tube and tap around the edges of the race:

Clean all parts with solvent. Test races for uniformity by seeing if they lie flat on glass or other smooth surface.

Reassembly: screw in threaded set races. For force set races use a wooden block (to avoid denting or bending the race) and hammer:

Make sure that it is seated fully into the frame. Use a wooden block also on the fork crown race if it is balky but be very delicate, and tap evenly all the way around the race.

Trouble-shooting

🚲 Fork tube is extremely loose in the head tube. May just need adjustment, but if things have come to this pass I suggest dismantling and checking condition of parts.

Adjustment does not work: top threaded race or fork is stripped. Dismantle and see. It is unlikely that this is the result of excessive tightening, and likely that the top threaded race was screwed down off-centre. When you have your new parts review General words, Threading, p 207, before starting.

🚲 Fork binds or catches, or makes grating and rasping noises when you turn handlebars. Adjust as per above. No go? Something is broken or bent, completely worn out, or there are too many or too few ball bearings. Review the possibilities. Has fork or headset been whacked severely lately? A couple of months ago? Did you or someone else service the headset and lose a bearing or two, or place too many in one race and not enough in the other?

Or perhaps the bike is simply ancient, and needs new races? In any case, disassemble, clean, and check all parts. Are bearings evenly distributed (ask your bike shop how many should be in your headset), and free of dents, cracks, and pitting? Do races lie flat on a glass surface? Replace defective parts and reassemble. If you can find nothing wrong, take the parts down to your bike shop and see what they say.

Forks

How they work
The fork holds the front wheel in place and allows the bike to be steered. The fork arms are curved, giving the axle drop-outs rake or trail from a line drawn through the fork tube. This rake or trail has two purposes: it makes the bike handle better and it helps the bike to absorb bumps and other road shocks. The amount of trail varies according to the purpose of the bike. Touring bikes have a

slightly longer trail for a softer, more comfortable ride. Racing and track machines have a shorter trail for greater efficiency in transmitting rider effort to the wheels. Additionally, the forks may be solid or tubular, the latter lighter and more flexible.

Lubrication and dismantling
Covered under Headset, pp 259–62.

Trouble-shooting
All problems with turning, grating noises, etc. are covered under Headset, above.

Bent forks: replace them. Bending fatigues metal and makes it weak. The weakness does not show. What happens is that the fork suddenly gives up while you are tearing along at 30 mph. This does not happen very often, but once is enough. Bicycle shops do have special tools for straightening bent forks and if the bend in yours is slight, you may want to try it. Be aware that you are taking a calculated risk, however small.

Tests for bent forks: the bike will ride oddly. If forks are bent to one side, the bike will always want to turn to the left or right. Test by taking your hands off the handlebars. Any decently set-up bike can be ridden hands off for miles. Forks which have been bent in, usually through a head-on collision, make the bike's ride choppy and harsh, and make it feel like it wants to dive in the corners. A sure sign of bent-in forks is wrinkled paint on the upper fork arms, or at the join of the fork tube and fork crown. Forks which have been bent out (rare) manifest themselves in a sloppy, mushy ride, and curious, long arcing turns. Again, there will probably be paint wrinkles at the bend point.

Otto Dicycle, 1880

4 Wheels

Wheel removal

Wheels need to be removed often, for a variety of reasons, and
sometimes on the road. So you can and will do this with a
free-standing bike, but it is much easier if it is hung up. Most
3-speeds and some 10-speeds can simply be turned upside down on
handlebars and seat, as long as cables or shift selectors are not
damaged. Bikes with calliper brakes in proper adjustment should
require some slacking of the brakes (see p 217) so that the tyre will
pass between the brake shoes.

Front wheel, any bike
Wheel will be held to fork by hex nuts, wing nuts, or a
quick-release lever:

For nuts, undo both simultaneously (anti-clockwise) and unwind a
turn or two. Levers, flip it. Remove wheel. Note washers go outside
fork drop-outs.

Rear wheel
10-speed bikes: Run chain to smallest sprocket. Undo nuts or lever
as for front wheel, and push wheel down and out. If you have a
free hand, hold back the derailleur so that the freewheel clears it
easily, otherwise just gently wiggle it by.
3-speed bikes: Shift to third gear. Disconnect shift cable at rear hub
by undoing locknut A and unscrewing adjuster sleeve B from pole
(see below).

Undo nuts simultaneously (counter-clockwise). Remove wheel, and note washers are outside drop-outs.

Single-speed coaster-brake bikes: Disconnect coaster-brake bracket from bike frame (metal arm at left end of rear axle), undo nuts (counter-clockwise), and remove wheel.

Replacing wheels

Front, any bike

Axle with nuts: Back off nuts a few turns and slip axle onto drop-outs. Washers go outside drop-outs. Set nuts finger tight and check that rim is centred between fork arms before snugging them down. Re-set calliper brakes if you have them.

Levers: Slip axle on to drop-outs with lever on left side of bike. If this is difficult, hold knurled cone with one hand and unwind lever a couple of turns with the other. Slip axle on drop-outs and wind lever down just short of finger tight. Check that wheel rim is centred between fork arms, and close lever so that it points upward and backward. It should be firmly shut but not hysterically so. Re-set calliper brakes.

Rear wheels

10-speed bikes: Work axle into drop-outs, slipping chain over smallest sprocket on freewheel. Set nuts or lever for light tension. Pull wheel towards rear of bike until right end of axle hits the back of the drop-out. Use this as a pivot point to centre the rim between the chain stays, and tighten nuts or lever. Re-set calliper brakes.

3- and 1-speed bikes: Work axle into drop-outs, slipping chain over sprocket. Lightly tighten nuts (washers are outside drop-outs), and pull back wheel so chain has ½-inch play up and down:

Centre rim between chain stays and tighten down nuts. Check chain tension. One-speed bikes: reconnect coaster brake bracket to frame. Three-speed bikes, with gear selector in 3rd: reconnect barrel sleeve to hub gear chain, and set locknut with cable slightly slack. Test gears and adjust if necessary (pp 312–14). Re-set calliper brakes.

Tyres

How they work
Any pneumatic tyre works by supporting a casing, the part touching the road, with an inside tube which is filled with air like a balloon. With tubular tyres the tube is fully encased by the casing; with wire-on tyres the tube is held in place by a combination of two wire beads which run around the outside edges of the tyre, and the rim sides:

Wire-on

casing   tube   bead   rim

Tubular

Air is pumped into the tube through a valve which comes in three types. Some wire-ons have Schraeder valves, the kind typically found on cars. Most have regular bicycle valves, requiring either a bicycle pump, or a special adapter for petrol station air pumps. Some wire-ons and all tubulars have Presta type valves, also requiring a pump or adapter:

Woods   Schraeder   Presta

'Presta' valves need to have the locknut A undone in order to be pumped up.

Tyre selection

There are tyres for nearly every purpose and condition: rain, mud, racing, touring, and carrying heavy loads. In tubulars heavy-duty 15-16 ounce tyres are about the only practical choice for touring and general use. Racers use lighter tyres which run 7 to 11 ounces. In wire-on tyres I suggest you explain your needs to a shop and try their recommendation.

Generally, 3-speeds are fitted with an all-purpose coarse-thread heavy-duty tyre, and 10-speeds with a lighter road pattern tyre. Better tyres cost only a little more and are worth it in the long run.

Routine adjustments

Tyre pressure

Use your own tyre pressure gauge (bike shops). Petrol station gauges are unreliable. When filling your tyres at a petrol station do it yourself. The proper pressure for your tyre may be as high as 100 pounds per square inch, but the total volume of air is small, and it takes only seconds to blow a tyre out. Some air pumps take a few moments to fill the tyre; others will do it instantaneously. Jab the air hose down on the valve for just a second, then release and test. Tyres should be hard enough so you can barely dent them with a finger, and bulge only very slightly when ridden. Consult chart below for proper pressure.

Bicycle pump : draw hose fitting out of pump handle and fit to pump and valve. Check connections periodically and as you pump. 'Presta' valve: undo valve locknut, push pump on valve, hold firmly to tyre with one hand, and pump with the other. Keep pump perpendicular to valve. Disengage with a sharp downward knock of the hand; wiggling will lose air and possibly bend valve.

Recommended pressures :
Note: for heavier loads increase pressure. The difference between pressure for a 125 pound rider and 200 pound rider is about 15 to 20 pounds per square inch.

Tubular 27 in	– Rear, 85 to 100; front, 75–90
Wire-on 27 in	– 50 to 90
Wire-on 26 in × 1¼ in	– 45 to 60
× 1½ in	– 40 to 55
× 1⅜ in	– 40 to 55
× 1¾ in	– 35 to 45
24 in	– 35 to 45
20 in	– 45 to 50
18 in	35 to 45
16 in	– 30 to 40
12 in	– 30 to 40

Check tyre pressure often. Tubular tyres 'breathe' air through the sides and need filling frequently. Hot weather in the eighties and upwards may require that you bleed some air from the tyre to avoid over-inflation and a possible blow-out.

Riding
Most tyre problems are the result of picked-up debris working into the casing as you ride. Going over rocks, through pot-holes, and on and off kerbs will cause ruptures. Cultivate an eye for these hazards, and if you are forced to go through a patch of broken glass, for example, check and see that the tyre has not picked any up. A useful gadget for tubular tyres is a nail-catcher (bike shops) which rides lightly over the tyre and brushes off particles before they can cause damage:

Keep oil away from tyres. It rots rubber. Grease, do not oil, bicycle pumps. Oiled bicycle pumps can vaporize and blow oil inside the tube. Check cement on tubulars about once a week.

Care and storage

Keep wire-on spares in a dry place. Tubular spares should be carried folded so the tread is on the outside and not folded back on itself. Under the seat is a dandy place. Secure with straps or rubber bands:

Every two weeks or so inflate a folded spare and let it stand for a while. Refold in the opposite direction.

Flats

Flats take the form of violent blow outs (rare), or punctures (common) which leak air with varying degrees of speed. Blow outs are usually terminal, doing so much damage that the tube and sometimes the tyre must be replaced. Punctures which are not gaping wounds can be repaired. There is debate as to proper policy for this and some bike shops maintain that any patching is 'temporary' and prefer to install a new tube. I suggest that you patch newish tubes and throw out older ones.

Wire-on tyres

You will need a tube patch kit containing patches, glue, an abrasive surface, tyre irons (the kind which hook on to spokes are handiest), and chalk.

First check valve by inflating tyre slightly and placing a drop of spit on the end of the valve stem. A leaky valve will bubble or spit back. Tighten valve if necessary with valve cap or suitable part of pressure gauge:

Hooray if the problem was a loose or defective valve. If not, spin the wheel and look for an obvious cause like a nail or piece of glass. Yes? Dig it out and mark the spot.

What you do next depends on circumstances. It is easier to work on a puncture with the wheel off the bike (see pp 267–9). However, you may not have the tools to accomplish this feat, or perhaps you know exactly where the puncture is. At any rate, the basic procedure is the same.

Deflate tyre and remove valve stem locknut if you have one. Work the tyre back and forth with your hands to get the bead free of the rim. If the tyre is a loose fit on the rim you may be able to get it off with your hands. This is best, because tyre irons may pinch the tube and cause additional punctures. To do this make sure that the bead is free of the rim all the way around. Take a healthy grip on the tyre with both hands and pull it up and off-centre so that one bead comes over the rim:

Then go around the rim working the bead completely off.

You will probably need to use tyre irons. Use tyre irons, not screwdrivers, as these are likely to cut the tube. Free bead from rim. Insert tyre iron under bead, being careful not to pinch the tube, and lever it over the side:

Insert second iron 2 in or 3 in away from first iron, and past where bead is over side of rim. Lever iron. For most tyres this will do the job. No? A third iron. If this doesn't work, use the now free 2nd iron for a fourth attempt:

and repeat process as often as necessary.

If you don't have tyre irons which hook on to the spokes, then you will need to use elbows, knees, etc. to hold down the irons as you work away. Be careful not to crush a spoke inadvertently, and keep your face away in case something slips and tyre irons start jumping about.

If you have only two tyre irons and need a third, scrounge something up. In the country a flat rock or a stick. In the city a pencil, a beer can-opener, or something from the garbage. Look around. At any hour there will be *something*. Prise up bead with a tyre iron. Insert foraged tool between bead and rim and wiggle iron out:

Use tyre irons to make two prises on either side of foraged tool.

One bead is off rim. Push valve stem up into tyre, and remove tube. Use chalk or eidetic memory to make note of which way tube was in the tyre. Inflate tube and rotate it past your ear. If you can locate the puncture through the hiss of escaping air, mark it with chalk. No? Immerse tube in water and look for escaping air bubbles. Dry tube with a rag while holding finger over puncture then mark with chalk.

Take sandpaper or metal abrader supplied with patch kit and rough up the area around the puncture. Spread a layer of cement over this area and let dry tacky. Peel the paper backing off a patch without touching the surface thus exposed, and press it firmly on the puncture. Hold for a moment next to tyre with valve stem alongside valve hole and note where puncture occurred. Set tube aside to dry.

If the puncture was on inside of tube probably a protruding spoke caused it:

File the spoke flush with the rim. Check other spokes.

If the puncture was on the outside of the tube find what caused it by rubbing your fingers around inside the casing. Check the rest of the casing for embedded particles, and for ruptures or breaks:

Replace the tyre at the first opportunity if it has these.

To install the tube, first inflate it slightly to prevent it from folding and pinching itself. Push the part of the tube with the valve stem into the tyre, and the valve stem through its hole on the rim. Fit valve stem locknut loosely. Stuff rest of tube into tyre being careful not to pinch or tear it. Check that valve stem is still straight.

Push valve stem part way out, and slip bead of tyre at that point back over the rim. It is important that you hold the base of the valve stem clear of the rim as you do this, or the bead may catch on it, creating a bulge in the tyre:

Work around the rim replacing the bead and always taking care not to pinch the tube. Ideally you do the entire job with your hands. Check that the valve stem is still straight. The last bit will be hard. Just keep working at it with your thumbs, first from one side, then from the other. When about 2 in of bead remains give it the grand mal effort. Don't wonder if it will go over; decide that it will. If you have to use a tyre iron, be very careful not to pinch the tube.

Tubular tyres

You will need: patches, needle, thread, rubber cement, sandpaper, talcum powder, chalk, screwdriver, sharp knife or razor blade.

Remove wheel (pp 267–9). Deflate tyre completely by opening locknut A on valve and holding down (see above).

Remove tyre from rim with your hands. Inflate and immerse in water a little at a time. Do not be misled by air bubbles coming out by the valve. Since the tyre is sewn, the valve hole and puncture hole are the only places air can escape. Hold finger over puncture when located, dry tyre, and mark puncture with chalk.

With a screwdriver or similar implement pry away about 5 in to 6 in of the tape of the inner side of the tyre at the puncture area:

Next cut stitching about 2 in to either side of puncture. Make only two cuts to avoid numerous bits and pieces of thread, and cut upward to miss tyre:

Gently remove tube and locate leak. A mixture of soap and water will pin-point elusive ones. Dry tube if wet. Abrade area around puncture with sandpaper. Apply cement and let dry. Peel protective paper from patch without touching surface thus exposed and apply to puncture. Dust with talc to prevent tube from sticking to casing. Get whatever caused puncture out of casing. Insert tube, inflate, and check for leaks. Do this carefully. You are going to be mad if you get it all back together only to discover it still leaks.

Thread the needle and knot the two loose ends of thread. In a tight situation, 12-pound linen thread or silk fishing line will do. Using the old holes, start with an overlap of about $\frac{1}{2}$ in, i.e. $\frac{1}{2}$ in past where thread was cut. Pinch the sides of the casing between thumb and forefinger to keep the tube out of the way:

Pull stitches firm, but not so tight as to cut casing. Finish with a $\frac{1}{2}$-in overlap into original stitching. Layer cement on casing and inside of peeled-away tape and keep apart until dry. Position carefully and press together firmly.

Mounting a tubular

New rims and tyres: inflate tyre, deflate, place on rim (see opposite page), inflate, deflate, remove.

Repaired tyres and/or old rims: clean off old cement from rim with shellac thinner or solvent (bike shops).

There are two methods of mounting a tubular.

(1) Slow but sure. Deflate tyre. Insert valve. Stand rim on soft surface with valve stem up, and working from above, work tyre down over rim:

Be careful to distribute tyre evenly around rim. Finish by grabbing with both hands and getting the last bit over by main force:

Check again that tyre is evenly distributed and centred on rim. Roll back a portion of the tyre and brush glue on rim and lining. Repeat all the way around and from both sides. Check again for evenness. Inflate hard. Allow half a day to dry before using or tyre may creep (bunch up in spots) or simply come off the rim in a corner.

(2) Fast method. Apply glue to rim and tyre and allow to dry tacky. Wear old clothes and assemble as above.

Road repairs: use the old cement on the rim and don't lean hard into corners going home. Double-sided rim tape (bike shops) is very handy.

Rims and spokes

How they work

The rim which supports the tyre is laced (held) in position by the spokes, which are held fast at the hub and screw into the rim, so that they are adjustable:

Adjustments

The tension on the spokes relative to each other determines both the strength and position of the rim. Positioning the rim correctly, both up and down, and side to side, is a long job requiring lots of patience and skill. Most times it is much more efficient to leave this to a bike shop. If you have no alternative however, or are determined to go it alone, here's how:

Hang up the bike or place the wheel in a jig. Spin the wheel while holding a pencil or something similar at a fixed point like the fork arm or a seat stay with the point near the rim to see how bad the wobble is. If it is over $\frac{1}{2}$ in, pack up the entire project and take the wheel to a bike shop. If they think they can save the wheel, fine, otherwise get a new wheel.

With a less than $\frac{1}{2}$-in wobble: deflate tyre. If job looks to be major, it will be easier if you just remove the tyre altogether. Pluck the spokes with your fingers – they should all 'ping' – and tighten any that are slack so that they all have an even tension. Spokes are tightened by turning *anti-clockwise*. If in the course of doing this you find spokes with frozen nipples (the part which holds the spoke to the rim) they must be replaced (see below). If it is more than three or four spokes I once again suggest resorting to your friendly bike shop.

Hold a chalk or pencil at the *outer edge* of the rim while you spin the wheel so that the high spots are marked. Working one-half to one turn at a time, tighten the spokes at the chalk mark (*anti-clockwise*) and loosen them opposite the chalk mark. Continue until wheel is round.

Hold pencil or chalk at *side* of rim so that side to side wobbles are marked. Working one half to one turn at a time, and in groups of four to six spokes, tighten up the spokes opposite the chalk mark and loosen the ones next to it:

Tighten or loosen the spokes which are in the centre of the chalk marks a little more than the ones at the edges of the marks. When you have finally succeeded, or compromised, run your finger around the rim and check for protruding spoke ends. File protruders down.

Replacing spokes

Remove tyre (pp 273–5). If you are dealing with spokes on a free-wheel-equipped rear wheel that go to the freewheel side of the hub, the freewheel will have to be removed (pp 309–10). Take broken spokes out of the hub and rim. Get replacements which are exactly the same; many different kinds are available.

New spokes should go into the hub so that head is on opposite side of hub from adjoining spokes and spoke is pointed in opposite direction:

Be sure that it is correctly positioned in the hub with respect to the bevels:

wrong   **right**

On almost all bikes the spokes touch where they cross. Weave new spokes through old as per other spokes on wheel. Place nipples on spokes and tighten. True wheel (see above), file down any protruding spokes which might puncture the tube, and remount tyre.

Trouble-shooting

🚲 For side-to-side wobbles and elliptical wheels see pp 280–81.

🚲 For bulges in the rim caused by piling into kerbs, stones, etc; you will need vice-grips, channel-lock pliers, or a **C**-clamp. If bulge is equal on both sides of rim, place implement over bulge and squeeze *gently* until the rim is even again:

If the bulge is on one side of the rim, distribute the pinching force of your implement on the non-bulge side with a block of wood or some such:

Fixing bulges almost invariably leaves a slight dimple because the metal itself was stretched, but the wheel will probably be usable.

Wheel building

You may want to go the whole route and build your own wheels. This is at once straightforward, and an art. A good book on the subject is *Building Bicycle Wheels*, by R. Wright (obtainable from The Cyclists' Touring Club, 69 Meadrow, Godalming, Surrey, GU7 3HS; £1.25).

New Rapid Tangent Wheel

Hubs

Excluded from this section are sealed bearing hubs. These are by definition maintenance free. When they do require servicing or repair often special tools and techniques are needed for each

particular make of hub. Consult the manufacturer for instructions
if you have sealed bearing hubs.

How they work
A hub consists of an axle, two sets of bearings, and a casing.
The axle is held fixed, and the casing, to
which the spokes are attached, spins around
it riding on the ball bearings:

Adjustments
Wheel bearings are out of adjustment if, with the axle held firmly
in place, the wheel can be wiggled from side to side (usually with a
clicking noise), or if the wheel will not turn easily. Wheels held with
nuts or lever nuts can be adjusted while on the bike. Generally
speaking however, the best procedure is to remove the wheel
(pp 267–9). Wheels with quick-release hubs must be removed.
You will need special thin hub spanners (bike shops).

Undo locknut A from cone B:

Holding axle or axle housing (quick-releases) still with spanner at locknut C (ten-speed rear wheels: if you can't get at it with a spanner use vice-grips or pliers), screw cone B fully home and then back off one quarter turn. Lock in place with locknut A. Test for side to side play. Wheel should spin freely, and on good hubs the weight of the tyre valve will pull the wheel around so that the valve rests in the six o'clock position.

On a three-speed hub this adjustment is made on the side opposite the hub gear chain and sprocket:

Loosen locknut A, turn cone B fully home, back off one quarter turn, reset locknut A.

On a Sturmey-Archer SC coaster hub:

loosen locknut B, then turn C clockwise to tighten, anti-clockwise to loosen. Re-set locknut B.

Front wheel 'dynohubs' are adjusted at the left side, away from the dynamo, while rear 'dynohubs' are adjusted at the left side next to the dynamo:

In both cases loosen locknut A, turn slotted washer B fully home, back off one quarter turn, and re-set locknut A.

Lubrication

Any front hub or 10-speed rear hub with oil clips or caps: $\frac{1}{2}$ teaspoonful oil a month. If a grease fitting, one or two shots of grease per month. Multi-speed rear hubs: 1 to 2 teaspoonfuls. Coaster brake rear hubs: if oil fitting, 2 tablespoonfuls per month; if grease fitting, two or three shots of grease.

Hubs need to be cleaned and re-greased every six months for bikes in constant year-round use, and once a year for bikes retired for the winter or used only moderately. This requires disassembly.

Disassembly and replacement

Remove wheel from bike (pp 267–9). Ten-speed rear wheels, remove freewheel (pp 309–10). Lay wheel down on rags or newspaper to catch ball bearings. Undo locknut A from cone B and remove both while holding on to axle at C.

Remove dust cover D. To do this, it may be necessary to let the axle drop in just a little way so you can prise the dust cover off with a screwdriver:

Prise out the loose or clipped ball bearings (or turn the wheel over and dump them out), count, and place in jar. Now slide axle all the way out and dump out remaining bearings. Garner and count. Undo remaining locknut and cone and remove from axle. Clean all parts in solvent. Examine bearings to see that they are not cracked or pitted. Clipped bearings should be secure in clip. Cups and cones should be even in colour all around where bearings run and free of pitting. Test axle for straightness by rolling on glass surface. Replace any defective parts.

Reassembly: pack cups with grease. Not too much, excess will attract grit. Replace and lock one cone and locknut on axle. Slip dust cover on axle. Pack bearings into cup on one side of wheel. Gracefully insert axle and turn wheel over. Pack bearings into cup, replace dust cover, screw on cone and locknut, and adjust as per above.

Trouble-shooting

If something goes wrong it is usually because (1) the hub hasn't been serviced, or (2) a cone and locknut have come adrift. In either case, if routine adjustment will not solve the problem, completely disassemble hub and replace broken or defective parts as per above.

The Omnicycle

5 Power train

Pedals

How they work

A pedal consists of a platform of metal or metal and rubber for the foot, an axle (called a spindle) which screws into the crank, and two sets of ball bearings on which the platform rides as it spins around the spindle.

Adjustment

If pedal can be wiggled back and forth on the spindle, it needs tightening. Remove dustcap A (prise with a screwdriver if it is the wedge type):

Undo locknut B from cone C. Screw cone C fully home and back off one-quarter turn. Secure with locknut B. Check for play and that pedal spins easily. Replace dustcap A.

Lubrication and disassembly

Pedals lead a hard, dissolute life and need cleaning and regreasing every six months, more often if you ride a lot or favour wet weather. This requires disassembly. Remove pedals from crank. *Note:* right-hand pedal has a conventional right-hand thread and unscrews by turning anti-clockwise, but left-hand pedal has a left-hand thread and unscrews by turning *clockwise*. Work with pedal over newspaper or rag to catch ball bearings. Remove dustcover A (see illustration above). Undo and remove locknut B and cone C while holding platform and spindle together with hand. Get all bearings out of dust cover end and place in jar. Remove spindle and place all bearings from crank end in jar. Clean all parts in solvent. Check ball bearings for pitting, cracks, disorderly conduct; cups and cones for uneven wear, pitting; spindle for straightness.

Reassembly: pack grease into cups on platform. Pack ball bearings into cup on crank side of platform (grease will hold them in place), and slide on spindle. Pack bearings into dust cover side cup. Screw down cone C fully home and back off one-quarter turn. Secure with locknut B. Check for play and that pedal spins easily. Replace dustcover.

Note: When replacing pedals on bike be sure that left-side pedal, stamped 'L' on end of spindle shaft, goes to the left side. It screws on *anti-clockwise*. The right-hand pedal is stamped 'R' (surprise!) and screws on *clockwise*.

Trouble-shooting

🚲 Pedal is tight to crank but askew. Bent spindle. Replace immediately.

🚲 Grinding noises, hard to turn pedal. Try routine adjustment as above. No? Something is probably broken. Disassemble as above and replace defective parts.

🚲 Loose pedal. Check that it is tight to crank. Left pedal tightens *anti-clockwise*, right pedal tightens *clockwise*. No? Loose bearings. Adjust as per above.

Cranks

Cranks support the pedals and transmit pedalling power to the front sprocket(s). They are attached to a bottom bracket axle which rides on two sets of ball bearings inside the bottom bracket shell. There are three types of cranks: one-piece; cottered three-piece; and cotterless three-piece;

one-piece   cottered   cotterless

Since one-piece cranks include the bottom bracket axle, they are covered under Bottom brackets. To test a cottered or cotterless crank for tightness, position the pedals equidistant from the ground. Press firmly on both pedals with hands and release. Rotate crankset

one half turn and press pedals
again. If something gives, one
of the cranks is loose.

Adjustment and removal
Cottered cranks : Support the
crank with a block of wood
which has a hole or V-notch
into which the cotter pin A fits:

Be sure that the support block touches only the crank and is firmly
in place. Otherwise what you do next will damage your bearings by
driving the balls into the sides of the cup and scoring it (called
Brinelling). Next: if you are tightening, give the head of the cotter
pin A two or three moderate blows with a wooden mallet or hammer
and wooden block combination. Then snug down nut firmly, but not
with all your might or you will strip it. If you are removing, undo
cotter pin two or three turns and then tap threaded end of cotter
pin. Repeat if necessary. Be careful not to damage the threads as you
will want to use the pin again. If you use a new pin and it does not
fit, file down the flat sides until it does.

Cotterless cranks : You will need a crank installer and extractor which
fits your particular brand of crank. Cotterless cranks are made of an
aluminium alloy called dural and must not be tightened with the
same force as steel parts.
To tighten or loosen, first
remove the dust cover A:

To tighten, apply socket of installer to nut B and turn down, wiggling crank arm to make sure it is seated all the way. For new cranks retighten every 25 miles for the first 200 miles of use.

To remove, first get chain out of way. Remove nut B. Back inner bolt A of extractor all the way out:

A

Screw extractor into crank, and then tighten down inner bolt A. *Do not do this with all of your might or you may strip the threads.* If the crank does not come loose with a firm tightening on the extractor bolt, give it two or three taps with a hammer, and tighten it one-eighth of a turn. Repeat until crank comes free. When replacing crank, be sure to wiggle it around a lot so that it is fully home before you give it the final tightening.

Trouble-shooting

🚲 There is a 'click' as you bring the pedal around on the upstroke and then a momentary dead spot and another 'click' as you push it down. It may be a loose pedal (p 292), bottom bracket (p 297), or crank. If it looks to be the crank, test and tighten if necessary as per above.

🚲 Stripped holding bolt on a cotterless crank. Get a new bottom bracket axle. If this is impossible, a machine shop may be able to re-thread the axle to accept a larger bolt. Be sure that the head of the larger bolt is small enough so that you can still use an extractor.

🚲 Stripped thread for the extractor on a cotterless crank. First ask your bike shop if they can solve the problem. No? You may be able to find a substitute tool which will do the job. I have one which looks like:

I have no idea what it is used for, although I think it has something to do with plumbing. It may be a flywheel remover. Anyway, the arms will hook on to the crank or sprocket while the bolt presses against the bottom bracket axle.

If you can't find a substitute tool you and a machine shop may be able to manufacture a new extractor. It will be some trouble, but at upwards of £40 for fancy new cranks it is probably worth taking a stab at saving the old ones. Take your bike to a machine shop and explain that you want a steel plate or bar threaded in the centre for an extractor bolt, and with holes drilled so that other bolts can be slid through and in turn be attached to metal plates which will hook behind the front sprocket:

Backyard special

If this Backyard Machine Shop Special Gizmo doesn't appeal to you, try jury-rigging your own conglomerate design of C-clamps, bolts, levers, bits and pieces and other materials. Just don't destroy your bike in the process.

🚲 Bent crank. Should be fixed by a bike shop with a special tool for the job.

Bottom bracket

How it works

The bottom bracket axle (called a spindle) spins on two sets of
ball bearings contained within the bottom bracket shell, and holds
the cranks. On the Ashtabula type one-piece crankset, the two
cranks and spindle are one unit. Three-piece cranksets (cottered
and cotterless) consist of two cranks and a separate spindle.
Although service techniques are fundamentally similar, we will
discuss one-piece cranksets and spindles for three-piece cranksets
separately.

Ashtabula one-piece crankset

Adjustment:
If axle is hard to turn, or slips from side to side in bottom bracket
shell, first remove chain (p 305). Then loosen locknut A by turning
it *clockwise*:

Use screwdriver in slot of cone B to turn it fully home
(*anti-clockwise*), and then back it off one-eighth turn. Resecure
locknut A (*anti-clockwise*), and check that cranks spin freely
without side to side play.

Lubrication and disassembly:
Bottom bracket axles should be cleaned and re-greased once a year.
This requires disassembly. Bearings for one-piece cranksets are
held in clips so don't worry about losing them. Remove left pedal
(*clockwise*) and chain from front sprocket (p 304). Undo locknut A
(*clockwise*), and unscrew cone B (*clockwise*):

A

B

Remove ball bearing clip. Slide all parts off crank and place in a jar. Now move axle to right and tilt to slide whole unit through bottom bracket and out of frame. Take right side bearing clip off axle. Clean everything thoroughly with solvent. See that ball bearings are secure in clips and free from pitting or cracks; cups and cones are even in colour where ball bearings run and free from pitting or scoring. If cups are deeply grooved, replace. Remove with hammer and steel rod or screwdriver:

and make sure the new cups are well seated by tapping them in with a hammer and wooden block:

To reassemble: pack grease into bearing clips and cups. Slide one clip on axle with solid side against right cone. Gracefully insert crankset through bottom bracket shell from right side. Slide on ball bearing clips with balls in, solid side out. Screw on cone (*anti-clockwise*), and turn it fully home, wiggling and spinning the crankset as you do this. Reverse one-eighth turn and secure with locknut (tighten *anti-clockwise*). Check that crankset spins freely without side to side play. Replace pedal (*anti-clockwise*) and chain.

Three-piece cranksets

Adjustment:

Bottom bracket axle (spindle) should be free from side to side play and spin freely. To adjust, first disconnect chain from front sprocket (p 304). Loosen notched lockring C on left side of bracket with a 'C' spanner (bike stores) or hammer and screwdriver combination (*anti-clockwise*):

Then tighten (*clockwise*) adjustable cup D fully home with a screwdriver or centre punch inserted in hole or slot and *very light* hammer taps:

Reverse one eighth turn and secure with lockring C. Check that spindle spins freely and has no side to side play.

Lubrication and disassembly:

Bottom bracket assembly should be cleaned and re-greased once a year. This requires disassembly. Remove chain from front sprocket (p 304) and cranks (p 294). Lay bike right-side down on newspaper or rags to catch loose ball bearings. Undo lockring C with 'C' spanner or hammer and screwdriver combination and remove. Carefully holding axle in place against right side bearings, remove adjustable cup D:

Look out for the ball bearings! Some will fall out, others will stick to various parts. Gather, count, and place in jar. Make sure you have them all. If your bearings are clipped, lucky you. Now pull spindle straight out. Garner all the right-side ball bearings and jar 'em.

There may be a plastic tube (E, above) inside the bottom bracket shell. This is to prevent grit in the frame tubes from falling into the bearings. Take it out and clean it off. Clean out inside of bottom bracket shell with solvent. Examine the fixed cup F with a flashlight. If it is unpitted and wear is reasonably even, leave it alone. Otherwise unscrew and replace. Clean all other parts in solvent. See that ball bearings have no pits or cracks, and, if clipped, are secure in retainers; inside of adjustable cup and cones on spindle also have no pits and wear is even; spindle is straight. Replace defective parts.

Reassembly: pack cups with grease. If ball bearings are clipped, pack retainers. Replace plastic sleeve. Pack ball bearings into cups. Grease will hold in place. Clipped bearings go with solid side on cone (balls face out). Carefully insert spindle, long end to sprocket side of bottom bracket shell. Without jarring loose ball bearings fit on adjustable cup and screw home. Rotate spindle as you do this to be sure it goes in all the way. Reverse one-eighth turn and secure with lockring. Be careful threading this on as it is easy to strip. Check that spindle spins easily with no side to side play. Replace cranks (p 294) and chain (p 304).

Trouble-shooting:

🚲 Tight or loose crankset, grinding noises. Try adjustment as above. No? Disassemble and replace defective parts as per above.

🚲 'Click' on pedal upstroke followed by dead spot and second 'click' on downstroke. Could be a loose spindle, but more probably a loose crank or pedal (pp 292, 297).

Front sprocket(s) (chainwheel)

The front sprocket is the business with all the teeth attached to the right crank which pulls the chain around to deliver power to the rear wheel.

Adjustment
The only maintenance needed is to check periodically for bent or chipped teeth. Remove chain (p 304). With a strong light behind the front sprocket, rotate it, looking from the side for chipped teeth, and from above or in front for bent teeth:

If teeth are chipped, replace sprocket (see overleaf). If bent, take an adjustable spanner, snug it down over the bent tooth, and bend it back:

It helps a lot if you can brace the sprocket as you do this to avoid bending it.

Replacement:

If it is necessary to replace your sprocket, take a look at the chapter on fitting and gearing. You might be interested in changing the number of gear teeth.

Ashtabula one-piece cranksets require replacing the whole unit (above).

1-speed and most 3-speed bikes have a one-piece right crank and sprocket. To remove see p 297.

10-speed bikes generally have a sprocket which is bolted to the right crank:

bolts

Simply undo the bolts (or Allen screws) to remove sprocket.

Trouble-shooting

🚲 There is a 'clunk' every time you bring the front sprocket around. One possible cause is a bent tooth. Check by hanging bike up and slowly running sprocket. If chain suddenly jumps up where it meets the sprocket – bent tooth. Fix as above.

🚲 Sprocket wobbles from side to side, hitting front derailleur cage or rubbing chainstays. If this is not due to incredibly loose bottom bracket bearings (p 299), the sprocket is warped. Fixing is a job requiring both great delicacy and considerable force. Techniques vary so much according to the exact problem that I strongly suggest you leave it to a bike shop.

Chain

The chain is that innocent and simple-looking business which transmits power to the rear gear(s). There are two kinds: one is used on non-derailleur bikes, is $\frac{1}{8}$-in wide, and held together with a master link:

which can be taken apart without special tools; the other for derailleur-equipped bikes, is $\frac{3}{32}$-in wide, and has no master link (it would catch in the rear gear cluster), so that a special chain riveting tool is needed to take it apart or put it together:

Removal and replacement

Chains should be replaced every two years on bikes that see constant use, and every three years on bikes that see average service. Although the chain may look perfectly sound, the tiny bit of wear on each rivet and plate adds up to a considerable alteration in size. A worn chain will chip teeth on (expensive) gear sprockets. To test for wear, remove chain (see below) and lay on table with rollers parallel to surface. Hold chain with both hands about 4–5 in apart. Push hands together, and then pull apart. If you can feel slack, replace chain.

Test also for side to side deflection. It should not be more than 1 in:

To remove and replace a master link chain find the master link and prise it off with a screwdriver.

To remove a derailleur chain drive out a rivet with a chain tool:

Be sure that the point of the chain tool centres exactly on the rivet.
Do not drive the rivet all the way out. Go only as far as the outside plate.
Stop frequently to check progress. Once rivet is near chain plate
I like to free link by inserting a thin screwdriver and twisting
gently:

Another method is simply to twist the chain. Be careful that you do
not bend the plates. To replace rivet, reverse tool:

Again, be careful how far you go, or the link will jam (see
Trouble-shooting to fix).

Fitting

Most new chains need to be shortened in order to fit properly. On a
non-derailleur bike it should be set so that there is $\frac{1}{2}$-in up and down
play in the chain with the rear wheel in proper position:

On a derailleur bike, the chain needs to be long enough to fit over the large front and back sprockets, and short enough to fit on the small front and rear sprockets. The less tension the better, but be careful the derailleur does not double up on itself. Remove links from end of chain that has two plates with no roller between them. Some adjustment can be made by changing wheel position with adjustable blocks on the rear drop-outs:

Lubrication

The scheme for lubrication depends on what kind of lubricant you use.

A dry film lubricant such as LPS-1 or (somewhat moist) LPS-3 is clean, does not attract dirt, and goes on in a flash. Apply every 1 or 2 weeks, and remove and soak chain clean in solvent every 2 or 3 months.

Oil is the common lubricant. The problem is that it attracts grit and the solution is to add more oil in the hope that it will float the grit away. Oil every link once a week, and remove and soak the chain clean in solvent once a month.

The most economical lubricant is paraffin wax, available in hardware shops. It is cleaner than oil. Remove and clean chain. Melt paraffin wax in coffee can, dip chain, and hang to dry so that drippings fall back into can. Once a month.

Trouble-shooting

🚲 Jammed link. Use chain tool to free tight links by working the rivet back and forth a quarter-turn on the chain tool at a time. If your chain tool has a spreader slot (handy), use that:

spreader slot

🚲 'Klunk' sounds and/or chain jumping sprockets. Test chain for excessive wear as per above. May also be a bent sprocket tooth (see p 301).

Rear sprocket

All chain drive bikes have a rear sprocket. On 1- and 3-speed bikes this is a single sprocket and is extremely simple. Derailleur-equipped bikes use several sprockets (also called cogs) mounted on a freewheel.

How it works

The freewheel is in two parts, and there are two basic designs:

C   B

The inside part B threads on the hub. Sprockets slide or are threaded on the outside part C. The freewheel is ratcheted so that when the outside part C is driven clockwise by the chain, the inside part B (and hence the hub) is driven too. But when the bike is coasting, with the chain stationary, part C holds still while part B spins merrily along. This ratcheting is accomplished through the use of a clever maze of ball bearings, pins, springs, and other minute and complex parts inside the freewheel.

Adjustment
Periodically check for chipped or bent teeth by looking at them in profile:

Replace cogs that have chipped or broken teeth, or an uneven U between teeth. Straighten bent teeth by removing cog (see below), gripping the bent tooth with an adjustable end spanner, and straightening:

Alignment between front and back sprockets is important.

Standing at the front of the bike and sighting between the two front sprockets, you should see the centre cog of the back gear cluster:

If back sprocket is too far out, so you can see the 2nd or 1st largest rear cog, the front sprocket must be moved out. This can only be done by installing a longer bottom bracket axle (p 300). If you have Ashtabula one-piece cranks (p 297) there is nothing you can do at all.

If back sprocket is too far in, so you can see the 4th or 5th largest rear cog, it must be moved out. This is done by removing the freewheel (see overleaf), installing a shim (bike shops), the freewheel again, and then possibly another shim so that the freewheel will clear the drop-outs. All this stuff usually makes it hard to put the wheel back in and may necessitate a little judicious bending. It is better to let a bike shop deal with problems of this sort.

Lubrication
A bi-weekly shot of petroleum distillate spray like WD-40 or LPS-3 is best. Remove freewheel (see overleaf) and soak clean in solvent once a year.

Oil: a few drops once a month. Remove and soak clean in solvent every six months.

Removal and disassembly
This requires a freewheel remover. There are two basic types, pronged and splined: but exact models vary according to brand of freewheel. Look at yours to see which kind you need. Remove wheel (p 267). Remove nut and washers from freewheel side of axle.

Quick release hubs: remove conical nut and spring from shaft of skewer and place spring in a jar. Fit freewheel remover. If it won't go on, you may have a spacer nut. Remove with a spanner while holding axle stationary with another spanner on the left-side cone or locknut. Fit freewheel remover into slots or splines. Replace nut on axle or skewer and screw down hand-tight. Use a spanner on the freewheel remover to break the freewheel loose (*anti-clockwise*). This may be difficult. As soon as it comes loose, remove freewheel and spin it off by hand.

Replacing freewheel. *Note:* a new freewheel or sprockets requires a matching new chain, especially if the existing chain is more than a year old. A stretched chain will probably kick up on new sprockets. Also, if you are getting a new freewheel, read the chapter on gears. You may be interested in changing gear ratios. If you do this, be sure to check chain tension after installing freewheel (p 306). To replace a freewheel, simply screw it on, being extremely careful not to strip the threads on the hub. Snug down with the freewheel remover secured by the axle bolt but do not bear down hard; it will tighten as you ride.

Changing cogs. For this you need a sprocket remover (bike shops) and, if you are removing all the sprockets, a freewheel vice (ditto). Incidentally, if you want a number of different gear ratios it is much simpler to have two fully set-up freewheels with different gear ratios than to keep diddling with individual sprockets. However, if you are experimenting to work out the combination of cogs which is best for you and are impatient with bike shops (they can do this job very quickly), then by all means proceed. Removing a cog is simple – it unscrews or slides off the freewheel – but tools for the job vary considerably in design. Follow the instructions given with your particular tool. If you change the small or large cog, be sure to check chain tension (p 306) after reassembly.

Dismantle freewheel. Uh-uh. This is another of those profitless jobs. If the freewheel goes, replace it.

Trouble-shooting

🚲 A 'klunk' two or three times per complete revolution of the front sprocket. May be a bent tooth on a freewheel sprocket. Check as per above.

🚲 Freewheel won't freewheel. Try soaking in solvent to free up innards. No? Replace it.

🚲 Freewheel turns but hub doesn't. Spin cranks while holding bike stationary and look carefully at freewheel. If both parts spin around the hub, threads on hub are stripped. New hub. If outside part of freewheel spins around inside part, freewheel is clogged up (frozen) or broken. Try soaking in solvent. No? Replace.

Gear changer systems

Except for the two-speed pedal-operated rear hubs, gear changer systems typically include a shift trigger, lever, or twist-grip, a cable, and the gear changing mechanism, of which there are two kinds, internal rear hub, and derailleur.

Multi-speed internally geared rear hubs

These come in 2-, 3-, and 5-speed versions, with planetary or sun gears inside the hub. I consider these units too complicated to be worth disassembling, and so does any bike shop I have asked about doing such work. Here, for example, is an exploded view of a Sturmey-Archer 3-speed hub and coaster brake combination (see overleaf). Believe me, if you run into trouble with your hub and can't solve it with routine adjustment or trouble-shooting (below), the best thing to do is remove the wheel (p 267) and take it to a bike shop. The chance of problems arising is quite small. A regularly lubricated hub should last the life of your bike.

Sturmey-Archer 3-speed hub

No adjustments are possible with 2-speed pedal-controlled hubs.
There are two major brands of 3-speed hubs, Sturmey-Archer, and
Shimano. Service techniques for both are virtually identical, and so
we will concentrate on one, the Sturmey-Archer.

How they work:
Shift trigger A connects to cable B, which in turn connects to toggle
chain C on hub.
Position of trigger determines gear.

Adjustment:
Three-speed hubs: To adjust a hub, first run the shift lever to 3rd or
H. Then take up slack in cable by loosening locknut A and screwing
down barrel sleeve adjuster B:

Leave cable very slightly slack. If barrel sleeve cannot do job, move the fulcrum clip which holds the cable housing on the bike frame forward:

thataway

Test gears. No? Check position of indicator rod by looking through the hole in the side of the right hub nut. With the shift lever in 2nd or N position it should be exactly even with the end of the axle:

indicator rod

Adjust if necessary with barrel sleeve. Test gears. No? Remove
barrel sleeve altogether. Check that indicator rod is screwed
finger-tight fully into hub. Reassemble and adjust as above. No?
Turn to Trouble-shooting, this section.

Five-speed hubs: For the right-hand shift lever, follow the same
procedure as for the 3-speed hub, above.

For left-hand shift lever, set it all the way forward and screw
cable connector to bellcrank B two or three turns:

Then run shift lever all the way back, and take slack out of cable
with cable connector. Secure with locknut C.

Lubrication:
A tablespoon of oil inside hub once a month. I strongly recommend
a quality oil such as is sold in bike shops and by gunsmiths. Some
household and other cheap oils leave behind a sticky residue when
the oil evaporates. This is the last thing in the world you want.
Once a month use a little petroleum distillate spray or a few drops
of oil on the trigger control, cable, and inside the cable housing.
LPS-3 is also a suitable hub lubricant.

Disassembly and replacement:
Hub: Remove wheel (p 267) and take it to a bike shop.
Cable: Needs replacement when it becomes frayed, the housing
kinked or broken, or exhibits suspicious political tendencies.

Run shift selector to 3rd or H. Disconnect barrel sleeve from indicator and loosen fulcrum clip (for illustration, see Adjustment above). To free cable from a:

Trigger: shift to 1st or L, prise up holding plate A with a small screwdriver, and push cable *in* until nipple clears ratchet plate:

and then pull cable out. Remove entire cable and housing assembly from bike and set aside fulcrum sleeve.

Twist-grip: first take off the spring S with a screwdriver:

Slide the twist-grip off the handlebar and catch the ball bearing B and spring SS if they fall out. Release nipple from slot, and remove cable and cable housing assembly from bike.

Top tube lever: undo the cable anchor bolt near the hub:

Unscrew the two shift lever halves A and B, and lift casing C away from bike:

Push cable in to free nipple from slot and thread out cable. *Note:* Take the old cable with you to the shop when buying replacement. This kind of cable comes in a variety of lengths. To replace a cable to a :

Trigger: place the fulcrum sleeve on cable housing and thread through fulcrum clip. Prise up trigger control plate, insert cable through hole in trigger casing, and slip nipple into slot on ratchet.

Run cable over pulley wheel if you have one, and attach to toggle chain. Shift to 3rd or H. Position fulcrum clip so cable is just slightly slack and tighten. Adjust if necessary as per above.

Twist-grip: insert nipple into slot. Grease and replace spring and ball bearing. Slide twist-grip on handlebar and secure with spring clip. Use a small screwdriver to work the spring clip in. Run cable over pulley wheel if you have one, and attach to toggle chain. Shift selector to 3rd or H and adjust as per above.

Top tube lever: thread cable through slot until nipple catches. Replace cable housing or run cable over pulley wheel, depending on the kind of system you have. Connect cable to anchor bolt, shift to 3rd or H, and adjust as per above. Replace casing, and screw together handle halves.

Shift control: If you have a bashed or recalcitrant shift control the best thing is to replace it. They are not expensive. To replace

Trigger: disconnect cable (see above) and undo bolt B:

Twist-grip or top tube lever: I recommend replacing with a standard handlebar trigger, which is a much better mechanical design and more reliable. To rcmove old unit disconnect cable (see above) and undo bolt B:

Trouble-shooting:

No gear at all (pedals spin freely) or slips in and out of gear.

🚲 Is gear in proper adjustment?

🚲 Is cable binding? Check by disconnecting barrel sleeve at hub and working cable back and forth through housing. Replace if it binds.

🚲 Is shift mechanism together and functioning? Stick and twist-grip models are especially prone to slippage after the track for the ball bearing becomes worn:

🚲 Insides of hubs may have got clogged through the use of too heavy or household oils so that pawls are stuck. Try putting in paraffin or penetrating oil and jiggling everything around. No?

🚲 Give up. Remove wheel (p 267) and take to a bike shop.

Derailleur systems

A derailleur system includes a shift lever, usually mounted on the down tube, but also on the top tube, or the stem, or at the handlebar ends,

down tube

stem

handle bar

top tube

a thin cable and (sometimes) cable housing, and a front or rear gear changer (derailleur) through which the chain passes. When the shift lever is actuated, the derailleur moves sideways and forces the chain on to a different sprocket:

Although we are dealing here with a system, it will simplify everything to take it piece by piece first, and then deal with it as a whole.

Shift lever:
How it works – Adjustment – Removal and replacement:
The shift lever should be set so that you can move it without undue strain, but be stiff enough to hold fast against spring pressure from the derailleur. This adjustment is made with the tension screw A:

Some tension screws have a slot for a screwdriver (or coin), others have wings, and others have wire loops. All function the same way. To dismantle the lever, simply remove the tension screw. Be sure to keep all parts in order. To remove a down-tube-mounted lever unit, undo bolt B above.

To make a top tube lever unit come off, remove the stem (p 254). A stem-mounted unit comes off by undoing bolts A and B (below):

A handlebar end unit requires first removing trim nut A (below):

then nut B and screw C. Then loosen Allen screw (6 mm) located at point P inside selector body, and remove unit.

Cables:
Adjustment:
Cables of derailleur systems are frequently exposed, thin, and take a hell of a beating. Check them often for fraying:

Adjustment is needed when the shift lever has to be pulled all the way back to engage the large sprocket. Place the shift lever forward so that the chain is on the smallest sprocket. Some systems have a barrel adjuster, either at the derailleur or at the shift lever:

Undo the locknut A and move the barrel adjuster up until slack is removed from cable. If this will not do the job, turn barrel adjuster back down fully home, and reset cable anchor bolt.

All derailleurs, front and back, use a cable anchor bolt or screw to hold the cable. Here is the location (CB) on four representative types:

D

CB

B

C

SB

CB

E

D

Loosen the bolt, take the slack out of the cable, pulling it through with pliers if necessary, and retighten bolt.

Removal and replacement:
Run chain to smallest sprocket. Screw home barrel adjuster, if you have one. Undo cable anchor bolt and thread cable out of derailleur. Check cable housings (not on all models) for kinks and breaks. Remove cable from lever by threading it out:

🚲 Reassembly: do not cut new cable to size until it is installed or it will jam when going into cable housings. If you are cutting new cable housing, be sure to place the jaws of the cutter *between* the wire coils of the housing:

wrong   right

Start by threading through shift lever, and then through down tube tunnel, cable stops, cable housings, and whatever else is in your particular system. As you pass the cable through cable housings, be sure to twist it so that the strands do not unravel:

Finish at derailleur. Move shift lever to forward position, make sure that cable housing ferrules (if you have them) are seated properly, and attach cable to cable anchor bolt.

Trouble-shooting:
Cable problems are evinced by delayed shifts, or no shifts at all. In any case, the procedure is the same: undo the cable anchor bolt and slide the cable around by hand, looking for sticky spots. Check carefully for fraying, and for kinks in the cable housing.

Derailleurs – front
How they work:
There is a metal cage through which the chain passes as it feeds on to the front sprocket. The cage can be moved from side to side, and by pressing on the side of the chain, shifts it from sprocket to sprocket:

Virtually all derailleurs are built as a parallelogram. Heh. This design is used to keep the sides of the cage A straight up and down as the cage is moved from side to side on the pivot bolt P:

The cage is moved by pulling with a cable at point B, and when the cable is released, spring tension pushes it back. Details may vary, but this is the basic design.

Adjustment:
The changer as a whole must be properly positioned, with the outer side of the cage about $\frac{1}{4}$ in to $\frac{1}{2}$ in above the sprocket:

Raise or lower the unit by undoing the mounting bolt (B). The sides of the cage should follow the curvature of the sprocket. Some cages are adjustable in this respect, others (perfectly good ones) are not.

Those that are usually swivel on a post between the cage and changer. Sometimes the post comes off the changer, and sometimes off the cage. Either way, there will be a locking bolt like C: Loosen, rotate cage to desired position, tighten.

Huret (front)

Side to side travel of the cage must be set. First check that cable is properly adjusted (above). Front derailleurs fall into two design categories, those with two adjusting screws, and those with one. Look at yours to determine the type.

One-screw derailleurs: Run chain to largest back and smallest front sprockets. The first adjustment is made with the cage positioning bolt C (above). Loosen it, and move the cage so that the left side just clears the chain. Tighten. Now loosen the adjusting screw D three or four turns. Run the chain to the smallest back and largest front sprockets.

Using the shift lever, position the cage so that the right side just clears the chain. Turn down adjusting screw D until resistance is felt, and stop.

Two-screw derailleurs: If you can't find your adjusting screws easily,

327

get down close to the unit and watch it carefully as you wiggle the shift lever back and forth. Each time the body of the changer reaches the end of its travel it will be resting on a spring-loaded screw or knurled ring:

On Campagnolo units they are the screws E and D:

Run chain to largest and smallest front sprockets. It should just clear the left side of the cage. Adjust left side (low gear) adjusting screw (D,) as necessary until it does. Now run chain to smallest back and largest front sprockets. It should just clear the right side of the cage. Adjust right side (high gear) adjusting screw (E,) as necessary until it does. Test operation of gears.

Sometimes it is necessary to set the high gear adjustment a little wide to make the chain climb up on the big sprocket – but be cautious, or the chain will throw off the sprocket.

Lubrication:
A little petroleum distillate spray or a few drops of oil on the pivot bolts once a month. If the unit becomes particularly dirty, take it off (see below) and soak it clean in paraffin or other solvent.

Replacement:
See above for illustrations. Remove chain (p 304) or alternatively, if your unit has a cage bolt A, remove it. Undo cable anchor bolt CB and slip off cable. Now undo mounting bolt(s) B and remove unit. Reverse to replace. Other units may have different mounting bolts but their function will be clear.

Trouble-shooting:
Most of the difficulties experienced with the front changer are actually caused by problems elsewhere in the power train. I am assuming that you have already set your changer as per Adjustment, above.

Chain rubs side of cage:
🚲 Is shift lever tight?
🚲 Can you stop rubbing by diddling with shift lever? For example, the amount of right travel necessary to shift the chain from the left (small) sprocket to the right sprocket may leave the cage too far to the right when the chain is on the large back sprocket, and cause the chain to rub the left side of the cage. In fact, it is frequently necessary with front changers to move the cage back just a trifle after a shift has been completed.
🚲 Is the sprocket warped? Or loose?

Chain throws off sprocket:
🚲 Is shift lever tight?
🚲 Cage travel may be set too far out. Adjust it slightly.
🚲 Is chain old? Test (p 304).
🚲 Are sprocket teeth bent?
🚲 Are front and rear sprockets in alignment (p 309)?
🚲 If chain continually over-rides big front sprocket, take an adjustable end spanner and bend the leading tip of the outside cage in very slightly – about $\frac{1}{16}$ in:

Delayed shifts or no shifts at all:

🚲 Are pivot bolts clean?
    Try a little spray or oil.
🚲 Is spring intact and in place?
🚲 Is cable sticking or broken?
🚲 If pivot bolts are adjustable, as P is on a Campagnolo unit,
undo locknut, back P off one eighth turn, reset locknut (see p 328).

Derailleurs – rear

How they work:
As the chain comes back off the bottom of the front sprocket it
passes through the rear derailleur on two chain rollers. The cage
holding the rollers is fastened to the main body of the changer by a
pivot bolt P, and is under constant spring tension so as to keep the
chain taut:

The lower roller is the tension roller (TR), the upper the jockey roller (JR). The position of the cage, and hence of the chain on the rear gear cluster, is determined by the changer body:

The changer body is under constant spring tension to carry it to the smallest sprocket. It is restrained from doing so by a cable and shift lever.

Derailleurs come in two basic designs, box, like the Huret Allvit or Simplex, and bare parallelogram, like the Campagnolo:

Campagnolo

Huret

Adjustment:

Position of changer with respect to bike: The body of the changer should form an angle with the vertical of about 20° to 30°. Many derailleurs are not adjustable in this respect and are held by spring tension against a stop (Campagnolo, Simplex). Others like the Huret Allvit can be adjusted by loosening locknut A and then pivot bolt P:

Chain rollers should align with the chain:

If your derailleur is fastened to a mounting plate, remove it, clamp in a vice, and bend it with an adjustable end spanner:

If your derailleur is bolted straight into the frame drop-out, snug spanner around the chain rollers and bend into alignment:

Bear in mind that this is a fairly drastic measure. I am assuming that the derailleur was bent in an accident, and that you have no choice. The alternative is replacement (see below), which you should consider if the old derailleur is on the way out. Box changers such as the Huret or Simplex are inexpensive and quite reliable, and a working derailleur, no matter how plastic and cheap, is miles ahead of a fancy job which is one shift away from disintegration.

Note: if it is a brand-new derailleur which is out of alignment, then the fault is with the frame drop-out. You can bend this into line yourself with an adjustable end spanner the same as you would bend the derailleur mount (above), but this is a very serious matter which should be left to a bike shop. Bending does cause metal fatigue, and if the rear drop-out were to shear unexpectedly you might have an accident.

Side to side travel of derailleur:

First check with chain on smallest rear and biggest front sprockets, and with rear derailleur shift lever all the way forward, that there is only a little slack in the cable. Take up or give slack through barrel adjuster and/or cable anchor bolt.

The derailleur needs to be set so that side to side travel is stopped short of throwing the chain into the wheel or off the small sprocket. This is done with two adjusting screws or knurled rings, and here is their location on six typical units (high gear – E, low gear – D):

If your derailleur isn't included here, get down close to it and run it back and forth, seeing which adjusting screw does what. OK, now: if derailleur goes too far, throwing chain off, set in position with shift lever so that jockey wheel lines up with sprocket on the side you are working on, and turn in appropriate adjusting screw or knurled ring until resistance is felt. Stop. If derailleur does not go far enough, back the appropriate adjusting screw off until it does. If this does not work, check to make absolutely sure adjusting screw is backed off. Yes? Turn back to Trouble-shooting for what to do next.

Spring tension for roller cage:

Spring tension on the roller cage should be sufficient to keep the chain taut when in high gear. No tighter. Excess tension will cause unnecessary drag and rapid wear. On the other hand, too loose a chain will skip. If you have this problem and the chain tension seems OK, check the chain itself for wear (p 304). Worn chains skip.

Adjustment procedure varies according to type of derailleur. Many have the spring set on a hook on the roller cage:

Move it carefully with pliers or screwdriver.

On a Campagnolo unit, first remove wheel. Then remove tension roller by undoing bolt G:

Use one hand to hang on to the chain roller cage and prevent it from spinning, and unscrew the cage stop bolt SB. Now let the cage unwind (about one-half to three-quarters of a turn). Remove cage pivot bolt with Allen key and lift off cage. Note that protruding spring end engages one of a series of small holes in the cage. Rotate cage forward until spring fits into next hole:

Replace pivot bolt. Wind cage back one-half to three-quarters turn and replace cage stop bolt. Replace tension roller and go back to the races.

On the Simplex, remove screw and dust cap (not on all models) from bottom pivot bolt A. Loosen locknut B, use a metric Allen key to turn A clockwise for more tension, counter-clockwise for less, reset locknut (see opposite).

B.

A

Shimano units: Remove wheel, tension roller, and cage stop bolt. Rotate entire cage one turn against spring. Replace cage stop bolt, tension roller, wheel.

The Madea Sun Tour V-Luxe can be adjusted as per procedure for Shimano units, but this is likely to produce too much or too little tension. For a finer adjustment, disassemble (p 349), noting the relative position of cage with respect to spring catch setting in crenellated nut. If the normal position is as A:

spring tension may be increased by moving spring catch to position B, and decreased by moving to position C.

Lubrication:
Petroleum spray: once a month on the jockey and tension rollers, pivot bolts, and cables. Once a year remove and soak clean in solvent.

Oil: a few drops monthly on chain rollers, pivot bolts, cables. Soak clean in solvent every six months. Regrease wheel bearings, if you have them (next page).

Removal and disassembly:
Disconnect cable from anchor bolt (p 322).

Remove tension roller by undoing bolt G (below, and pp 337, 341). Undo mounting bolt B (Campagnolo) or slacken axle nut and remove adapter screw AS (Huret Allvit) according to how your unit is mounted (opposite and next pages).

Disassembly: the parts that need this regularly are the chain rollers. Otherwise do it only to replace parts. Chain rollers: take off jockey roller (tension roller is already off).

On the Campagnolo this is done by undoing the jockey roller bolt just like the bolt for the tension roller. On the Huret it is necessary to first unsnap the cage spring:

and then unscrew the cage mounting bolt CB:

Be careful of those shims and whatnots! Keep track of their order.
There are two kinds of chain rollers, those with washers and a metal sleeve, and those with a hub and ball bearings:

If you have the ball-bearing type, disassemble the hub and remove the bearings. Both types: clean in solvent. Ball-bearing type reassembly: lay one cone flat on table, place chain roller over it. Apply petroleum spray or grease. Put in ball bearings. More lubricant. Screw on second cone.

For the rest of it, the degree of disassembly possible, as well as the technique, varies somewhat from model to model. We'll do six: the Hurct, Campagnolo, Simplex, Crane, Eagle and Sun Tour V-Luxe.

The Huret Allvit:

Undo locknut A and remove pivot bolt P with Allen key (previous page). Keep parts in order. Next: undo the upper lever arm bolt D:

and then lower lever arm bolt E. Remove lever arm, and use pliers to prise spring S off changer body. Then remove bolt F to remove spring S. Replace any parts to be replaced. Clean everything in solvent.

Reassembly note : Be sure to set all locknuts with sufficient play for smooth derailleur operation. Assemble movement arm spring S, bushing, spacer, at housing and insert bolt F, secure with locknut. Replace spring hook on changer body. Put lever arm in place and secure with bolts D and E.

Reassemble cage (see p 341 for illustrations): mounting bolt CB, outside cage, jockey roller, inside cage (has hooks for cage spring – these face changer body), washer, cage spring and bushing, washer; screw this assembly into the cage mounting plate. Set cage spring with screwdriver. Replace pivot bolt, stop plate, mounting plate. Mount derailleur on frame. Replace tension roller. Re-engage cable. Adjust side to side play as necessary (p 334).

The Campagnolo :

Hang on to chain roller cage to prevent it from spinning and remove cage stop bolt SB. Let cage unwind (about one-half to three-quarters of a turn). Remove cage pivot bolt A with Allen key and lift off cage. Slide out pivot bolt A and spring. Back off high gear adjusting screw E to minimize changer body spring tension, and undo spring bolt SS. Replace parts, clean everything in solvent.

Reassembly: screw in spring bolt SS while holding changer body spring R in position. Replace cage spring and slide in pivot bolt. Put cage on changer with two half-moon sides next to changer. Put nut on pivot bolt. Rotate cage back one-half to three-quarters of a turn and screw in cage stop bolt SB. Replace jockey roller. Mount derailleur on frame. Replace tension roller, cable. Adjust side to side travel as above (p 334).

The Simplex

Remove dust caps from pivot bolts A and E. Spring off clips C
(not all models). Undo locknut B for main arm pivot bolt A and
remove bolt and spring. Ditto for locknut D and cage pivot bolt E.
Some Simplex models have a circlip which can be removed so the
anchor bolt F will slide out:

344

G

F

circling

With the outer arm hinged up to relieve tension, unscrew the spring pivot pin G.

Other models lack this feature, in which case prise the spring up with a screwdriver:

G

and then unscrew spring pivot pin G. Clean everything in solvent and replace defective parts.

To reassemble: Put main body spring in place and screw in spring pivot pin. Push down outer arm and secure with anchor bolt and circlip, or set spring in place with screwdriver. Put in cage pivot bolt and spring. Put on locknut and cage, and give cage pivot bolt one-half turn to right for proper spring tension before setting

locknut. Repeat process for main arm pivot bolt, spring, and
locknut. Fasten jockey roller to cage. Mount derailleur on frame.
Mount tension roller, and then connect shift cable. Adjust side to
side travel of derailleur as necessary (p 334).

Singer 'Velociman'

The Crane : The mounting bolt B has a spring. To get at it, prise off
circlip C with a screwdriver or similar implement. It will come apart
quickly. Clean parts in solvent, replacing spring if necessary, and
grease. Reassemble by fitting spring, placing the head of bolt B
on a hard surface, and twisting bracket A anti-clockwise while
simultaneously pressing downwards. When it clicks into place,
hold it firm with one finger, and with the other hand fit circlip C.

To get off the cage pivot bolt D back it off slowly with an Allen
key, and when the cage stop catch SC clears the little bump on the
frame, let the chain roller cage unwind. Finish backing off bolt D.
Remove spring, plate bushing PB, and bolt D. Clean and grease,
replacing parts if necessary. To reassemble, fit bolt D, spring, and
plate bushing PB. Fit roller cage to bolt D and turn down $1\frac{1}{2}$–2 turns.
Wind cage clockwise until stop catch SC passes bump on frame,
secure bolt PB.

Eagle SS:

To undo mounting bracket
pivot bolt PB, remove dustcap D
by twisting off or prising up with thin
screwdriver, prise off circlip C, and
unwind bracket gently. When reassembling,
be sure that CC catch on mounting bracket
plate is wound past the corresponding catch
CD on the derailleur body.
To get off the cage bolt CB do exactly the same thing as above.

Madea Sun Tour V-Luxe:

To undo mounting bracket pivot bolt PB, slack off locknut N and then back out bolt PB.

To remove cage bolt CB, first undo cage stop screw SS and allow cage to unwind. Next, while holding cage and main body together, undo cage bolt CB and withdraw. Note position of spring S in slots of cage axle A, and of cage relative to main body. Separate cage and main body. Withdraw spring S, noting which of two holes the end catch fits into. Clean and grease, replacing parts as necessary.

Reassembly: place in spring S, fitting to appropriate hole. Refit cage. If the spring tension of the cage has been weak, start from a position anti-clockwise of the original, and if it has been too strong, from a position clockwise of the original. A little diddling will achieve what you want. Fit cage bolt CB. Wind cage clockwise until cage stop screw SS can be fitted.

The Positron

The Positron is a semi-automatic derailleur utilizing a twin cable control.

Mount derailleur on dropout and axle. Move unit by hand until index pin lines up with numeral 3 on derailleur body:

Check that guide pulley is aligned with the centre sprocket of the freewheel:

If it is not, turn the adjusting screw in or out until the two parts align.

Thread through the chain:

And affix the shifting lever.
Loosen the cable fixing screw on
the lever:

Fit the cable end with the head
into the slot provided on the cam
plate, and the cable end with
no head through the cable
adjuster:

Thread cable through anchor bolt, pull tight with pliers, and snug
down anchor bolt. Move shift lever to 3 on lever plate and tighten
cable fixing screw. Check operation of unit. If necessary, adjust in or
out with adjusting screw. After about 50–100 miles of riding, check
the cables for slack.

Cable replacement:
Undo cable fixing screw and cable anchor
bolt (preceding illustrations). Slide out
old cable. Use the end of the new cable to
poke through the hole in the side of the
shift lever and move the cable fixing
plate back:

Thread cable through housings:

Fix and adjust as per instructions above.

Disassembly:
Remove chain or remove tension roller by undoing bolt 14. Slack off rear wheel axle bolts, undo adapter screw and nut 11 and 12, and remove unit from bike. Undo jockey roller bolt 14.

Prise off dustcaps 1. Remove circlips 2. Pull out cage plate 15 until cage stop catch clears main body of unit and allow to unwind. Separate. Ditto procedure for adapter 10.

Clean all parts in solvent. Be sure main body is thoroughly dry before lubricating. Assembly is reverse of above.

Trouble-shooting
Derailleur is sticky, won't always shift, sometimes shifts unexpectedly:
🚲 Is shift lever working smoothly but with enough friction to hold derailleur in place (p 322)?

🚲 Are cables sticking (p 321)?

🚲 Are pivot bolts lubricated and clean? On some models (Campagnolo, Huret, among others) these bolts can be adjusted:

Undo locknuts for bolts
D, E, and F, undo bolts
one eighth turn;
reset locknuts.

Derailleur will not go far enough:

🚲 Is cable slightly slack with shift lever all the way forward (p 334)?

🚲 Are adjusting screws properly set (p 334)?

🚲 Does cable slide easily (p 331)?

🚲 Is pivot or main changer spring broken?

🚲 Are chain rollers lined up with chain (p 333)?

🚲 Try to wiggle the derailleur unit by hand. Can you push it to the desired position?

Yes: works are gummed up. Clean in solvent and lubricate with spray or oil. Adjust (not possible with all models) by undoing pivot bolts one eighth turn and resetting (see above).

No: if it won't reach the big rear cog, remove mounting plate and bend it in a vice.

If it won't reach the little rear cog, bend mounting plate, or put in shims at the mounting bolt.

Chain throws off cogs:

🚲 Are adjusting screws set properly (p 334)?

🚲 Are any teeth worn or bent (pp 301, 308)?

🚲 Is chain good (p 304)?

353

🚲 If chain is skipping, is spring tension for roller cage sufficient (p 337)?

🚲 Is roller cage aligned with chain (p 333)?

Power train – trouble-shooting index

Noises

First make sure that noise is coming from power train by coasting bike. If noise continues it is probably a brake (p 212) or hub (p 266) problem. If noise persists, try to determine if it comes from the front (crankset), the chain, or the rear sprocket(s). Do this by disconnecting the chain (p 304) and spinning the various parts.

Grinding noises

Front:

🚲 Bottom bracket bearings OK (pp 297, 299)?

🚲 Pedal bearings OK (p 292)?

🚲 Chain rubbing derailleur?

🚲 Front sprocket rubbing cage or chainstays (p 303)?

Back:

🚲 Wheel bearings OK (p 284)?

🚲 Freewheel OK (p 307)?

P is the chain pulley, one being placed at either end of the crank-shaft, and capable of freely revolving thereon, except when jambed by the shallow rollers, R. These rollers lie in a cavity formed by a circular recess in the pulley and a steel disc, D, which is shaped off on four sides so as to form alternately hollows and wedges. The disc, D, is a fixture on the crank-shaft. When the latter moves forward in the direction shown by the arrows, the rollers, R, are jambed between the disc and the inner surface of the pulley, P, and the whole of the parts, pulley included, run solid. The machine is then driven. On the contrary, when D is turned in the opposite direction, the rollers pass into the hollow spaces, and there simply rotate without jambing. This also happens when the crank-shaft, with the disc D, is held stationary as in running down hill, in which case the pulley P runs on, rotating the rollers in the hollows as already explained.

Clicks or clunks

One for every revolution of crankset:

 Pedal tight (p 292)?

Crank(s) tight (p 293)?

Bottom bracket bearings OK (pp 297, 299)?

Are teeth on sprocket(s) bent (pp 301, 308)?

Two or three for every revolution of the crankset:

Are teeth on rear sprocket(s) bent (p 308)?

Is chain worn or frozen (p 304)?

No go. Pedals and chain spin uselessly:

3-speeds, see p 318.

10-speeds, see p 310.

Delayed shifts, no shifts, or not all gears:

3-speeds, see p 318.

10-speeds, see p 352.

For all other problems consult the trouble-shooting section for the part which is malfunctioning.

Tricycle carriers like this late 1800s model are what we need now

6 Service interval chart

Service interval chart

Part	Weekly	Bi-weekly	Monthly	Bi-monthly	3 months	6 months	Yearly
General	Clean with cloth and toothbrush		Nuts and bolts secure?			Wax or coat with LPS-1	Leather saddles, dress with neatsfoot oil from underneath
Tyres	Check pressure and for embedded glass						Give thanks
Brakes	Check cable and shoe adjustment		Oil or LPS pivot bolt adjustment				Dismantle, clean and regrease or LPS
Rims	Check for truth and even spoke tension						
Chain	Oil, if in hard service	Oil or LPS-3	Check for play	Remove, clean and re-oil	Remove, clean and re-LPS-3		

Derailleurs	Oil or LPS	Chain roller wheels – dismantle, clean and regrease or LPS	Dismantle, clean and regrease or LPS
3-speed hub	Oil		
Hubs	Oil, check adjustment	Dismantle, clean, regrease	
Bottom bracket	Oil, check adjustment	Dismantle, clean, and regrease (hard service)	Dismantle, clean, and regrease (ordinary service)
Headset	Check adjustment		
Pedals	Oil, check adjustment		
Cables	Check for fraying	Oil or LPS-3	Dismantle and regrease or LPS

7 Dream–Ramode–Sunfighter–Dream–Birthright

Everybody has dreams and here is one of mine: motor cars are banned from central areas of all major metropolitan regions. Each city provides free bicycles (with adjustable seats and handlebars) or recumbent tricycles (fitted with weather protection screens and large-load luggage carriers), scattered about to be used as needed. There are repair centres throughout town, as well as special racks in which machines in need of servicing can be left.

A dream? Perhaps. This is the age of the automobile, but the ecological and economic extravagance concomitant with the use of motor vehicles for private transport is so tremendous that they will of necessity go the way of the Dodo bird. In China, a country trying to embrace the fruits of technology as quickly and as efficiently as possible, there are 22,535 people for each motor vehicle, as against 3 people per motor vehicle in Great Britain or the United States.* In China, people ride bicycles or use public transportation. The saving in money and energy expenditure at every level is gargantuan. A bicycle factory, in comparison with an automobile factory, is a low-technology operation far easier to initiate and maintain. Bicycle production and use does not require vast support industries in petroleum, metals, rubbers, plastics, and textiles. Petrochemical and cement road building industries are minimal. There is no need for traffic regulation or vehicle registry, and little need for courts, solicitors, and expensive insurance. There are no hundreds of thousands of maimed people requiring expensive hospitalization, emergency, and other medical services.

A dream? The forecast is that Great Britain will have 27 million motor vehicles by the end of this century.† Already the motorways and roads regularly jam to surfeit with motor vehicles carrying just one human each. The sheer waste of it all is absolutely fantastic. In terms of time, trouble, and expense, we do not own our motor

* Heilman, Gail, *Bicycling!* June 1977.
† Bendixson, T., *Instead of Cars*, Penguin Books Ltd, Harmondsworth, Middlesex, 1977.

vehicles; they own us. Eventually motor vehicles have to go. When is a matter for speculation and debate, but it is highly unlikely that it will come to pass before the end of this century.

In consequence the immediate solution is to design total transportation systems in which the needs of all road and path users are met separately and without conflict. This is done by creating independent roads for motor vehicles, cyclists, and pedestrians. Use of one particular type of road is not obligatory; the charm of the system is that it works so well that most road users prefer to use the carriageway designed for them.

A dream? It has been done. Stevenage, Hertfordshire, a town of some 72,000 souls sequestered 32 miles north of London, is a transportation dreamworld, a kind of magical Walt Disney fantasy in which everything flows with perfect smoothness and problems evaporate. Stevenage was the first designated New Town under the provisions of the New Towns Act of 1946, which allows for development financed by the state with 60-year loans. Most or all of the credit for the design and engineering of Stevenage, and in particular its transportation systems, goes to Eric Claxton, now retired as Chief Engineer for the Stevenage Development Corporation, and a man who must be reckoned a one-of-a-kind genius.

With a population of 72,000 on 6,000 acres, Stevenage has a population density greater than that of Central London. Yet there is not one single traffic, cycle, or pedestrian stoplight or sign in the entire town. The flow of these different kinds of traffic, even at rush-hour periods, is so smooth and even that there does not appear to be anybody around. What rush hour? One asks, looking around for lines or packs of traffic. There are none. There is no congestion because nothing ever holds still.

The Stevenage system succeeds because it is a *total* transportation system. Roads for pedestrians, cycles, mopeds, and motor vehicles are separate and never conflict. It is possible to drive a motor car throughout the town without once encountering a cycle or pedestrian. As a result the average speed of rush-hour traffic is 20 mph, double the average of other cities, and better still than the average in major metropolitan regions such as London. You are guaranteed a parking space right near your destination except on the two Saturdays before Christmas. Bus services operate to and from the absolute centre of town, literally only steps away from shopping and municipal centres. There are no dwellings more than a 5-minute walk from a bus stop. Most are much closer.

If you are cycling it is also possible to go anywhere you wish in town via the cycleways or footpaths (on which pedestrians, cycles, and mopeds have mingled freely and without incident for over 20 years), and never encounter a motor car. For pedestrians, in addition to a comprehensive network of footpaths, the town centre and many subcentres are completely pedestrianized, with no vehicle traffic and complete protection from the weather.*

The official cycleway system is 25 miles long, and is shared by all types of cycles, mopeds up to 50cc capacity, and pedestrians. The cycleways frequently run alongside main roads but are separated by grass verges and trees from both the roads and footpaths. There are in addition a number of crosstown cycleway links which run independently of roads. Some were originally country lanes from which vehicular traffic has been withdrawn. Additionally, cycles make free use of over 100 miles of footpaths so that most cycle journeys are door-to-door. There are no rules or regulations (and hence no need for the police to concern themselves with traffic regulation) governing the use of the cycleways and footpaths, no 'cycles must or must not'. Cyclists are free to use the vehicle carriageways if they prefer. The existing cycleway system is so attractive, however, that only the odd racer in training buzzing along at 25-mph-plus chooses to mix with the cars.

The different types of roads are kept separate through the generous use of underpasses. These are a study in sensitive design and architecture. An overpass for cycles must rise at least 16 feet over the road, necessitating either a long or steep gradient. An underpass for cycles only requires 7 ft 6 in of headroom; and by excavating to a depth of only 6 feet, and using the excavation material to gently raise the road 3 feet, the differences in gradient are still further minimized. The cycleways are normally 12 feet wide and carry two-way traffic. Construction is similar to a footpath, with minimal lighting and drainage. The main costs derive from the earthworks and concrete underpasses needed at intersections to keep cycleways and motor roads apart.

* Traffic bans increase business in shopping areas. The Organization for Economic Cooperation and Development reports that vehicle bans increased business by 25–50% in Vienna, 15–35% in Norwich, and 10–15% in Rouen (1972).

Equal in importance with underpasses to the success of the Stevenage system is the frequent use of ingeniously improved roundabouts described here as part of the 'Good Ideas To Keep In Mind' campaign.

In the classic roundabout vehicles must fairly well stop before entering, and the tendency is for paths through the circle to conflict, creating four crossroads where formerly there was only one:

When the right of way of vehicles already in the circle is observed, traffic flow is improved, but heavy traffic from one road will impede lighter traffic from another for long periods of time. Enter the Stevenage traffic circle:

Under this system the crossroad conflict points are replaced by weaving areas. Before arriving at the circle the motorist positions him/herself in the correct lane for the intended route. It has been found that at busy periods most of the motorists know where they are going. Those few who need to read signs before selecting a lane can manage a shuffle without difficulty.

Vehicles then enter the roundabout at between 15 and 25 mph, the same speed (by design) as traffic already in the circle. Merging is simple, and under the Stevenage system vehicles may go before or after vehicles already in the circle as long as there is no abrupt dislocation. Vehicles turning left have no problem at all and can just motor through. For sceptics, I can only say that I have tried this system myself and it works like a charm.

The benefits of a system such as Stevenage's are often intangible and not easily reckoned on a balance sheet. What is the worth of never, ever, having an obstruction or aggravation in travelling? That whole series of abrasions, conflicts, and problems for which most of us armour up each day just doesn't exist in Stevenage. What price a mother's peace of mind, knowing that her children can walk or cycle anywhere – and never encounter a motor vehicle? Sixty per cent of the workers in town go home for lunch. How do you measure the value and effect of this increased home life? These are alterations in the quality of life, perhaps describable as similar to the relaxed pastoral peacefulness of a 'primitive' society – but with full technological benefits! The worth of this sort of thing can only be determined by each individual.

Other benefits are more tangible:
The cycleways serve the interests of a large segment of the population aged 6 to 16 who cannot drive cars. Of 16,760 children, 1,420 (8.4%) cycle daily to school. This figure is low, because Stevenage's primary schools are located within easy walking distance of home. Of secondary school children, 17.4% cycle to school.

Such few accidents as do occur on the cycleways are minor. Pedestrians, cyclists, and moped riders are all equally vulnerable and take equal pains to avoid each other. Stevenage's safety record is 4 casualties per 1,000 population per year as against a national average which is more than 50% greater. The direct saving in medical service costs is considerable, to say nothing of life and limb.

By encouraging cycling and walking, the Stevenage system promotes mild exercise. There are 4,000 regular cyclists, about 11 per cent of the people working in Stevenage, and 10,000 recreational and shopping cyclists. This health benefit may seem minor, but for many people it is the only exercise they get, and as such may extend their longevity up to five years.

An immense amount of time is saved. There is a car ownership rate per household of .80, which is high. People walk and cycle because it works better than using cars.

As a New Town, Stevenage has had considerable freedom in designing and implementing a transportation system. But the difficulties encountered with already existing towns are also surmountable. For example, Peterborough is currently creating a 72-mile-long system of four types of cycleways: cycle path, completely separate from motor traffic; cycle lane, by the side of a road and separated by a painted line or curb; cycle route, low-traffic streets marked with signs giving priority to cyclists; and cycle trail, through park, countryside, and forest, utilizing bridle paths, disused railway tracks, and footpaths. The proper cycle path is the ideal, of course: at one-sixth the per square yard cost of a road, with a 12-foot-wide cycle path yielding five times the carrying capacity of a 24-foot road, it is a bargain. In existing built-up areas, however, cycle lanes, routes, and trails are often a better compromise. Construction of a proper cycle path can await general redevelopment although sometimes, if there is no suitable alternative, it cannot. This costs, but in the end a lot less than sticking with what we have; also, expenditures can be spread out over a period of time. For the most part, a great deal of special provision for cyclists can be made right away, with minimal construction and expense.

The first step is to arm yourself with information. A first-rate book is *The Bicycle Planning Book*, by Mike Hudson (Open Books, London, 1978; available for £1.95 from Friends of the Earth, 9 Poland Street, London WIV 3DG). It is essential reading. *A Handbook for Bicycle Activists*, by Ernest Del, *et al* (Stanford Environmental Law Society, Stanford Law School, Stanford, CA 94305, USA; $2.95), is an excellent book about dealing with American institutions and authorities. Many of the techniques discussed could be adapted for use here. *Cyclateral Thinking* (Urban Bikeway Design Collective, W20-002, MIT, Cambridge, MA 02139, USA; $3), and *The Cycling Traffic Engineering Handbook*, by John Forester (Custom Cycle Fitments, 782 Allen Court, Palo Alto, CA 94303, USA; $12), are both full of nitty-gritty particulars on bikeways design.

Action. Write to your local authority and ask them what they are doing to encourage cycling. What about cycleways? What about parking for cycles? Sixteen cycles will fit into the same space as one car.

Design a cycleways system for your area. Mark on a map all the schools, factories, offices, shops, and places of interest that need to be served by a cycleway. Work out routes from residential areas to these areas which are as direct as possible, going along back streets, footpaths, bridlepaths, etc., and necessitate the minimum of construction. Some conflicts are unavoidable, and once the plan is accepted, will be resolved with traffic lights, bridges, or underpasses. Provide for recreational cycling and access to leisure facilities and the surrounding countryside. Cycle the routes yourself. Note where parking should be provided and what major problems, if any, exist. You can get help and advice with this project from:

The British Cycling Bureau,
Stanhope House,
Stanhope Place,
London W2 2HH;

and do not hesitate to call on them, because promoting cycling is their job.

Once you have completed your plan/proposal, send it to your local authority asking for their comments, and send copies to The British Cycling Bureau and your local newspapers. If you have done your homework – and the books listed above plus material from the British Cycling Bureau will give you a blizzard of information on the advantages of cycleways – you should get some action. If not, stir things up. Organize a bicycle demonstration/rally. Make sure the newspapers and TV stations know about it. After a ride around town, have the rally end at the offices of the local authority for a formal presentation of the plan together with a demand for a comment by a specific date. You may be fobbed off with some meaningless statement such as: 'We have the matter under study.' Keep pushing, and keep emphasizing the advantages of a cycleways system to the community as a whole. Demand that the authority create at least one experimental cycleway as a test. This has happened in many areas, and can happen in yours if you do something about it.

Such activity is valuable, but there are some other things to keep in mind. An integrated traffic system such as Stevenage's is a masterful study in efficiency where each modality of transport complements the other. The question arises: should efficiency be the prime value? What about the need to preserve health, or to expend energy wisely? Stevenage clearly shows that the car is not the enemy of the bicycle unless they share the same road. Create an integrated system, and this problem evaporates. But the car remains an enemy of man, a tool with a backlash of millions of dead and grievously injured. More Britons have died in accidents since the inception of the auto than in World War II. The simple fact is that humans cannot master the safe operation of motor vehicles. And even if they could, the motor vehicle is interdictable on account of air and noise pollution and energy waste.

We may mourn the loss of an early morning run into a rising sun, the thrill and satisfaction of fast motoring, the love and fury we feel for our machines – but the price is too stiff. There is a curious rationale: the actions of a Jack-the-Ripper style sniper or mass murderer, while a predictable outcome of the society, are seen as aberrant and 'unacceptable', whereas the thousands killed and mangled by motor vehicles are seen as unhappy but necessary by-product casualties of transport needs.

Bilge. It is not a necessity on two counts. One, that we do not need such mobility, and two, even if we insist on having it, there are other, safer ways to get it.

Let us start with the idea of banning the motor vehicle as an unwarranted assault on human rights and life. Many must feel that such an action would have a severe price in depreciated quality of life, and is completely unrealistic. Not so. The precise point is that an excess of transport efficiency is not good for us, but bad. We do not own our transport; it owns us.

Mobility and the nuclear family are factors of alienation, concomitants of an industrial society. The extended kinship family is not necessarily the model for relationships, and relationships are not needed by everyone, but relationships must exist for most people most of the time. An industrial society, particularly a hyper-industrial society such as ours, inhibits relationships. Men and women are sorted into worker and non-worker groups. Employability is privileged, and non-workers, who include females, the old, the foolish, the poor, the incompetent, and the uncooperative of whatever form and for whatever reason, are discriminated against. They simply have fewer human rights.

It is the nature of industrial processes that it is difficult to employ groups or families or even couples. For the sake of worker mobility, males are given the dominant central economic role in a nuclear family, and females, less desirable in the labour pool, are made accessories.

So there is a situation where a large segment of the society has been relegated to inferior status and rights, and where even the structure of relationships is subordinate to industrial needs. And the reward is not job satisfaction, or a furtherance of the interests of the society, but consumerism. The use of the products and services created by this particular method of organizing society. And, quite simply, we have no choice. We do not reap benefits; rather, we are compelled to adopt certain behaviours if we wish to live. We do not own the machines and the technology and the products therefrom; they own us.

It is my feeling that some loss of mobility would be a good thing. Negatively, in that employment for the sake of consumerism is worthless and destructive; and, positively, in that it may encourage relationships and foster wholesome goals together with greater self-awareness. The consumer society is built on promises and a hoax of future progress. Expectancy blinds us to the realities of the moment. The 'primitive' societies that functioned without technological innovation or expectancy that the future would be different enjoyed a far richer here and now.

But it goes deeper than not perpetuating the evils of consumerism. If the members of the society are to engage management and share privileges and responsibilities, there must be a relative equality of experience. The creation of privilege – in this example, mobility – for the purpose of administering, coordinating, or whatever worthwhile activity, is a terrible mistake which confers discriminatory power. And power corrupts and perpetuates. It is more important to maintain power-equality.

Ivan D. Illich in his wonderful book *Tools for Conviviality* (Calder & Boyars Ltd, 18 Brewer Street, London w1; £2.25) says that the upper limit of transportation technology should be the bicycle. A genuinely socialist society cannot support anything more advanced. Properly limited technologies 'serve politically interrelated individuals rather than managers'.

THE ANCHOR, RIPLEY

The point of this discussion is to show that 'alternate transportation' does not necessarily mean just another way of doing the same thing. This is more than a matter of perspective, because the form of our transportation is related to the content of our culture. The car, for example, is a tool of alienation. Giant shopping complexes are created to promote the use of cars. Gone is the local butcher, fishmonger, greengrocer, and frequent contact with known people, replaced by uniform packaging and uniform employees who work with customers the same as a nut-and-bolt assembler on a production line. If we are conscious of the desirability of other goals besides employment, mobility, and consumerism – goals such as human contact – then transportation design may be influenced in evolution.

But I. D. Illich directs his ideas towards influencing the lifestyle possibilities of countries which have not yet industrialized. No one standing by the endless streams of cars blaring through our cities and countryside can realistically hope that it will end quickly. In one important sense the energy crisis is a boondoggle, a hoax, not the harbinger of a new and different time, but a manipulation by the petro-chemical companies and governments to maintain consumerism – and power. 'Shortages' are basic operations of a 1984 Fascist society. We may need to want the things now in short supply about as much as rectal cancer, but it is just too much to expect that the hyper-industrialized society, in dying, will do anything but promote to the utmost the values which have preserved it in the past.

No major concessions will be made to cyclists and human beings as long as the automotive and petro-chemical industries hold the economic clout. A glimpse into the future was provided a while ago in France.

Paris is famous for traffic. Cars are everywhere, moving in a constant rushing stream, and creating an incredible din. Cars have the right of way and pedestrians have to fend for themselves. In Paris the auto is king. M. Pompidou once even announced, 'We must adapt Paris to the automobile and renounce a certain aesthetic idealism.'

Not all Parisians agree. They want alternate means of transportation and an end to noisy traffic jams. On 23 April 1972, the Organizations Les Amis de la Terre, Comité Antinucleaire de

Paris, Comité de Liberation, Ecologique, Etre, Objectif Socialiste, and the Federation of Users of Public Transport staged a massive bike-in to dramatize their demands. It was beautiful.

Some 10,000 bicycles of every conceivable type and condition rendezvoused at Porte Dauphine. A few forward-looking Frenchmen showed up on roller skates! Harried police tried to route the demonstrators to exterior streets, but the procession went straight down the Champs Elysées to the Place de la Concorde, up the Blvd St Germain, and on to Bois de Vincennes (a park). Bus loads of riot police tried to stem the tide on the Champs Elysées but failed, possibly because they did not want to be violent in full public view. As the procession wound along replete with signs and streamers, some sympathetic motorists blocked side streets with their cars to add to the confusion, and pedestrians shouted 'Bon Courage!' One spoilsport who refused to be stymied ran into several bicycles with his car. Surrounded by several thousand angry bicyclists he paid damages on the spot.

When the cyclists reached Bois de Vincennes, they were greeted with victory hymns by the Grand Magic Circus troupe. An hour of dancing, singing, and good times followed. Then the CRS riot police arrived. Helmeted troops on motorcycles charged the crowd and tear gas flew. Efforts at reason failed. About 50 people were arrested. The CRS used the shelter of the woods to smash up bicycles with their night-sticks.

Now Les Amis de la Terre and other groups are pressing on with their demands: the creation of pedestrian streets; one million free bicycles at the disposition of Parisians; non-polluting public transportation à la Rome; the closing of Paris to more automobile traffic, and a halt to the creation of inner-city expressways. *Yeah!*

The French experience points the way to real victories. Theirs was an *ecological* demonstration stressing the needs of both pedestrians and bicycles. Bikeways are not enough. What is needed is the elimination of polluting transportation. In urban areas the car accounts for up to 85% of the air pollution, and for 85% of the noise pollution. In Vienna the intra-city ban has reduced air pollution levels by 70%; a 1971 closing of New York City's Madison Avenue resulted in a threefold drop in carbon monoxide levels. The absolute elimination of internal combustion engines from urban areas is the practical solution which benefits everybody.

And the curious thing is, if we do define mobility as a prime value, then in urban areas a car is the last thing we need. It just does not work. George Washington, riding a horse, made better time between his home in Alexandria, VA and the Capitol, a distance of some six miles, than today's Washingtonian does driving a car. Trains, buses, bicycles, roller skates, steam- and electric-powered delivery vehicles are more than adequate – they are better. At present motor vehicles are very heavily subsidized by the general public, and if the users of this form of transportation were to pay the full cost they could not afford it. Support must now go to alternative (and cheaper) methods. Trains and buses must have racks for the free carrying of bicycles. Stations, terminals, businesses, and residences must have cycle parking facilities. There must be a comprehensive system of cycleways serving not only industry and consumer outlets, but areas of recreation and sport. It has to be possible to go anywhere in the country on a bicycle without getting involved with motor vehicles. No road or street should exist without a corresponding cycle path. Instead of squandering funds on motorways and traffic regulation, cities must provide free, simple, easily adjustable bicycles for intra-city use. And as for the car and lorry, in urban areas – Ban it!

Which is of course easier said than done. The industries with a vested interest in maintaining a motor age are large and powerful to the extreme. Petro-chemical companies are a law unto themselves. Steel, mining, rubber, textiles, cement, and plastics are automotive-related industries, each with a profit and make-work situation to protect. Each, curiously enough, is a major pollutor in its own right. Ultimately, the only solution to this vicious conglomerate of vested interest and power will be to take the profit out of their activities by nationalizing all transportation – bicycles, cars, trucks, buses, trains, aeroplanes – and all related service industries: economic and psychological revolution, and in the immediate prospect, hardly likely.

What we are more likely to see is a long series of minor reforms, tokenism, and other concessions to public unrest. One day there might be a major smog disaster in which thousands of people will suddenly all die at once, instead of piecemeal as they do now. This might spur improvements which would ultimately save more lives than were lost. But the power of vested interests in maintaining a motor age is such that there will probably be a long-drawn-out struggle, and concessions will not be won without a fight.

So don't be too surprised if you are beaned at a bike-in by a club-swinging bobby who calls you a dirty communist, and don't back off because of it. *You have a right to live.* Arguments which present the bicycle as economic, efficient, etc. are well and good, but the situation is extremely simple : motorised transport is filling the air with deadly fumes and noise and recklessly wasting a dwindling supply of natural resources. *People are being injured and killed.* The right to live is your birthright – but you will have to fight for it.

The opportunity for radical change and transformation, of revolution, of destruction, reorganisation, and creation – if it comes at all – is a matter of individual assessment and decision. We all move according to our best understanding of right and wrong, and ability to act. If the chance comes your way,

Take It.

Index

AN AWKWARD CORNER.

The author

Richard Ballantine has no academic education he considers worth
mentioning. He has engaged in, for greater and lesser durations, a
stimulating variety of occupations and professions, among them busboy,
chef, shooting gallery attendant, electronics technician, door-to-door
salesman, book editor, community organizer and anarchist. He is the
co-author, with John Cohen, of *Africa Addio* (1966), a noble attempt to
rationalize a bloodcurdling film of the same title; and, with Joel
Griffiths, of *Silent Slaughter* (1972), a survey of radiation hazards, with
emphasis on emissions from electronic products such as radar, television
sets and microwave ovens. Mr. Ballantine is fond of skiing, travel
and photography. He is the happy co-owner of a home-built
34-ft Wharram catamaran, which he hopes some day to sail with his
wife and children to South America and points beyond, completing
en route his *Richard's Boat Book* In the meantime, the family make
their home, together with a *mélange* of dogs, chickens, ducks, geese,
sheep, and a cow on Dartmoor in the West Country.